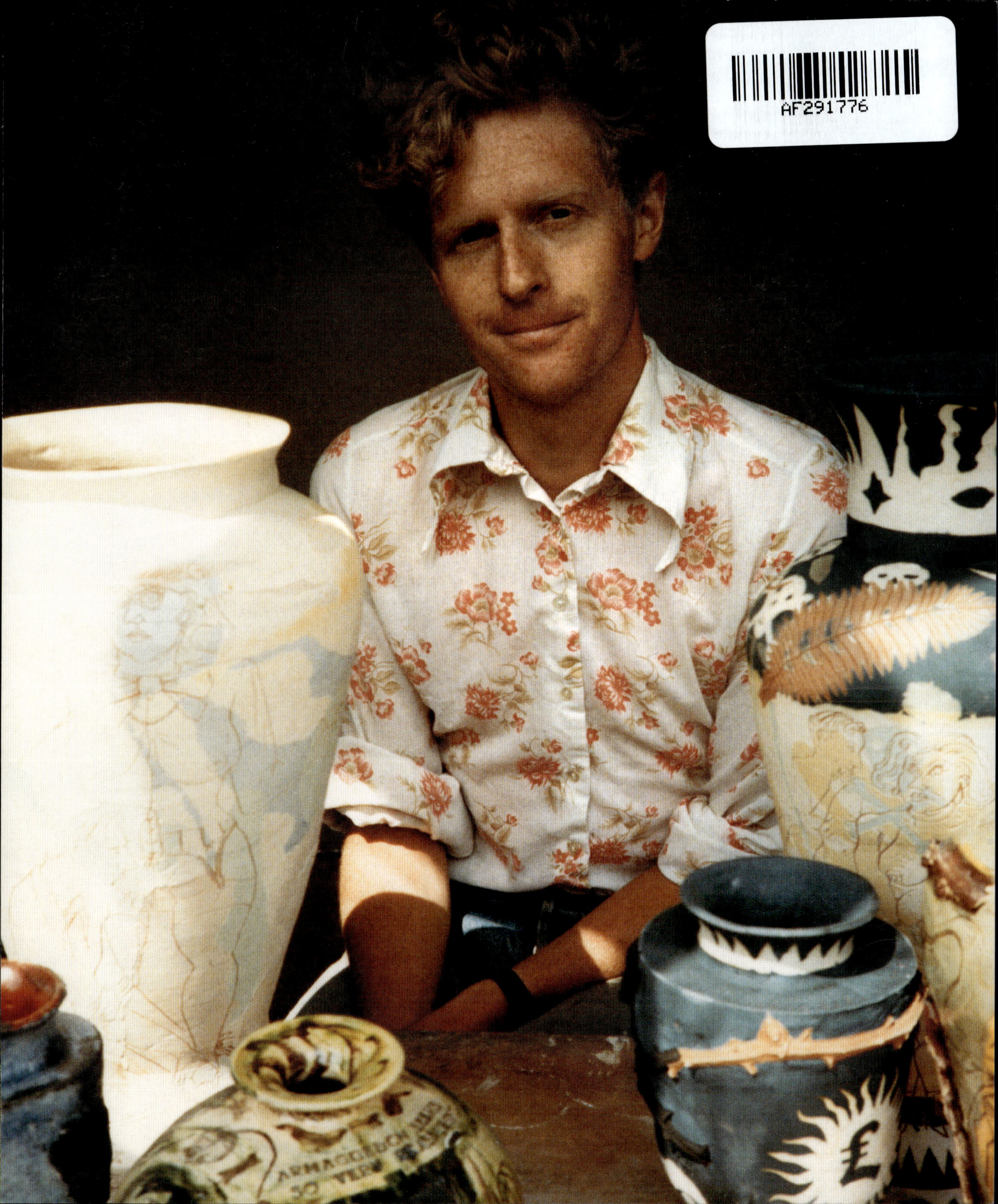
AF291776

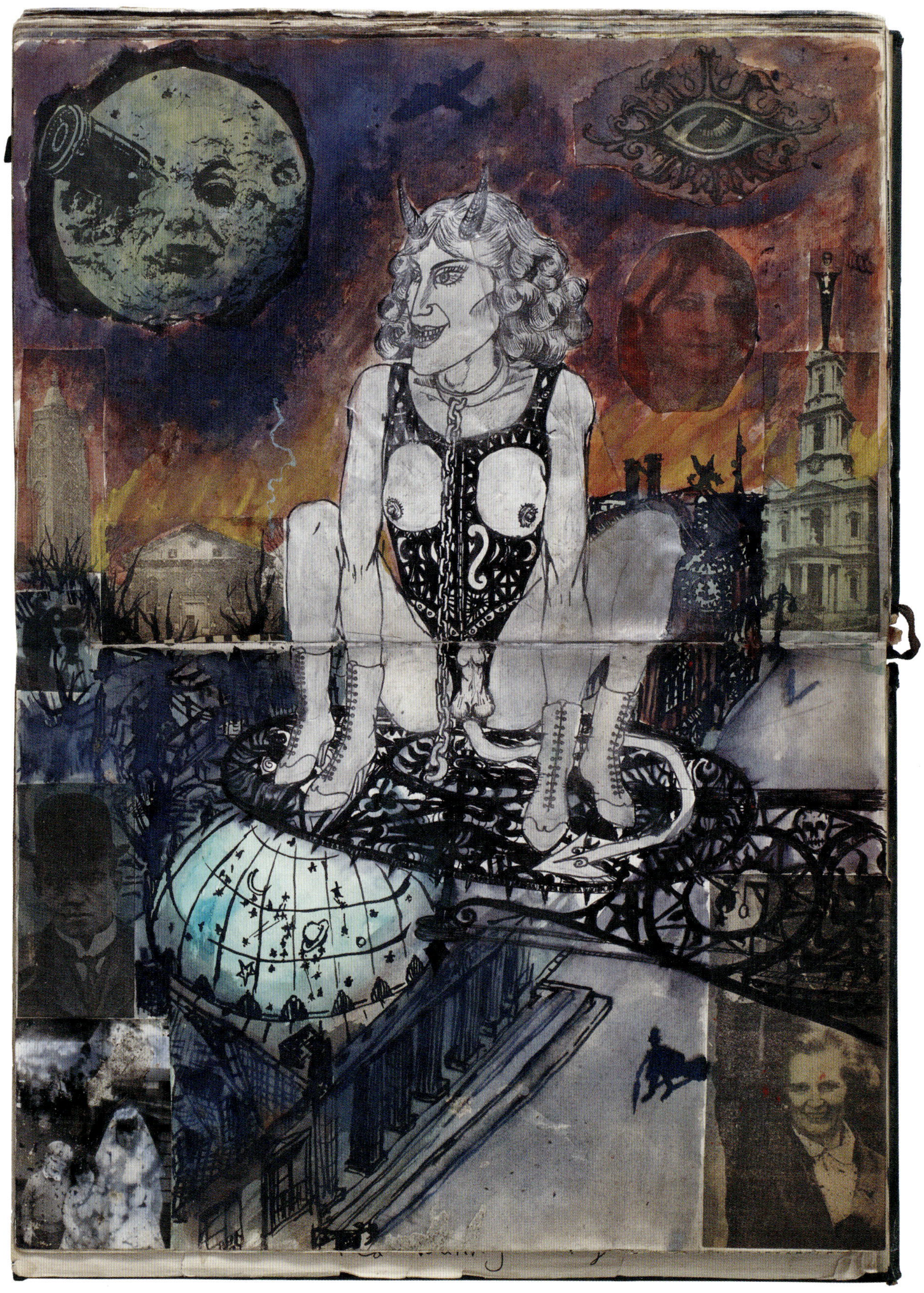

GRAYSON PERRY

The Pre-Therapy Years

Edited by Catrin Jones and Chris Stephens

with 148 illustrations

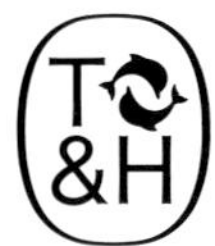

THE
HOLBURNE
MUSEUM

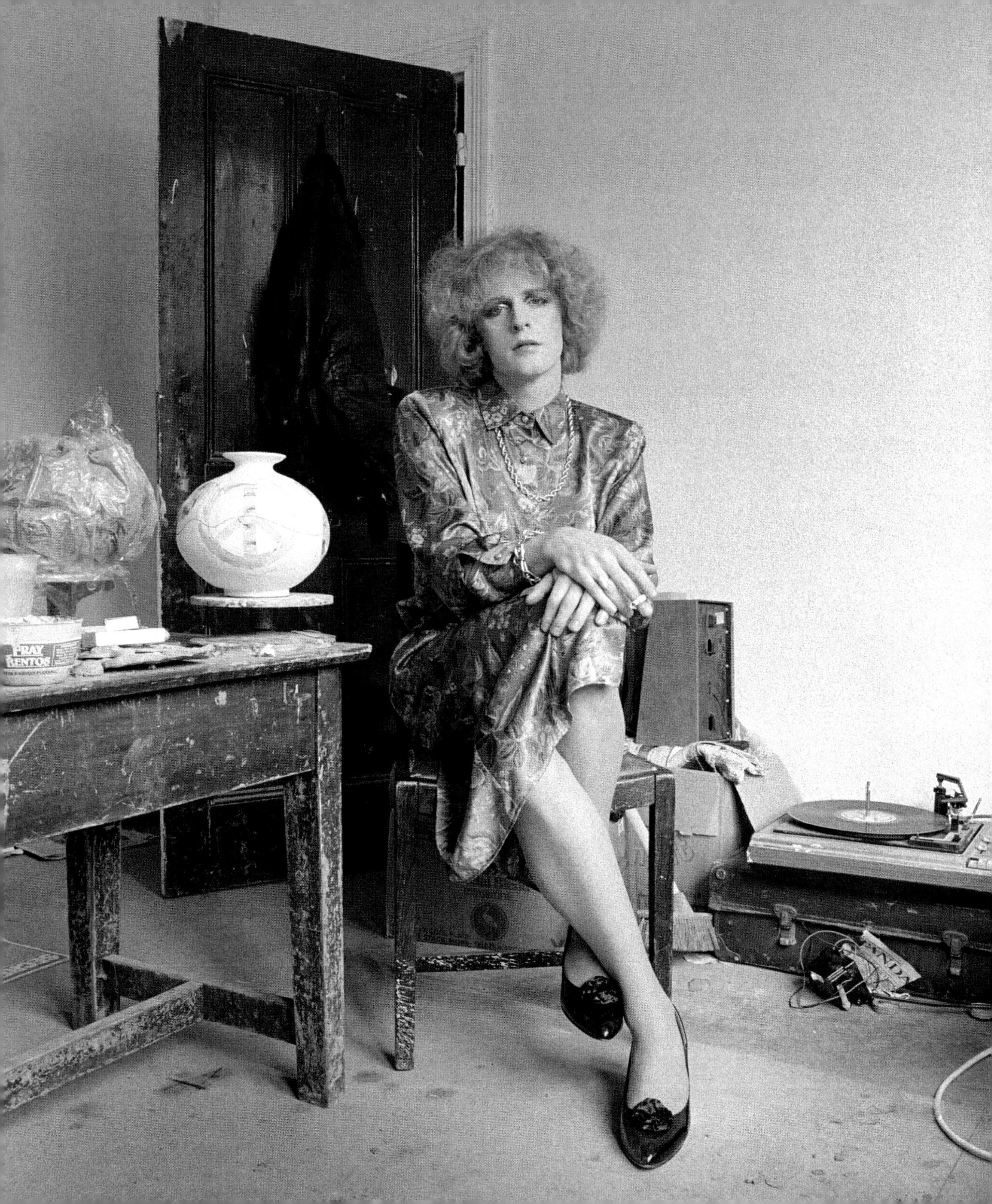

FOREWORD

Chris Stephens

Grayson Perry is one of a tiny group of living artists whose names and reputations extend beyond the narrow fraction of gallery-goers into a wider public realm. In the past decade, he has written and presented numerous television documentaries, including several series that have dealt, especially, with class, taste and masculinity. He has, in addition, appeared on several television chat shows and topical quiz programmes. More than simply a famous artist, more even than a household name, Perry has become for many a national treasure. In his broadcast work, Perry has combined an engaged and empathetic approach with a subtle intellect and a sensitivity informed by his own origination from a suburban, working-class background. What makes his popular success both remarkable and especially heartening is the fact of his prominent transvestism. His alter ego, Claire, is as recognizable as his other self. As Grayson observes elsewhere in this book, he has a unique 'brand' as 'the transvestite potter' but it seems remarkable that it is precisely his unconventional identity and the complex subconscious that underlies it that determine those qualities that have made him so popular. It might not always have seemed possible.

As is often the case with those few artists who reach broader audiences than most of their peers, Perry has occupied a space somewhat outside the mainstream art world. When he won the Turner Prize in 2003 – the premier recognition of success in the British contemporary art scene – there was a sense in some quarters that his victory was an inappropriate intrusion. Perry was never considered part of the loosely defined group that during the 1990s became known as 'Young British Artists' (YBAs) despite the fact that his work included the elements of shock and profanity that seemed, to many, to characterize the movement. The definition of such cultural phenomena often depends on social networks as much as on historical developments. It is also the case that even in a period when increasingly artists felt free to employ an eclectic range of media, whether it be painting, drawing, sculpture, film, video or installation, Perry's use of ceramic – generally in its traditional forms of the vase and the plate – set him apart. The distinction between fine and decorative or applied arts has long been challenged but it certainly remained resolutely in place in the late 20th century regardless of what we consider its current status to be.

This book has been produced in conjunction with an exhibition originated at the Holburne Museum in Bath. The Holburne has a notable collection of European and East Asian ceramics and there are interesting resonances between Perry's work and those earlier examples, most especially with the narrative imagery of Italian maiolica. Certainly, as Catrin Jones demonstrates, the history of ceramics is one of the many conventions that Perry has sought to challenge. As a historical museum, we felt there was a valuable project to be undertaken to revisit the early career of a major artist who had, perhaps, become known for work somewhat different from that which had first secured his reputation.

When we approached Grayson we were delighted with – and a little surprised
by – the enthusiasm with which he responded to our proposal to mount an
exhibition of his early ceramics. The sense of the project being one of research
as much as of display reinforced its value: in unearthing those early works, many
of which the artist had lost track of, we also felt we were excavating the history
of an important period of British cultural history.

In considering the art of the 1980s we are looking back an entire generation,
opening up a history unfamiliar to many. In that conflicted decade we might
see, inevitably, the seeds of many of the political and ideological tensions
that characterize the UK in the late 2010s. The process of de-industrialization
undergone in the 1980s, with its attendant social unrest, and the move towards
an economy based on service and finance provided a context for the booming
art market of the 1990s in which the YBAs played such an important part. The
political consequences of the impact those changes had on many are only now
being fully recognized. In another vein, however, it was hard to imagine the
popular success of a prominent transvestite during a period in which sexual and
gender politics were dominated by the AIDS crisis and a government initiative
to prevent the normalization of same-sex relationships through Section 28 of
the Local Government Act that prohibited the 'promotion' of homosexuality.
Attitudes to mental health have, similarly, evolved and this project's highlighting
of the therapeutic function of creativity fits well with the commitment that the
Holburne shares with many of its peers to promoting the relationship between
art and wellbeing.

In our initial discussions, we sought to define what we meant by Perry's 'early
work'. We agreed that the primary emphasis would be on ceramics, though we
would include a selection of the complementary sketchbooks and the films that
were important in his artistic formation. The end date was less easily arrived at but
a helpful suggestion was Perry's first exhibition at the Anthony d'Offay Gallery in
1994, the transfer to d'Offay marking a move from the fringes to the Bond Street
heart of the art market. The date also, helpfully – perhaps tellingly – seemed to
coincide approximately with a shift in the aesthetic of Perry's pots. When we then
proposed 1994 as the terminal point of the show it was Grayson who laughed and
observed those were the 'pre-therapy years'. Even if it was actually in 1998 that
he embarked upon a course of psychotherapy, the observation seemed pertinent.
In 2013, Perry produced a self-portrait in the form of a map, setting out graphically
the idea of one's self as a disparate, multi-faceted and contingent entity in contrast
to the notion of identity as singular and fixed with an essential core at its heart.
That is clearly a post-therapy understanding of subjectivity and one might imagine
the imagery which is explored through the early ceramics presented here as an
unconscious attempt at a similar mapping of identity. There is, most notably, a lot
of anger and a clear desire to shock through challenges to the most fundamental

Chris Stephens

of contemporary standards. Graphic and sometimes violent and perverse sexual imagery is a prominent feature. Similarly, the recurrence in a number of works of Nazi imagery, especially the swastika, can be read as a strategy of offence similar to that employed a few years earlier by such Punk icons as Sid Vicious and Siouxsie Sioux. Deliberately offensive such imagery might be, but we should be wary of seeing it in those terms alone given the artist's fascination with fetishism and what we might think of as sexual or gender power relations. Indeed, as discussed later, from an early age pottery and fetishism were conflated in Perry's mind.

I am incredibly grateful to Grayson Perry for the opportunity to explore and present his early achievement and we have benefited from his engagement and generosity throughout. At the Holburne, the project has been led by Catrin Jones, supported by Sylvie Broussine and Nina Harrison Leins, with particular skill. I was delighted that Andrew Wilson, a great expert on the work of Grayson Perry and the cultural histories of the period, agreed to join Catrin in writing this book. Both exhibition and book have been generously supported in all sorts of ways by Grayson's gallery, Victoria Miro, and I am hugely indebted to Victoria herself and her team, especially Erin Manns, Valeska Wittig and Hannah van den Wijngaard, for all their help. A major part of our research was a public call for Grayson's early work and I must thank all the different owners who responded to that appeal not only with works in their possession but also often with associated stories. We are especially thankful for the encouragement and advice of James Birch, who played such a key role in Grayson's early career, and to Louisa Buck. Finally, it is good to be working once again with Roger Thorp and with the rest of the team at Thames & Hudson.

Numerous things are striking about Grayson Perry's early work. Angry, ironic and frequently shocking it may be but the wit and humour are equally powerful and give the clue to some of the qualities that have subsequently won him such widespread admiration. The iconography and meanings are compelling in their layered complexity, subtlety and empathy. The graphic qualities of some of the imagery is frequently offset by the dry humour of Perry's distinctive tone of voice. It is true that to explore these works is to enter back into a particular subculture of the 1980s and early 1990s but what strikes me most in reviewing the images is how they retain their power and relevance over thirty years after they were made.

PAGE 10: Grayson Perry filmmaking at Birling Gap, East Sussex

PAGE 11, FRONT: Christine Binnie, Jennifer Binnie and Grayson Perry at London Zoo, 1982

PAGE 11, BEHIND: Party, 1984

PAGE 12, FRONT: Jennifer Binnie's 30th birthday celebration and unveiling of a portrait by Andrew Logan, Crowndale Road, 1986

PAGE 12, BEHIND: Grayson Perry at Crowndale Road, 1983

PAGE 13: Grayson Perry at Crowndale Road

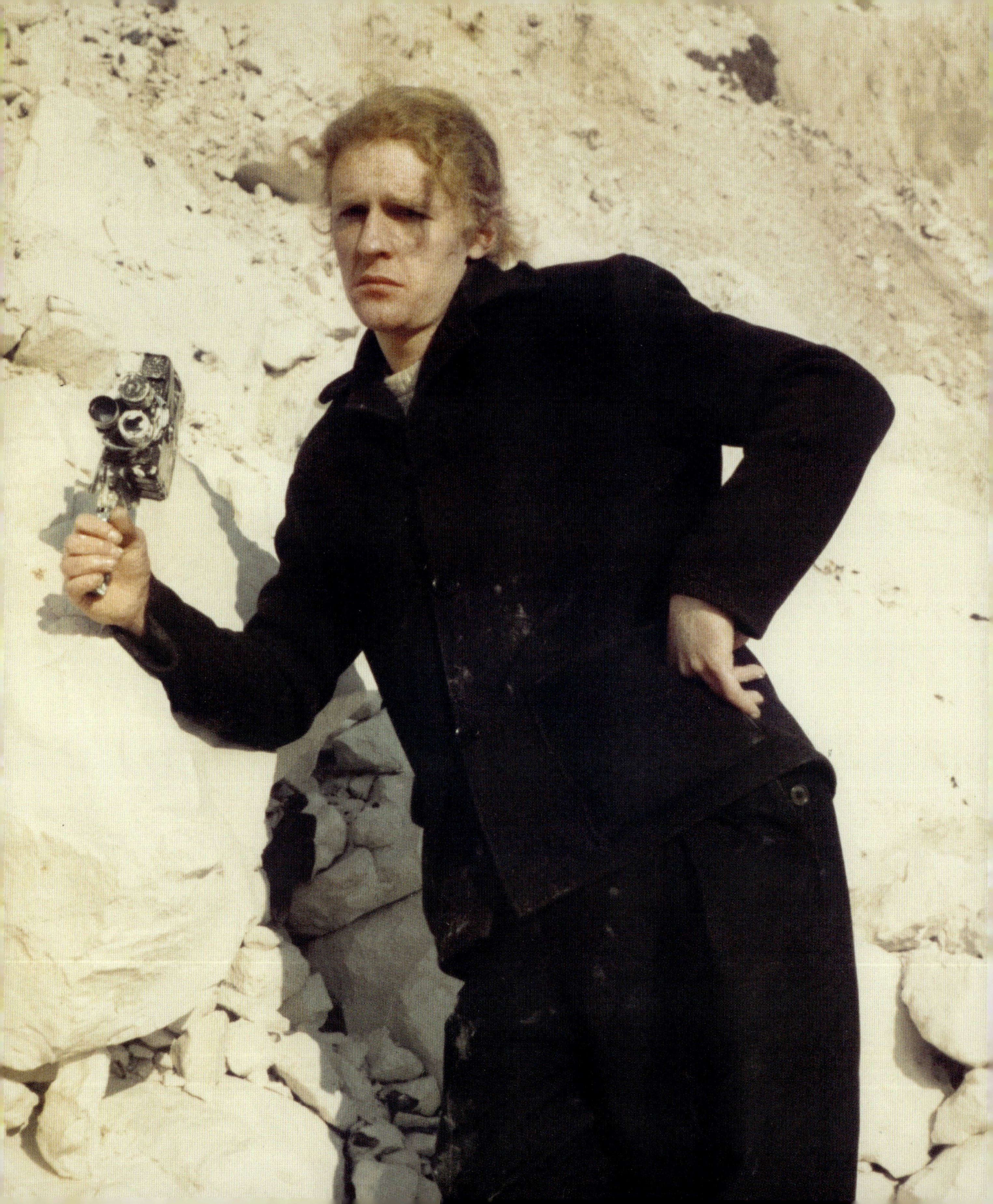

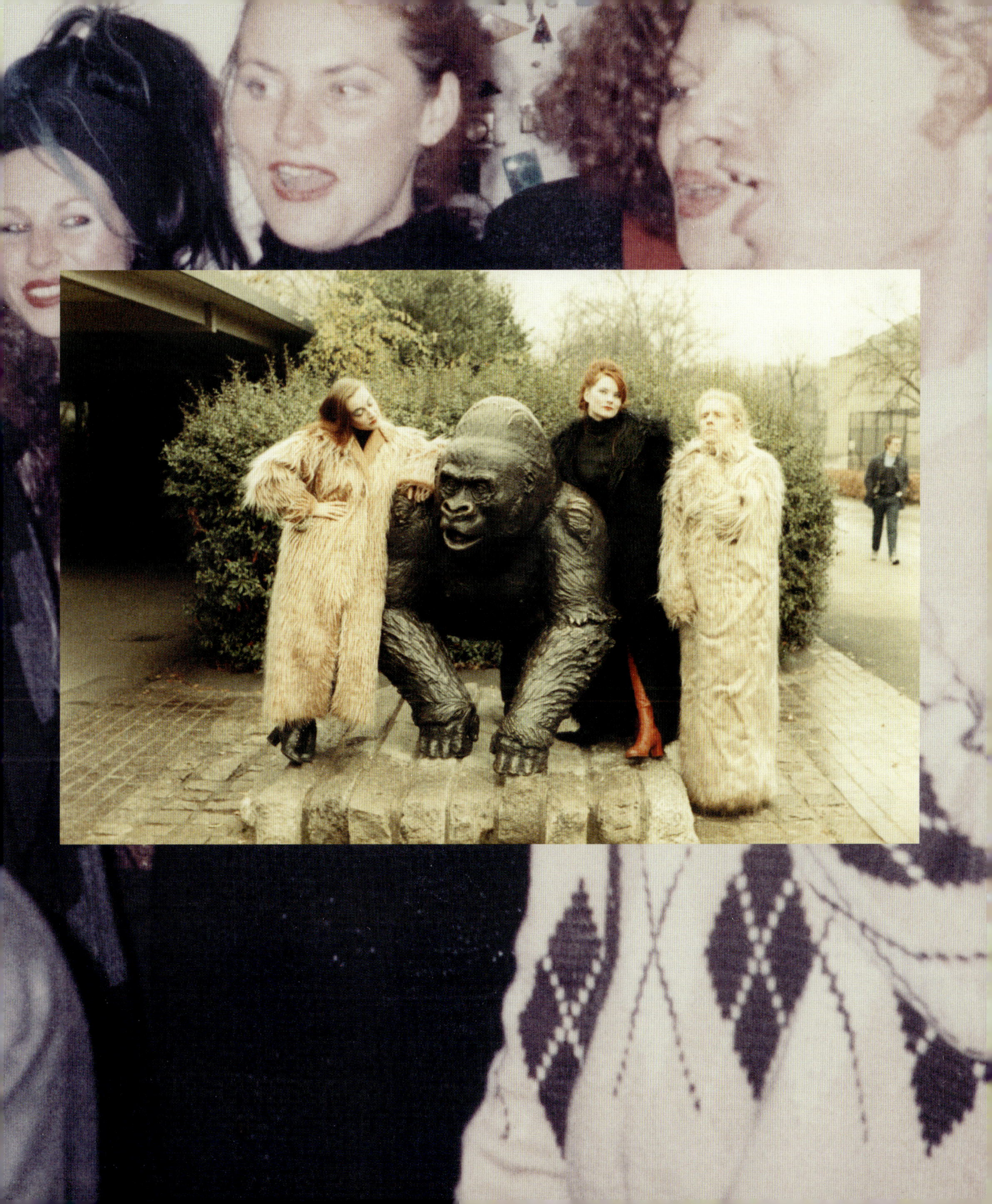

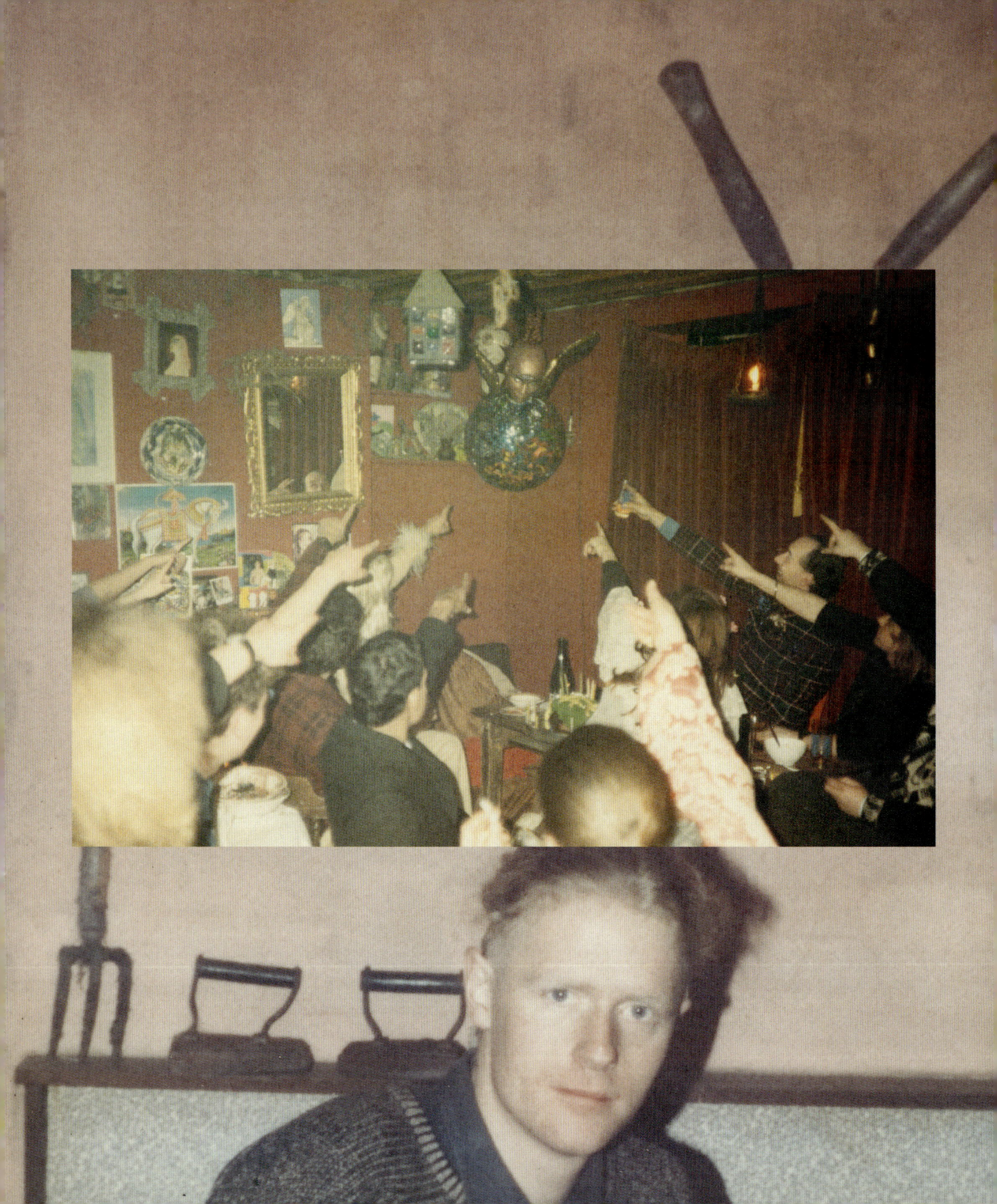

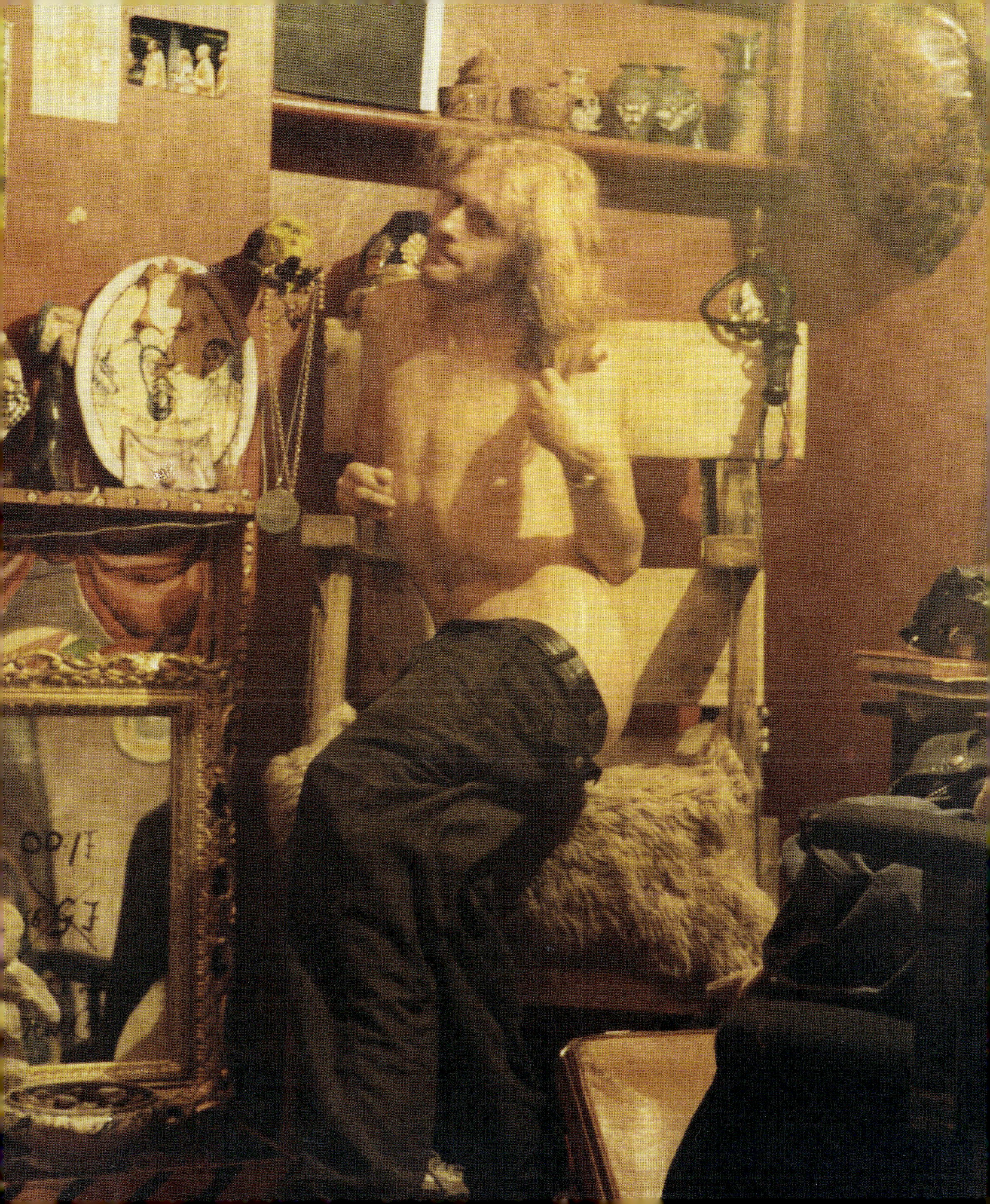

TOWARDS
A PRE-HISTORY
OF GRAYSON
PERRY

Andrew Wilson

Asked why he decided to be an artist, Grayson Perry recalled how his art teacher
at school had told him that he had a facility for drawing and asked him if he had
ever considered going to art college. It was an odd suggestion, perhaps, to someone
who as a child 'lived in a culture-free zone with no books and no paintings'. But
the logic of this equation – you're good at drawing, you should go to art college
– was to become coupled in Perry's head with what it could offer him in terms
of the possibility of continuing with a fantasy life, or more particularly how art
could provide 'a way of accessing the engine of that fantasy life'. He could, he
said, 'remember a day in my teens when I couldn't play a fantasy game anymore,
which was pretty late for a child. In a way, art is not a way of getting in touch
with fantasy life, but the muscles that developed from a very strong fantasy life
can be used, kept going.'[1]

The fantasy life that Perry created as a child and teenager was largely about
finding safety – the significance given to his bear Alan Measles as a father-figure
cannot be over-stressed given the difficult family life he experienced, with
a violent stepfather and a mother he became estranged from. His mother had
an affair with the milkman and when his father moved out the milkman moved
in to become Perry's stepfather. He was uncommunicative yet violent, a wrestler
as well as a milkman. Another part of Perry's fantasy life took one of its essential
aspects to a logical if transgressive end. Dressing up as a transvestite became an
essential part of Perry's make-up. From the age of 13 he started to wear his sister's
clothes and within two years he was walking around the fields in them – in public,
but privately. In December 1975, he left home to live with his natural father but
within a few months his stepsister discovered his diary in which he had written
about his transvestite adventures and fantasies, and his stepmother threw him out;
after a few days of homelessness, he was taken back in by his mother. From one
point of view, being a transvestite was about making up an alternative family by
being another sister or mother; more essentially, it also entailed a recognition that
identity was both something you were born with and something that could be
made and played around with. It is about the view inside yourself and about what
could be projected or communicated. This is why the example of the transvestite
in terms of its explicit contradictory coding has been so useful subsequently
to Perry as an artist. When he dresses as a woman, he isn't becoming a woman,
despite his adoption of the persona Claire, and he has used the language of craft
in a similarly transvestite way.

In 1988, at the time of his fourth solo exhibition in London, at Birch & Conran
Fine Art, and a year after he had bought his first kiln, Grayson Perry described for
Ceramic Review magazine his first experience of ceramics:

One afternoon when I was eight or nine years old, I was given my first
pottery lesson at Woodham Ferres C of E School, Essex. To protect our

clothes we were made to wear long-sleeved smocks made of light blue
rubber. I can vividly recall mine being too small as the pretty teacher did
up the snap fasteners down the back. I became very excited at the feeling
of the tight smooth material. In this state I made my first ever pot, an ashtray
for my dear mother. We all grow with the friendship of pots in our homes.
A pot has no pretensions of becoming a great public work, we know where
we stand with a plate or a vase.[2]

Perry's retrospective account of this childhood moment twenty years earlier
is revealing on a number of counts. The pot is a product of a normal family life,
its domesticity defines it as unremarkable, without pretensions regarding taste
or significance. In this respect the pot is a little-noticed aspect of home furnishings.
For the artist that Perry became, it could be not only the container but also the
motor of communication for the subject matter of his art. Comfortable in its
position on a mantelpiece, the pot can therefore become a potent material and
stage for subversion and transgression – for the contradictions that are manipulated
in turning worlds upside down. For Perry his memory of the pottery lesson was
inextricably bound-up with his growing obsession with his sexual identity and
fetishism, the first stirrings of his transvestism; this all went hand in hand from the
beginning. Perry first wore a dress because he was initially excited to wear a dress
– an excitement that was autoerotic. Being a transvestite is one aspect of his wider
obsessions. As he admits, 'I am obsessed with fetishism on a personal level. That's
why I make the work. Like other people are obsessed with cars or landscape,
I am obsessed with sexual fetishism.'[3]

Ten years after making the ashtray for his mother – a simple vessel unadorned
save for a feminine yellow glaze – Perry was at art college in Portsmouth, and
less than five years after that, and a year before his first solo exhibition, he
inhabited a milieu in London in which he felt comfortable describing himself
as a 'poet, filmmaker and general artist'.[4] Later that year, in September 1983,
he started to attend pottery evening classes, encouraged to do so by the artist
Christine Binnie, the elder sister of his girlfriend Jennifer Binnie. One of the
earliest products of the evening classes was a plate, *Kinky Sex* (1983) (p. 70),
which continued the narrative that Perry had first initiated as a child with *Yellow
Ashtray* (1968). At first glance, *Kinky Sex* looks antique and one reference point
is to 17th-century slipware portrait dishes made to celebrate marriages, yet
the ritualized image on Perry's plate is altogether different in tenor. Two heads
in profile attend to and observe a long-haired, sexually ambiguous, crucified
Christ dolly-figure, additionally wounded over crotch and chest by a melted
coin providing an image of ejaculation. *Kinky Sex* shows victim and perpetrator,
degradation and fulfilment. Making a plate such as this was one way for Perry
to externalize his fantasy world.

Andrew Wilson

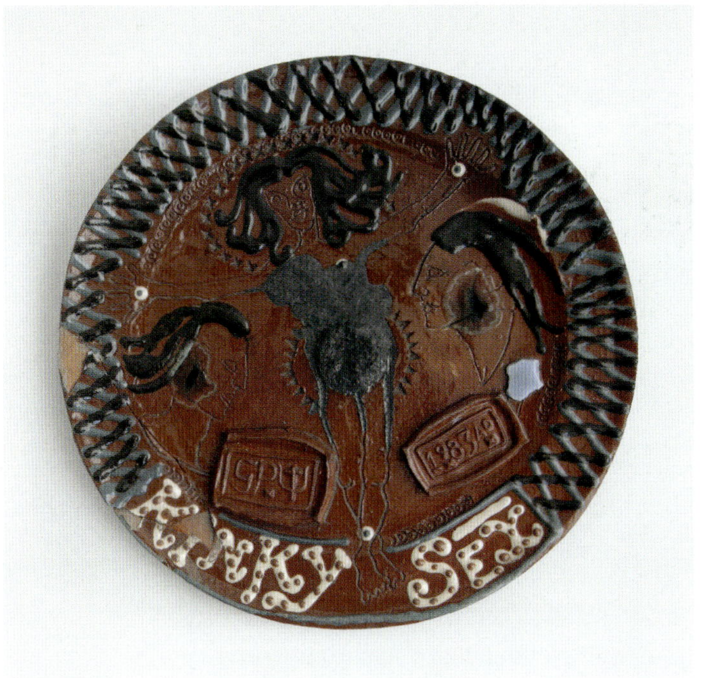

Kinky Sex, 1983

If there is a correlation between Perry's transvestism and his adoption of craft practices it poses a question of authorship as much as about the uses he makes of ceramics. For Perry, his fantasy life, embodied by his transvestism, is clearly no pretence or masquerade. He is 'dressing up in the heraldry of my subconscious'[5] and Perry's initial attraction to craft is as a manifestation of this declaration: 'Craft is seen as a female thing and as a tranny I have got a high tolerance for the suburbanness of craft.'[6] By deploying aggressive and transgressive sexual imagery under the cover of a normality communicated by a row of plates proudly displayed on a Welsh dresser, Perry's pottery became an extension and result of a fantasy life realized. Here, however, Claire is not the suburban housewife that Perry often became but rather a visualization of its other manifestation as sado-masochistic dominatrix or victim.

Following the advice of his art teacher at school, in 1978 Perry had gone to Braintree College of Further Education for his foundation art course and near the end of this year, after he had been accepted for Portsmouth Polytechnic, he made a visit to London with his lecturer to see the *Outsiders* exhibition at the Hayward Gallery. This was an exhibition of untutored artists and was a revelation to Perry. The exhibition's subtitle was a provocation to the young art student – 'an art without precedent or tradition' – and one artist in particular caught his fascination. From the age of 8 Henry Darger had grown up in an institution for 'feebleminded' children until he ran away at the age of 16; for the rest of his life he had a sequence of janitorial jobs in hospitals. He was a compulsive churchgoer but otherwise was isolated, socially starved and remained locked-in as an emotional adolescent who created a fantasy world he ceaselessly documented, first in writing and then in images, under the descriptive title of 'The Story of the Vivian Girls, in What is Known as the Realms of the Unreal, of the Glandeco-Angelinnean War Storm, Caused by the Child Slave Rebellion'. Perry's identification with Darger's work was immediate: 'I felt that they were like one of my pots rolled out. He retreated into his imaginary world full time, but his paintings are visually very sophisticated and not repetitive like a lot of outsider art: spatially, compositionally, stylistically and colour-wise they change drastically.'[7]

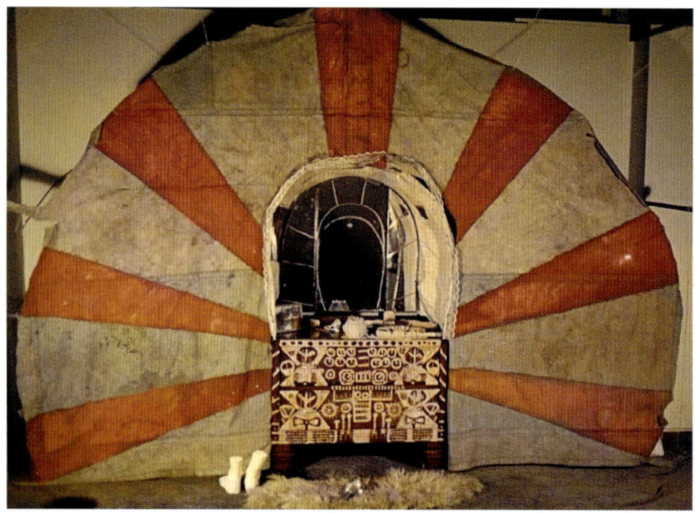

Transvestite Jet Pilots, c. 1980–81

Darger was an artist whose work allowed full rein to the expression of a fantasy life but, even as a student, Perry was aware of tradition and precedent, and was producing work for an audience, not solely for his own gratification. Yet the fundamental lesson of the exhibition, reinforced a few years later after leaving Portsmouth, was the recognition that being an artist was not a job, not something that you do and then switch off (like working in a biscuit factory, as Perry had once done) – it is who you are.

The timing of the *Outsiders* exhibition was also symptomatic of a cultural shift at the end of the 1970s as the certainties and dominance of modernism were fully recognized to be redundant. That essentialist master narrative was swapped for a postmodernism where irony and scepticism fuelled an artistic language that at the end of the decade embraced expressions of individuality and complexity, and tradition could be followed and refused in equal measure. Conceptual art's strategies of analysis and textuality, rather than visuality, had characterized the dominant form of postmodernism in the early 1970s. By the time Perry arrived at Portsmouth with the example of the *Outsiders* exhibition planted firmly, if subconsciously, in his head, the primacy of the pictorial, the expressive and expansive potential of media (paint and ceramics as much as performance or video), and the relevance of individuality and subjectivity dominated artistic discourse. Neo-expressionist painting, framed by Joseph Beuys's mantra of 'everyone an artist', became a direct influence on the young student – A. R. Penck, Markus Lüpertz, Georg Baselitz, Anselm Kiefer, Jörg Immendorff – and, looking forward to his evocation of the Essex landscape in such later works as the press-moulded *Commemorative Plates* of 1985 (pp. 86–87) or *I was Just an Ordinary Person* (1988), there is a scorched quality to his line that is especially reliant on Kiefer. Yet the expression of personal fantasy and ritual echoed Darger's world, and that of many of those gathered together as outsiders, and exerted an even more profound grounding effect on Perry's work.

During his first year at Portsmouth, Perry also found a comfortable environment in which the private world of his transvestism could be nurtured and accepted, initially through his relationship with Jennifer Binnie, a painter a year above Perry. The following year this was realized artistically in the installation that marks the beginnings of his life as an artist: *Transvestite Jet Pilots* (*c.* 1980–81). Darrell Viner, Perry's tutor, had set him the task of writing about himself and to make a work

Andrew Wilson

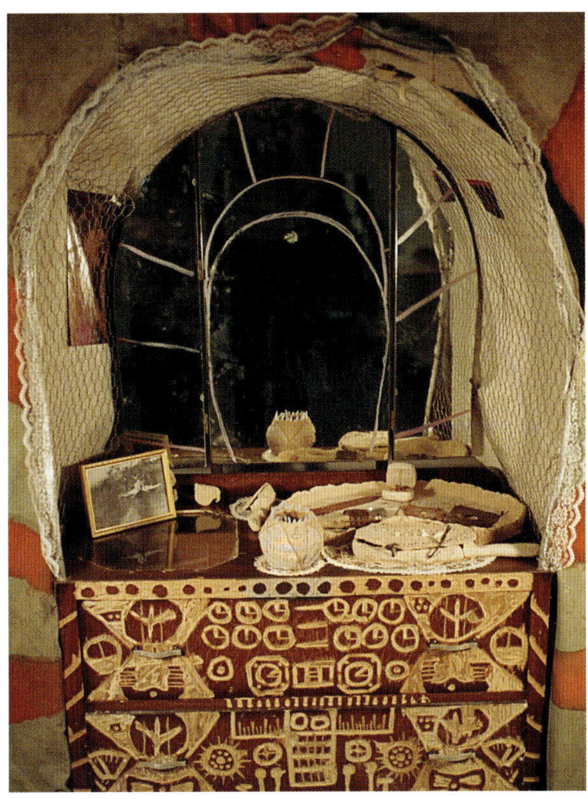

about what he had written, and this was the result. It is a cockpit of identity where the references to technology and conflict usually implicit in the world of the jet fighter pilot are exchanged for a feminized domesticity; the cockpit canopy is the taped-up glass mirror of a dressing table that provides the ground into which Perry has carved the plane's controls to look like ritualized hieroglyphs. The dressing table – gendered as cockpit – is the locus of shifting identity, of doing your hair and putting your face on. Pulling out the lower drawer of this table reveals a sequence of photographs encased in clay, like a film strip with images moving from Michelangelo's *David* (a pose that Perry has returned to many times as the artistic epitome of a certain masculinity), a naked Grayson, a naked Grayson with Claire's hair, Grayson in Claire's underwear, and then finally transforming into Claire.

This image of an 'Oxfam Auntie' was hidden in one drawer, the drawer above contained a single image of Claire peering through a frame of ceramic tiles and a pot in the shape of a hairy pair of testicles, while on top of the dressing table were brush, comb and hand mirror 'moulded from clay alongside dinky pots decorated with penises – I made caveman versions because my skills were crude'. The dressing table was then surrounded with a parachute painted with sunrays to look like an altarpiece. Looking back, Perry recognized the work's significance: 'It was a mishmash but it had an energy to it which none of my previous work had had. Art was no longer something I did for the lecturers, nine to five. Now I wanted to make art about me.'[8]

Ideas within *Transvestite Jet Pilots* are consistent within Perry's subsequent work – the tension of identity within transvestism, the use of the vessel as a reliquary within which those tensions can be played out, the domestic as a site for celebration, subversion and satire – but the work can also be seen in the context of shifts in sculpture at the time. It had been admired by Helen Chadwick, a visiting lecturer at Portsmouth. Chadwick's own work sought to highlight and complicate conventional situations – in the home and workplace – concerning the objectification of women. Two years previously, she had created the performance sculpture *Train of Thought* (1978–79), a fairly realistic

slice of a London Underground train carriage, which provided the stage for
a performance that she said was about 'the conflict between strangers. The
way a female might react inwardly to a male on the Tube. It was very much
a sexual arena – harassment a-gogo. The way a kind of formal public place
like a Tube train can suddenly precipitate into a very intimate, disturbing
contest.'[9] Chadwick's work shifts between sculpture and performance. This
is a distinction that Perry would later play with in his use of ceramics, not
just as an extension or reflection of performance, but also in terms of the way
he has consistently framed his turn to ceramics in relation to his transvestism,
dressing up in the clothes of another. As sculpture, however, both Chadwick's
Train of Thought and Perry's *Transvestite Jet Pilots* mark a move towards the object
as an image communicating narrative, symbolization and subjectivity in ways
that sculpture had shied away from since the 1960s when process, materials
and abstraction were the norm. Many of the visiting tutors at Portsmouth –
including Chadwick, Edward Allington, Nicholas Pope and Anish Kapoor
– illuminate different reactions to this shift, which, alongside the *Outsiders*
exhibition, demonstrably established the tone of Perry's artistic voice.[10]

This voice was additionally supported by what Perry described as 'a crash
course in bohemian lifestyle', in early 1980s London.[11] Perry's memoir of
this period reveals how first his girlfriend, Jennifer Binnie, and Veronica,
their flatmate in Portsmouth, and then Jennifer's elder sister, Christine,
created a mood in which everything was up for question:

> 'Dare I take anything seriously?' because Jen and Veronica would pounce
> on me if I did. It was an extremely creative ambience because it meant
> I questioned what I was doing until it stood up to a very rigorous test of their
> acerbic wit. I revelled in the masquerade of us being cruel to each other. Nor
> were we frightened of being naff, which was being prepared to be unstylish
> and old-fashioned in order to be personally expressive – naff became a strong
> force in my creativity… [Christine] was the first person I knew who liked
> ABBA in a postmodern way. They were at the tail end of their success, but
> [Christine], before they'd even come to an end, was being ironic about them,
> enthusing, 'Wow! ABBA! Oh, I love ABBA!' which was uncool, because
> everyone else was raving about punk rock. ABBA was in opposition to punk.
> The flip I got from the sisters was to kick against the pricks, twist things round
> and say, 'This could be funny if we just turn it over'.[12]

Twisting things round and turning them over was to become the basis for
Perry's developing identity as an artist. As a student Perry concentrated on
drawing and sculpture but the purchase of a camera – encouraged by one
of his tutors – led to the first photographs of Claire. Then, in 1980, he and

Andrew Wilson

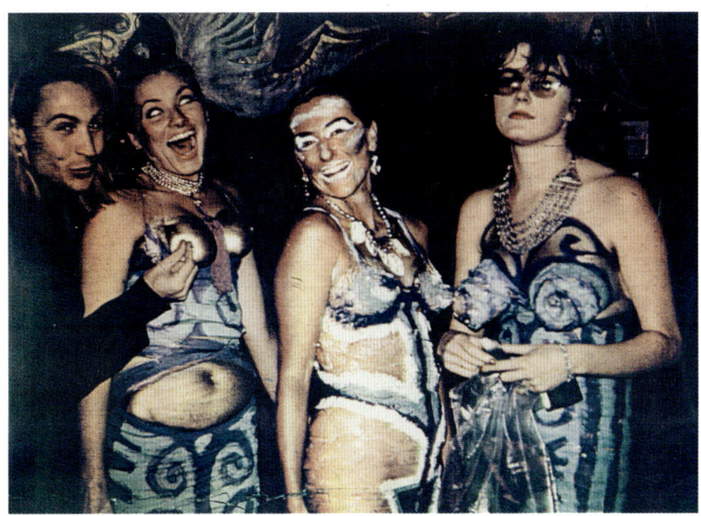

Marilyn, Jennifer Binnie, Christine Binnie and Wilma Johnson, Sellotape Dresses at Crowndale Road, 1984

Jennifer spent the summer in London visiting Christine who lived in a squat in Carburton Street near Warren Street with a pre-Culture Club Boy George, Marilyn, Princess Julia and others.[13] Earlier that Easter, Christine, Jennifer and Princess Julia had presented a performance at the Blitz Club that was a foretaste of what would, the following year, become the Neo Naturist Cabaret. Singing *Death Where is Thy Sting?* beside Iain R. Webb as St Sebastian, the sisters, wearing sack dresses, handed out Cadbury's creme eggs to assembled clubland communicants. The squat and the Coffee Spoon café, set up by Christine, became the site for similar events that then also spawned performances and fancy-dress parties back in Portsmouth the following year.[14]

Fancy-dress, performance and the growing normalization of Perry's transvestism coincided and was strengthened by his contact with the nascent New Romantic scene centred on the Coffee Spoon:

There were occasional cabaret evenings at the café, where we took it in turns to put on a performance. John Maybury had been honing his film-making skills while befriending Derek Jarman and showed a super-8 film of his pretty boyfriend dancing at Andrew Logan's studio while reflected in a cracked mirror. His other reel was of [Christine] dancing. In the film she was running toward the camera and at the exact moment she actually burst through the paper screen dressed in the same clothes.[15]

The performance that Perry and Jennifer presented there was the first time he had dressed as a transvestite for an audience – as the imperious television cook Fanny Craddock arriving into the café on his motorbike to cook banana flambé with her sidekick Johnny (Jennifer). The Coffee Spoon, the squats nearby and St Martin's School of Art provided co-ordinates for the New Romantic club scene. Steve Strange, progenitor and club promoter, described the defining dandyism caught in his own club nights at Billy's and Blitz:

Boy George was there in his kimono, Stephen Linard in his Culloden outfit, Marilyn, Claire the Hair and Tranny Paul. Pinkietessa…dressed like an all-pink, home-made version of Bo Peep…. Everyone made an effort to look as different as possible, drawing influence for their looks from the unlikeliest

of places. One night David Claridge and Daniel James turned up as
characters from Thunderbirds. St Martins was at its height of creativity,
and the bright sparks of the fashion department seemed to be using the
club as its common room. People stood in the Soho rain in gold braid
and pill box hats, waiting to get in. Cossacks and queens mingled happily
as narcissism ran riot. Billy's attracted a clique of outrageous people like
a magnet. It was bizarre. All these people were dressed like royalty, while
in reality they were just ex-punks running up the clothes on their mum's
sewing machines at home in the suburbs or living in the nearby squats
in Warren Street and Great Titchfield Street.... Every week the clothes
would be different, as people constantly tried to outdo each other.[16]

The Neo Naturists grew out of Christine Binnie's experiences as a life model
at St Martin's as much as out of cabaret entertainments she had started staging
at clubs such as Blitz and St Moritz in 1979. Paradoxically both innocent and
contrived in character, the performances of the Neo Naturists – which also
included the painter Wilma Johnson alongside Perry and Jennifer Binnie
at its core – represented the Binnies' 'sensible girl upbringing: things like
don't waste anything and learn to use Calor gas to cook your dinners as
that will always be useful for the rest of your life. Being sensible and being
sensible doing something really stupid (but it wasn't really stupid) was a
really important aspect of Neo Naturism.'[17] It invoked a mix of retro sixties
hippiedom, a clash of town with country (or at least a suburban countryside),
the aesthetics of the 'bring and buy' or village fete, Girl Guideish sensibleness,
and became increasingly structured around culinary ritual (usually involving
Calor gas camping cookers).[18] The aim was for 'an honest revival of true sixties
spirit – which involves living one's life more or less naked and occasionally
manifesting it into a performance for which the main theme is body paint'.[19]
Articulated by its Girl Guide camp outlook, Neo Naturism brought William
Blake and Samuel Palmer, Cecil Collins and the Neo-Romanticism of the
1940s into direct collision with the slick gesturing of New Image Painting
and Neo-Expressionism, the world of Haysi Fantayzee's song *John Wayne
is Big Leggy* and the clubland post-punk New Romantic outlook that had
emerged and then flourished at Billy's, Blitz, Hell, Cha Cha Cha and Taboo.

In the summer of 1982, Perry finished college, and left Portsmouth for
London, arriving in time for one of the defining Neo Naturist performances
– a week-long residency at the B2 Gallery in Wapping run by David Dawson
and Roger Ely. The gallery was completely taken over for the week, with no
distinction between sleeping, eating, planning performances, going to the
Prospect of Whitby pub for refreshment and the performance itself. They built
environments in the gallery and at low tide performed on the beach outside;

Andrew Wilson

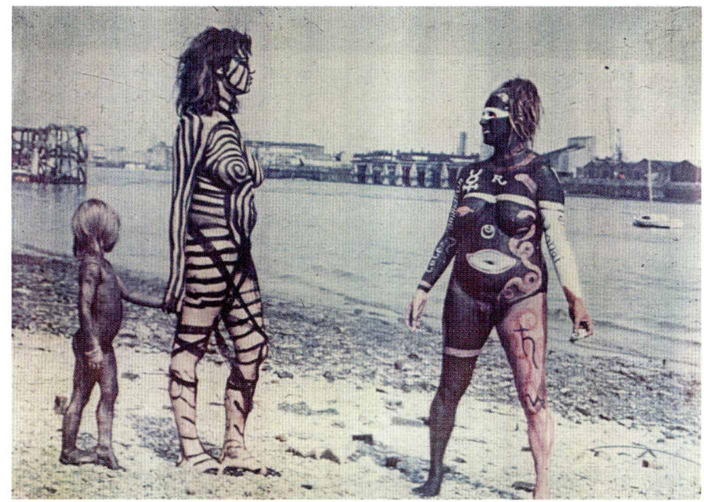

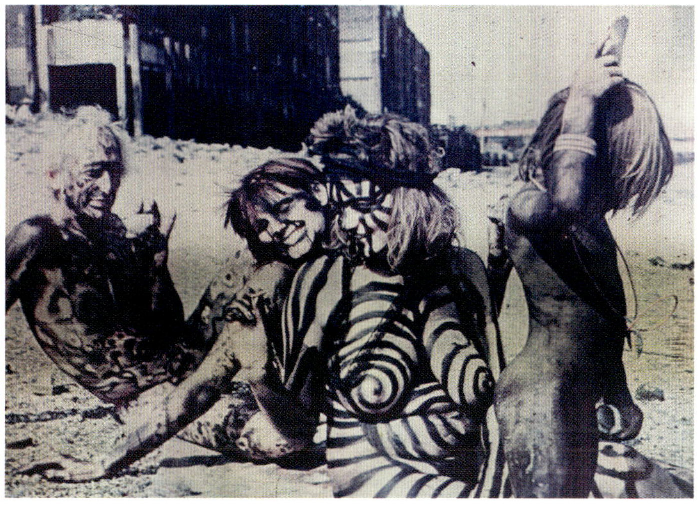

they made a huge bed where they slept in long lines. Each day of the residency took a different theme: Art, Fashion, Macbeth, Black Rapport, and Punk. For Macbeth Day, Perry was outside the gallery with other members collecting the Forest of Dunsinane. The evening included a short ten-minute version of the play 'with seven witches because they were the favourite part. [Christine] was Mrs Macbeth: she had an industrial cooker on stage and spent most of the performance draped in tartan, frying Scottish pancakes. I was the forest of Dunsinane, holding up a bundle of buddleia that I'd ripped up from an old East End bomb site, and covered in body paint that was mixed with Scottish oats so I had a crusty tree trunk texture all over me. The porridge set hard…clinging to the hairs on my body…. It was very painful to move…. After the performance we were directed to sprint out of the gallery screaming, so I hobbled down the road feeling quite vulnerable.'[20]

By 1982, much of the scene around Carburton Street in 1980 had moved to another squat that straddled Warren Street and Euston Road, where David Holah and Stevie Stewart of the fashion label Bodymap, John Maybury, Cerith Wyn Evans, Geoffrey Hinton and Christine Binnie lived. Early in 1983 Perry and Jennifer Binnie moved into the burnt-out basement of a house that Marilyn had previously squatted at Crowndale Road near Mornington Crescent in Camden. Christine Binnie took over the top floor; Wilf Rogers and Jackie had the upstairs room; the filmmakers Cerith Wyn Evans and Angus Cook (with Sophie Muller they styled themselves as International Film and Video) had the ground floor. The artist Firewolf lived nearby in a house from which he had removed all the floorboards.[21] At the corner of Crowndale Road was a squat run as a gallery by Slim Barrett, which occasionally showed work by both Perry and Jennifer Binnie. The Crowndale Road squat continued until 1986 – and marked the period of greatest activity for the Neo Naturists – performances with Michael Clark, for Bodymap fashion shows, for the launch

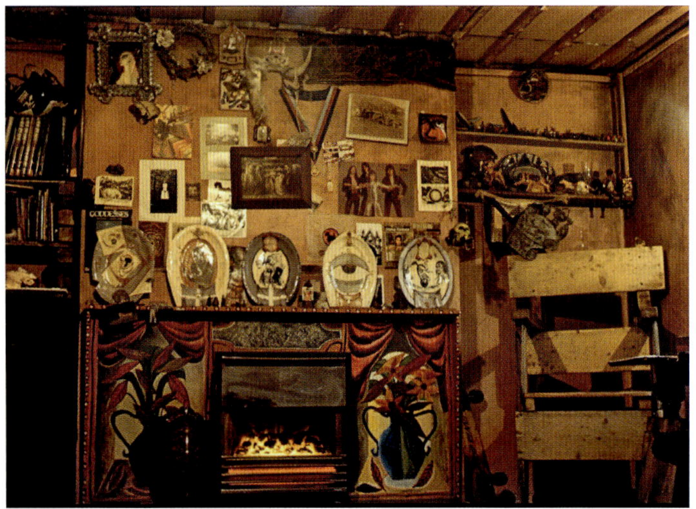

43 Crowndale Road,
Camden Town, 1983

of Derek Jarman's book *Dancing Ledge*, for the openings of exhibitions and for Andrew Logan's Alternative Miss World as well as performances at the Zap Club in Brighton, Notre Dame Hall, Riverside Studios, B2 and the James Birch galleries, the Fridge, the Dome, Centre Point fountains and Henley Regatta, among many other venues.

The Neo Naturists took their place among the extreme personae found in London's New Romantic clubs, which, Robert Elms has observed, weren't places 'for those who dressed up for the occasion but for those who dressed up as a way of life'.[22] This chimed absolutely with the Neo Naturist aesthetic as explained by Christine Binnie, that 'if everyone is dressing up in very theatrical outfits, it was taking it as far as you could to paint the clothes onto your body and have a different outfit every time you went out'.[23] Despite this, the Neo Naturists enacted a distinct clash of cultures: between their resolute unfashionability (all patchouli and body paint) and the studied fashionability of the post-Punk New Romantic club culture they moved through; between an already discredited sixties communal rustic new-ageyness and the first glimpses of an eighties self-regarding urban Thatcherism. The contemporaneous performances of 1960s veterans Bruce Lacey and Jill Bruce, for instance, had strong links with shamanism, attracted the attentions of occultists and connected with beliefs of earth-magick and witchcraft.[24] Yet, even if the Neo Naturists performed with similar materials alongside Lacey and Bruce and others, their outlook was one that found its authenticity and core elsewhere.[25] A constant source of 'reality' was its amateurish spirit. As Perry remembers, 'Christine never capitalized on Neo Naturism. It was frowned upon to optimize the career chances of things, she never repeated things and she never compromised on the un-entertainingness of it. She wasn't one to have had a rehearsed show in the eighties – she thought that would be really selling out to do a rehearsal because that would smack of entertainment.'[26] What the Neo Naturists enacted was not so much performance (that would ordinarily call for rehearsal) but ritual based on everyday actions, such as cooking and cleaning, or bodily process, through which they celebrated nudity and the Mother Goddess.

From 1982, Perry took part in many of the Neo Naturist performances though the ideas behind Neo Naturism and the direction it took were almost exclusively the concern of Christine Binnie and Wilma Johnson. Nevertheless, the experience acted as a springboard for Perry's filmmaking, which became his

Andrew Wilson

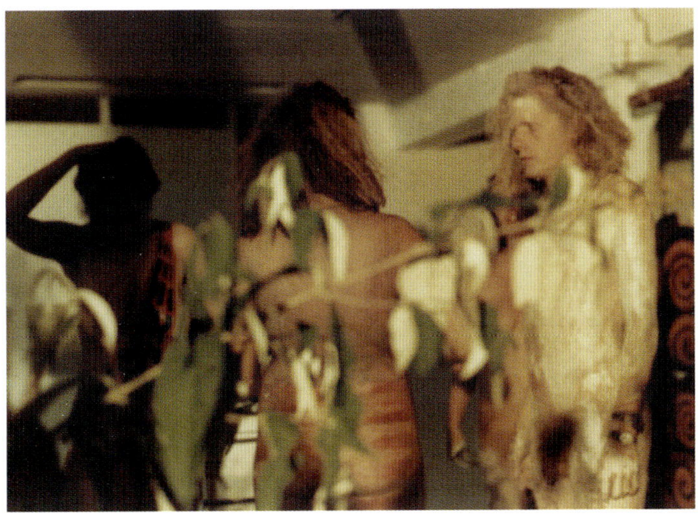

Macbeth Day, B2, July 1982

primary medium until about 1985. Like his contemporaries John Maybury and Cerith Wyn Evans, as well as Derek Jarman, Perry looked in part to the work of Kenneth Anger for an approach to his subjects. Yet his films, imbued with the village fete spirit of the Neo Naturists, were more 'Inauguration of the Guest Bedroom' than 'Inauguration of the Pleasure Dome'. *Bungalow Depression* (1981) shows a day in the life of a Women's Institute member set in Wannock, a suburban village near Eastbourne where Jennifer and Christine Binnie's parents lived and their mother was a leading light in the local WI. Perry acts out this figure as Claire through nine episodes from breakfast to evening sherry. In many respects this is a counterpart to Jennifer Binnie's earlier film, *Wannock Weekend*, in which the Binnie sisters, with Johnson, Perry, Wyn Evans and others spend a weekend on the South Downs in an evocation of both the romanticism of Blake and Palmer, and the Neo-Romantic, pastoral surrealism of Cecil Collins. *The Green Witch and Merry Diana* (1984) provides an account of a woman cursed with a tail, set in London and the Sussex Downs, while *Odd Steve 'n' Steven* (1984) is a story of love, marriage and the happy birth of a devil child. In this film, Angus Cook's alchemical cooking of lead and his Buddhist toast and honey tea ceremony in the back garden of Crowndale Road becomes more powerfully magickal because of their ordinary domesticity; in Perry's films alchemical ritual is shown to be more like high tea than something more mysteriously shadowed and troubling. Ultimately, the films parody the seriousness in which Anger's work was held at that time and were, as Perry has admitted, 'almost like one long in-joke about the time and the naffness of new-ageyness and mysticism'.[27] This is, however, to deny them their very real power that was enhanced by their suburban, slightly comic narrative representation as well as by the balance of innocence and contrivance, which forms the basis of Perry's home-made film aesthetic.

If the years at Warren Street and Crowndale Road mark one highpoint for the Neo Naturists, for Perry they also mark a clear turning point. In the late 1970s Christine Binnie had completed a ceramics diploma at Eastbourne College of Art, so it was natural for her in 1983 to encourage Perry to accompany her to the Central Institute's ceramic evening classes that she was attending. Although the focus of Perry's practice at Portsmouth was film, he had used ceramics and within a year the balance had shifted to pots. Pots could be seen as existing between sculpture and performance in ways that the assemblages that Perry had continued

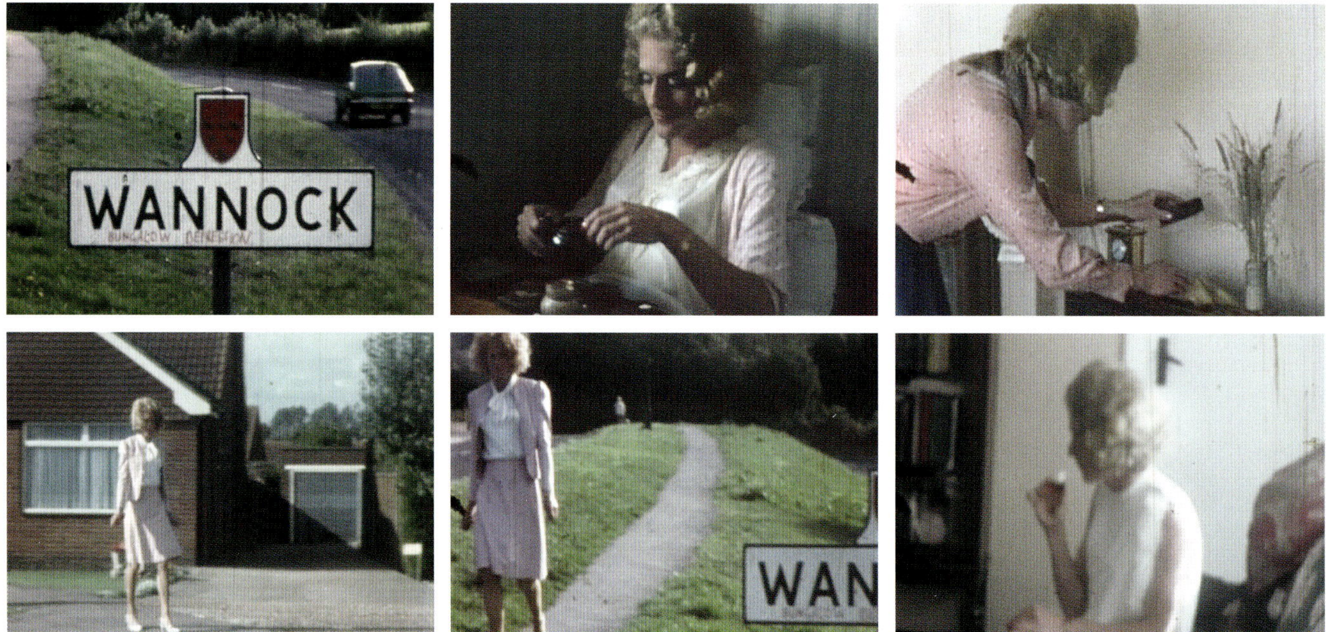

Bungalow Depression, 1981

to make in London, such as a chicken-footed sculpture of a shed – *Baba Yaga's Hut* (1983) – just did not. The connections between Neo Naturism and transvestism could be easily transmitted through his quickly developing attitude to ceramics. As Perry has outlined:

> The Neo Naturist spirit helped me handle the naffness that pottery was seen as, it gave me the tools to handle things that were seen as really uncool. Anybody that cared about fitting in and doing the right thing were mods and in that sense we were the rockers. We let it all hang out and we didn't really care. We just wanted to express ourselves and yes, we made some mistakes, but so what, and that was our ethos. What I picked up from the Neo Naturists, more than anything, was the spirit of the occasion and the freewheeling ability to flip things. I called it going with the line of most resistance: choose the thing that people will find the most ugly and then find a way to make it beautiful.[28]

The Neo Naturists found beauty in representations of ugliness, naffness and home-made amateurishness; their work was not entertainment or a rehearsal but instead the realization of life adorned. Perry equally embraced this sense of ugliness as a means to find beauty in life. Just as Christine Binnie was vocal in her adoration for ABBA, Perry sought out 1970s nylon shirts from charity shops.[29] Although all of this could be construed as a desire to be different and show off, as was the norm for the New Romantic, it was also echoed in the out

    Andrew Wilson

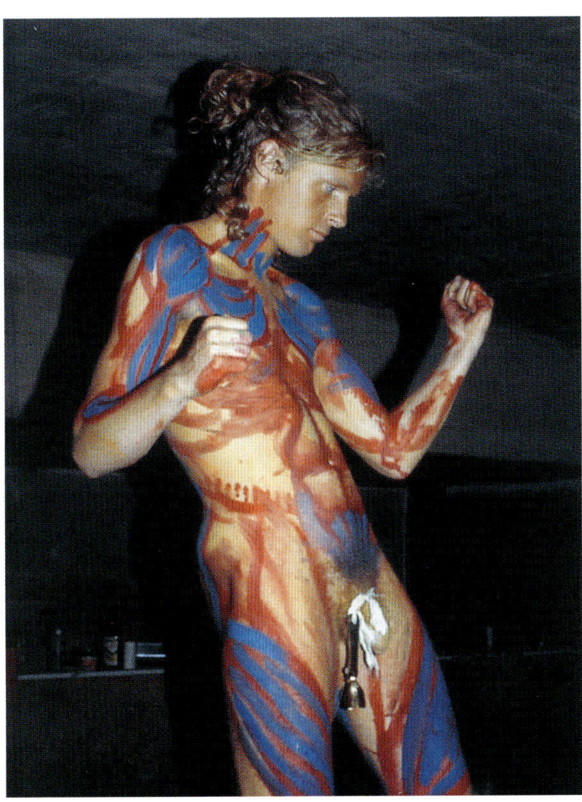

Grayson Perry in Neo Naturist 'Punk Keep Fit' performance at The Fridge, Brixton, London, 1982

of kilter appearance of his ceramic work, as well as the character of the Neo Naturist Cabaret. The development of Claire's persona as a suburban aunt figure also connects directly with this outlook. The significant reference here is to the body: the pot as body, a body to be adorned or dressed. Perry quickly recognized the pot's potential to become a costume and be suggestive of an accompanying and generative activity – positioned between craft, domesticity and ritual activities – as much as something to be dressed by him (a distinction that is significant given Perry's transvestism). The pot is not decorated in an additive manner, but becomes an integrated ground for an image-system of grotesques that challenges the norms of life. It is in the nature of the image-system that Perry's pots move away from an identification with Neo Naturism.

One of the abiding principles of Neo Naturism for Christine Binnie was a lack of danger – which for an avant-garde art practice held its own dangers. This went hand in hand with the village fete, handmade, amateurish approach that valued authenticity over slickness. Perry took this further, explaining, 'When I started making plates, it was about how I could wind people up…. I'm attracted to things that make me feel uncomfortable, that make me think, "Oh my god I've stepped over the mark here". So I started using sexual and fascist imagery.'[30] Perry's description of his second exhibition in 1985 as 'satanic and suburban'[31] went against Neo Naturism, as Christine Binnie explained: 'Neo Naturism hasn't got anything to do with S & M – well, its sensible – it's much more C of E.'[32] Reiterated by Jennifer Binnie's assertion that 'the main point is that we're in the nude but we're not in black leather and stuff like that. We're not sexy and that's shocking in itself…. I think it shocks people that we're naked and do things like cooking.'[33] Their rituals were neither confrontational nor titillating, as Christine said – they may have been naked but they weren't 'sexually packaged'.[34] However, neither were the Neo Naturists expressing prelapsarian innocence and Perry's masculine presence had set up a natural tension: 'I was always nervously aware that the dangling presence of a male member painted blue with a bell tied to it lent the performance an extra edge to which some of the crowd could take exception.'[35]

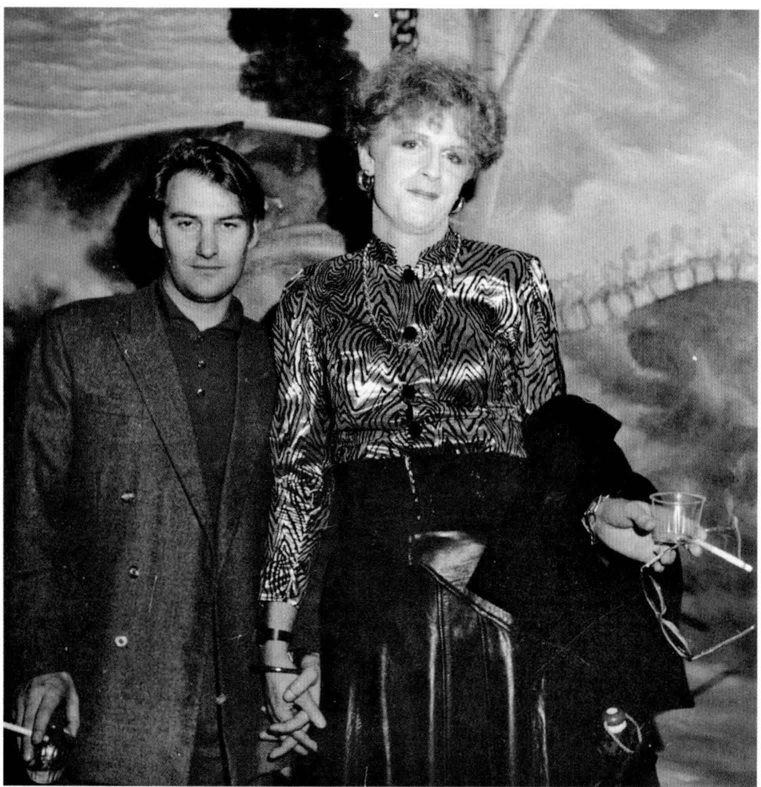

James Birch and Grayson Perry
as Claire, 1987

At a time when studio ceramics was still in thrall to the formal idea of a subject matter being defined by the well-made pot, a realization of a truth both to materials and process, Perry located authenticity elsewhere: not in the material of clay or full attention to the processes of making, but in the ways to make a pot have a purpose and meaning as a carrier of more subversive themes. Part of this revolved around the base form of his pots – not created by throwing clay on a wheel, but instead summoned up by coiling – in which the world of the artist is replaced by the different intensities of the hobbyist or obsessive outsider. Alongside Perry's use of coiling, the decoration of his pots by sprigging (the application of press-moulded elements), the scratching of images into the pot's surface, the stamping of inscriptions, slip trailing to provide a decorative or inscribed raised surface on the pot, utilize the decorative vocabulary of small-scale English vernacular country potteries, and especially those that looked to medieval or Roman models such as Edward Bingham's 19th-century Castle Hedingham Pottery in Essex, close to where Perry grew up. The realization of these intensities in ceramics – the obsessive, the hobbyist and the country potter – initially manifested itself as a form of shock. At evening classes he decorated his pots with swastikas and other images designed specifically to provoke outrage from the middle-class middle-aged ladies who worked beside him.[36] Perry's elaboration of a private magickal and mystical language for his ceramic work brought together masonic and Tarot imagery (Christine Binnie read Tarot cards at that time) with a mythic understanding of the spirit of place realized in images of Essex, overlaid by all manner of brutal perverse sexualized imagery.

Perry's imagery and strategies seemed at home in the context of the James Birch Gallery and Birch & Conran Fine Art, where he exhibited between 1984 and 1990. Alongside Jennifer Binnie (whose first exhibition there was a few months before Perry's), the programme included the surrealism of Eileen Agar, Reuben Mednikoff, Grace Pailthorpe and John Banting and the rituals

Andrew Wilson

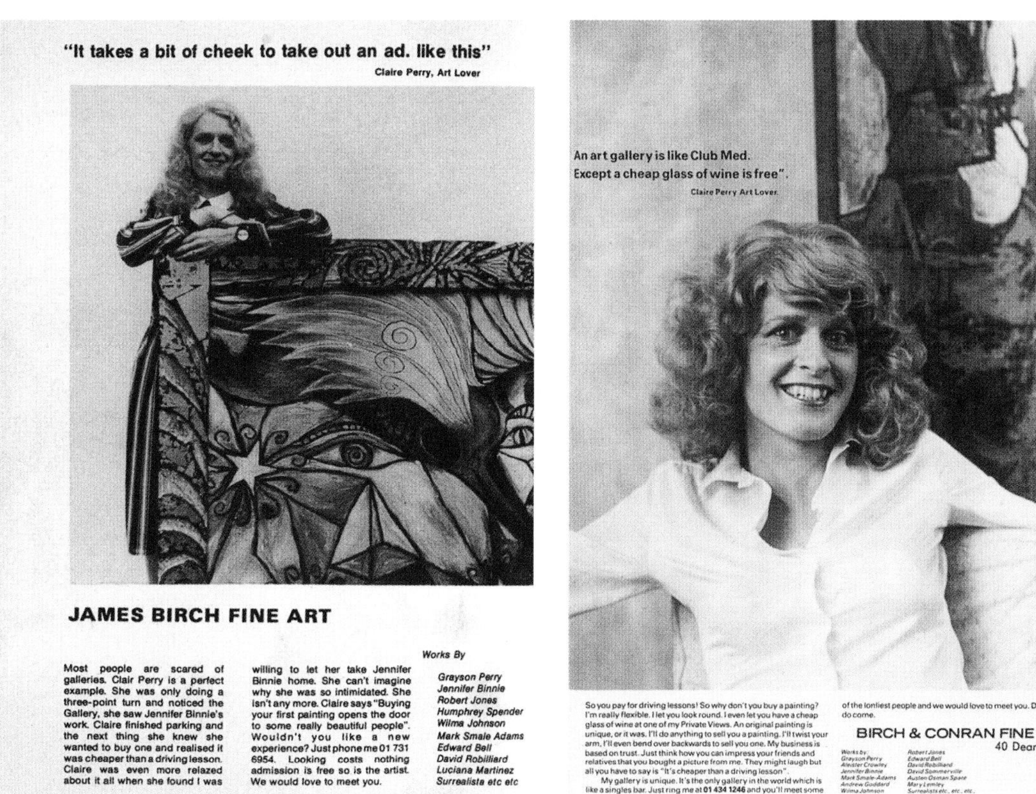

James Birch Fine Art and Birch & Conran Fine Art advertisements in *The Fred*, 1985 and 1987

and paintings of Bruce Lacey. Perry was fascinated by shamanism and folk ritual, the heraldry of the masonic movement and the occult. Near to Blitz was the Freemasons' Hall of the United Grand Lodge of England and the surrounding streets between Holborn and Covent Garden were also home to shops supplying the regalia of the movement. One friend, Timothy Prus, an associate of David Dawson's at B2, gave Perry a bag full of this regalia that was then made into sprig moulds, which found their way onto his plates and pots. This loaded imagery took its place within an anti-fashion sensibility that mixed suburban Essex with a blighted landscape of witchcraft and turned Perry's autobiography of disturbed childhood and transvestism into a mythic narrative that formed a frame for a portrayal of perverted sexuality.

The printed catalogue list for Perry's first exhibition at the James Birch Gallery in 1984 is framed with a nod to the Arts and Crafts movement of William Morris: faux medieval borders to the sheet are initialled G and P; pottery is described as 'The Oldest of the Arts' and in the centre of the sheet are two images – both inscribed 'Grayson Perry' – one depicting artisanal potters of a bygone age and the other a dominatrix giving pleasure, the oldest of the arts. The exhibition sold well for the Christmas market and was made up entirely of plates, pots and little sculptures, including a small ceramic throne to coprophilia, *Saint Diana (Let Them Eat Shit)* (pp. 72–73). They were all made at evening class and communicated Perry's dominant trio of subjects: the shock tactic of sexual perversion, money as a central preoccupation of the 1980s, and the flat, unromantic, suburban landscape of his childhood Essex. The majority of the works were press-moulded plates – such as *Kinky Sex* or a series of oval dishes, some flat-ended and intended to be stood on end (a photograph of his room at Crowndale Road shows them arranged on the mantelpiece). Essentially he was making objects for display rather than use and it is apposite that for his last film, the feature-length *The Poor Girl* (1985) (p. 94), he created the name of Welsh Dresser Films, and not just because the film was largely funded by the sale of his ceramics. For his second exhibition the same year, Perry had even hoped to display his ceramics on a dresser as a way of emphasizing the country vernacular dimension within the work.

In 1986, Perry left Crowndale Road for Leytonstone, where the following year he installed his first kiln. This cemented his identification with ceramics, just as *The Poor Girl* ended his relationship with film. Yet however tempting it might be to compartmentalize Perry's work by medium – sculpture, film, ceramics, textile, photography and performance – that would not adequately describe its ambition. His work and an understanding of its subject matter cannot be approached strictly as a direct product of one medium or another. However pretentious the term 'General Artist' might seem, it describes the intention of the work more exactly than the medium-specific 'poet', 'filmmaker' or 'potter'. Just over fifty years before Perry described himself in this way in *i-D* magazine, the surrealist John Banting had adopted the same epithet on a business card that listed the effects and techniques he could bring to bear in his work as 'General Artist'.[37] By contrast, Perry's post-therapy adoption of the term 'Transvestite Potter' has occurred more recently and is recognition of the way his public persona, particularly since winning the Turner Prize in 2003, is identified both with ceramics and with his transvestism. In the 1980s, his active transvestism, though it formed the basis of his approach to ceramics and had been a subject of films, was still a more privately expressed obsession and was yet to result in the public persona Claire has now become.

One assessment of Perry's work, looking back over the last thirty years, might point to his evolving and developing skill – how his bombs of content have been becoming ever more stealthy. Another would attend to his growing public persona, his popularity as a kind of spokesperson for contemporary issues, largely through television. Yet another would be to look to Claire and recognize that since therapy, as Perry admits, she has blossomed.[38] The position that Claire held within his work undoubtedly started to change prior to his embarking on therapy. In the 1980s Claire could occupy a position separate to the work, even if the principle of transvestism was central to the way he approached ceramics

Andrew Wilson

and she figured as a subject. However, in the mid-1990s a definite transition started to unfold with his growing awareness that there was a possibility for Claire's personality and identity to come even more to the fore as a form of work herself. This coincided with the first studio visits by the gallerist Anthony d'Offay, who started to show Perry at this time, yet 'spent more time looking at my photo album of Claire than he did at my work'.[39] This process led naturally to *Claire's Coming Out Speech* in 2000 – a performance ritual slide show at the Laurent Delaye Gallery in which she clearly stated: 'I don't want to be a woman. I am a transvestite.'[40] Perry linked this both to his childhood experience and his life as an artist. Post-therapy, Claire has become a kind of a guide and a witness – a Virgil-like character – within Perry's world-view, just as she had been there on Perry's early teenage walks around the fields and woods. As the fulcrum for a carnivalesque turn-around, Claire has figured publicly both as ordinary and suburban, as well as magickal; she reveals honesty as much as contrivance, perversion and transgression as much as an acceptance of everyday conventions.

It is with this ideal of Claire that the potency and strengths of Perry's work, and what sets him apart from many of his contemporaries can be identified. Claire is who Perry is, just as his art is him and not just something that he does. Perry recognized this with Henry Darger as he was also finding it for himself. If the 1980s had been characterized by forms of transgressive play, the 1990s adopted a veneer of professionalism for its art; the street met the seminar room. Perry could never be mistaken for a YBA – not quite young enough, too naff, too expressive, too involved with narrative and crucially not strategic (other than pursuing the line of most resistance). He may have been collected by Charles Saatchi; he may have moved from James Birch to Anthony d'Offay, but there was no game being played to achieve this. When Perry stood up as Claire in 2003 to accept the Turner Prize and announced that it was about time that a transvestite potter won the Turner Prize, it was indeed as 'freaky'[41] a result as artist and critic Matthew Collings judged it to be. Freaky because Perry seemed to be and has remained as far removed from what was then becoming academic about YBA as it was possible to be. Freaky because Perry has always been uncomfortable with work where the concept might be too neatly sewn up, finding unhealthy the kind of professionalism where 'you know what you are doing and know what you are doing in your work'. As he says it, 'An artist should be searching.'[42]

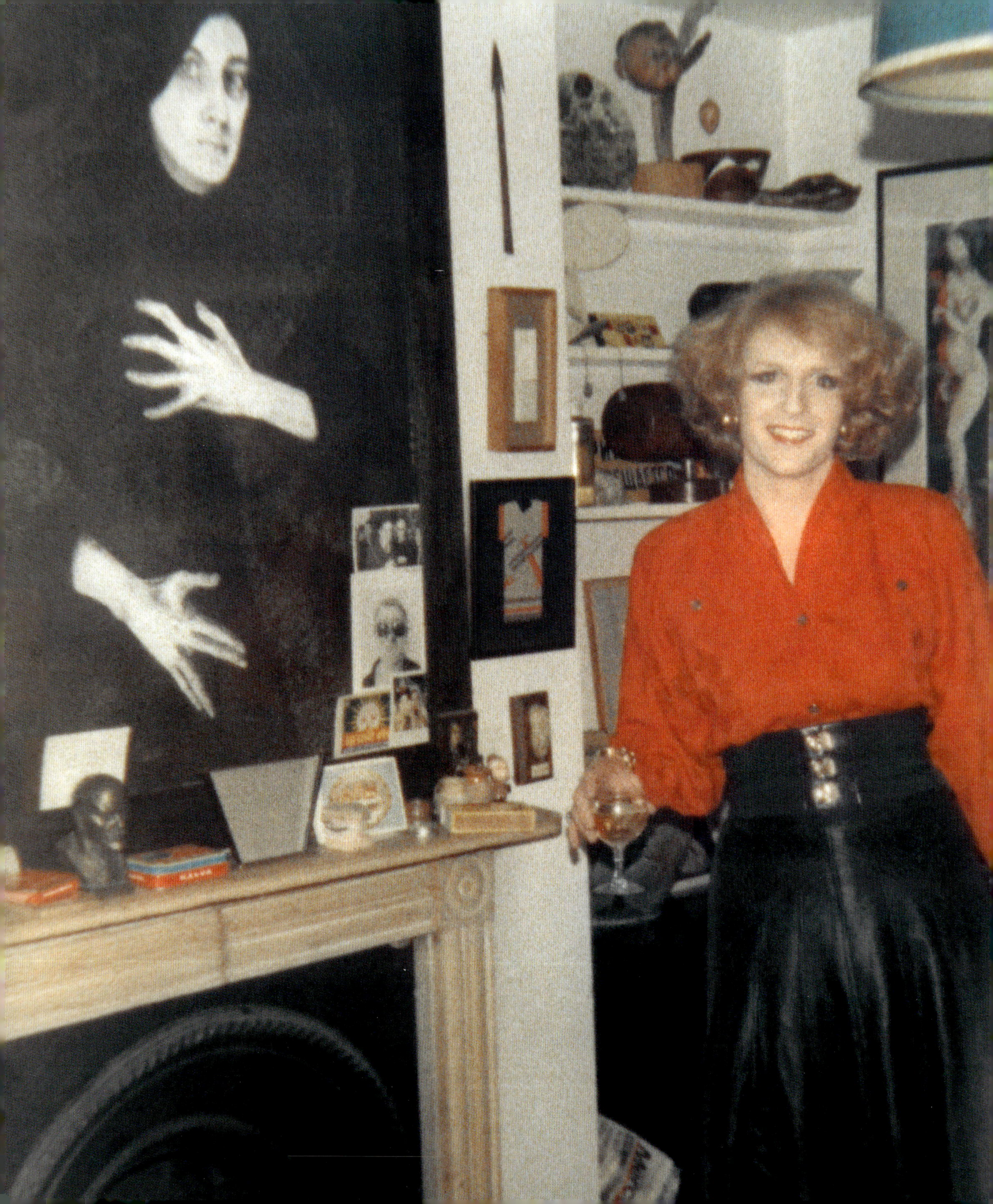

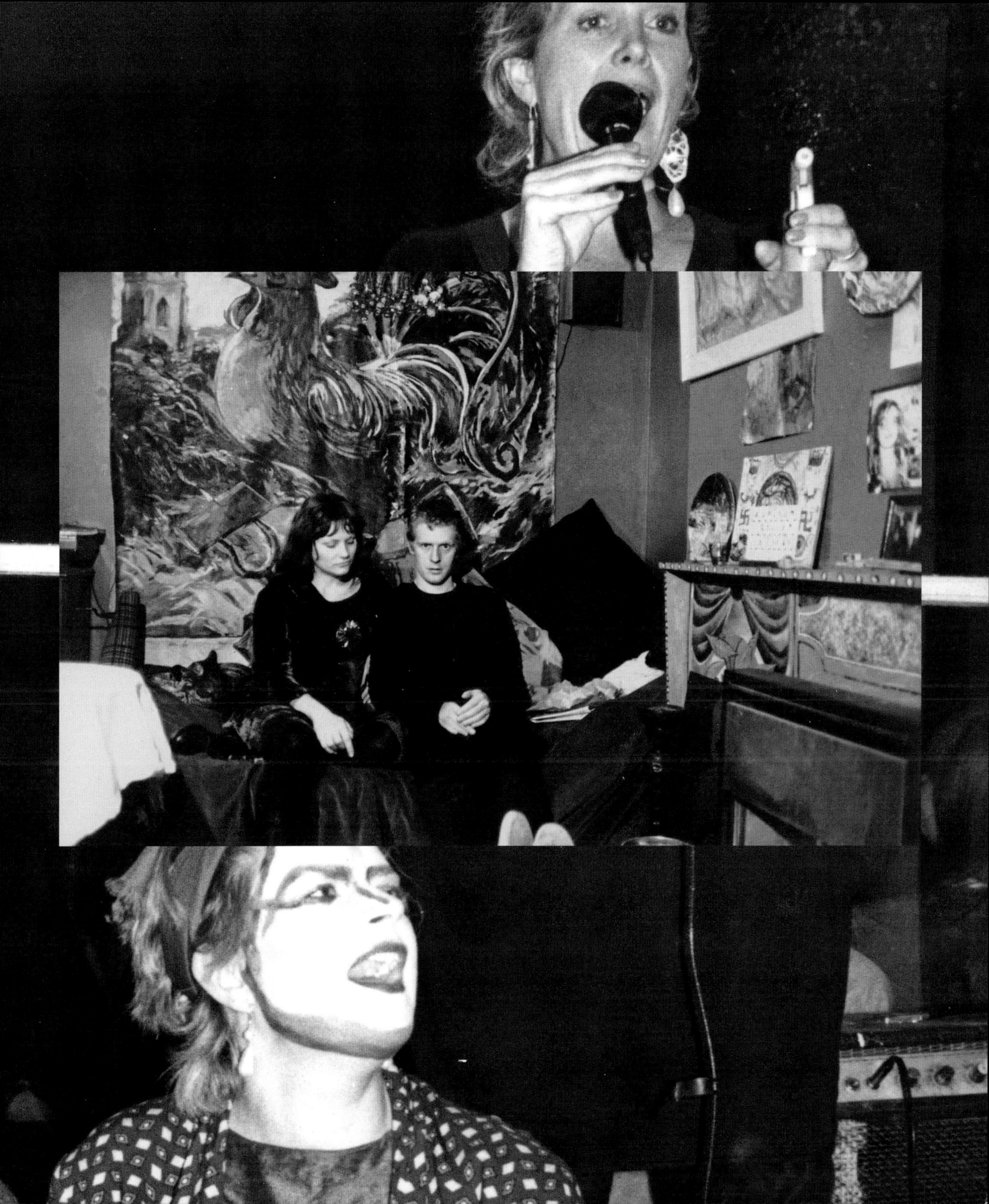

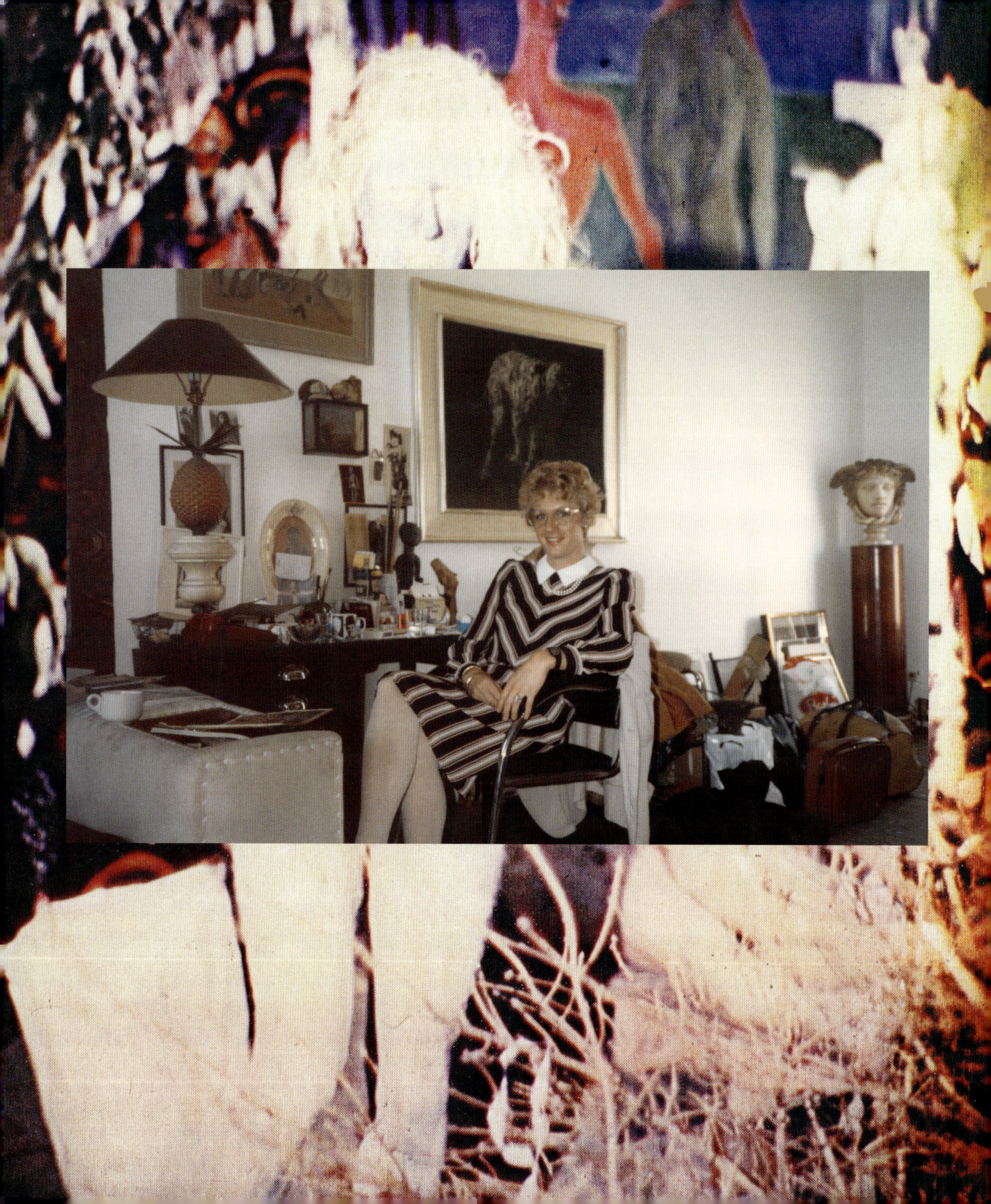

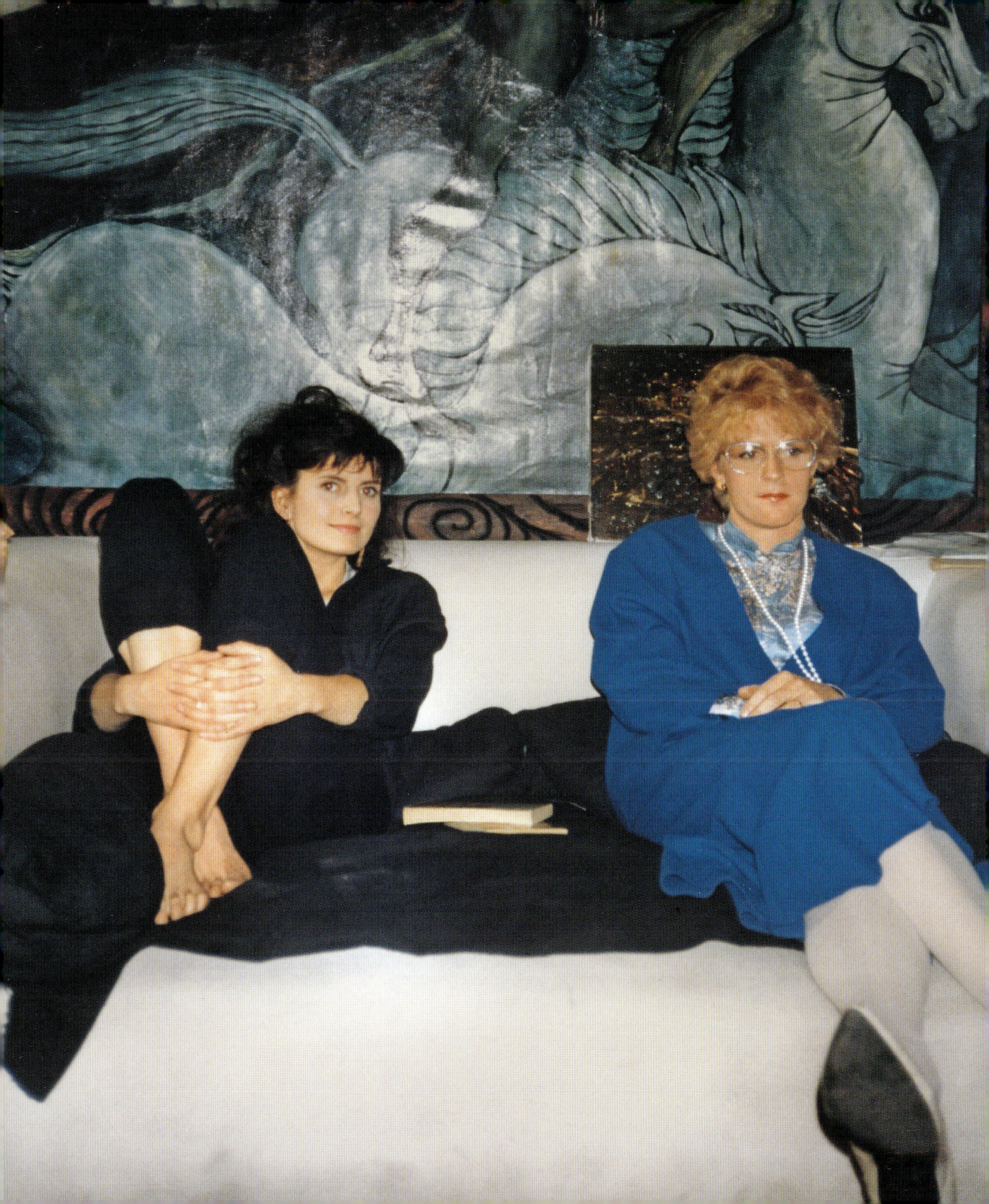

THE ICONOGRAPHY OF GRAYSON PERRY'S 'PRE-THERAPY YEARS'

Catrin Jones

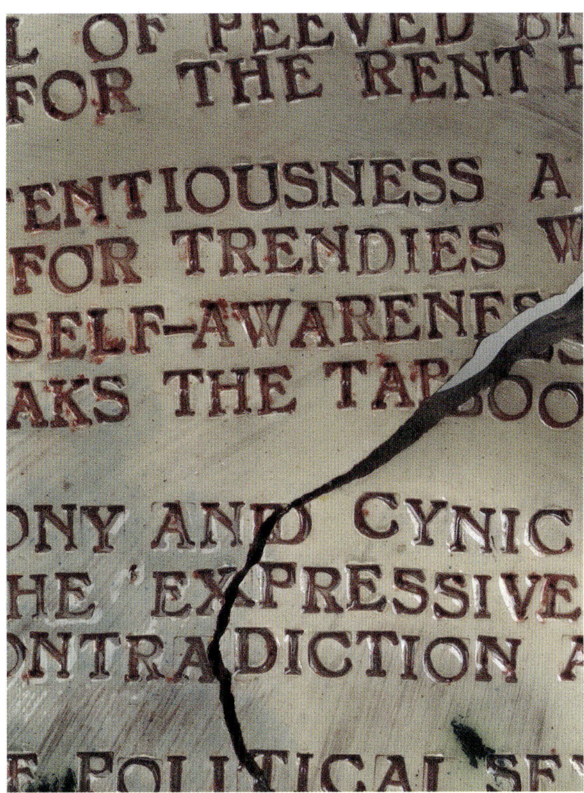

Detail of *Self Portrait Cracked and Warped*, 1985

Grayson Perry 'makes pretentiousness a virtue and makes pots for trendies who hate ceramics, turns self-awareness into a dirty word and breaks the taboo of being original. In his hand, irony and cynicism become as hackneyed as the "expressive brushstroke", compromise and contradiction abound. A true eighties artist. Callous use of political, sexual and moral issues as surface decoration.'[1] What might sound like a particularly savage critical review is in fact the artist's acerbic inscription on *Self Portrait Cracked and Warped* (left and p. 98), a plate from one of Perry's early solo exhibitions. At once mocking his own artistic endeavour, commenting on the context in which it was made, and knowingly distancing himself from the complex decisions involved in creating his work, this pronouncement introduces many of the themes that Perry would continue to explore through his art of the late 1980s and early 1990s.

As the artist would describe it, the early years were also 'the Pre-Therapy Years'.[2] Perry's collaborator on his autobiography *Portrait of the Artist as a Young Girl* (2006), Wendy Jones, noted the contrast between his account of his past in the year 2000, and post-Turner Prize win, when Perry's work had captured the public imagination and he was well on his way to so-called 'National Treasure' status: 'it was a past formed, fired and polished into something smooth.'[3] Like his life story, Perry's art prior to his beginning psychotherapy in the late 1990s has a rawness, often technically as well as in terms of content, in comparison to later pieces. What Perry's early work, whether in clay, film or his sketchbooks, reveals is that all the ingredients that still define his striking and varied practice were there from the outset. The iconography is frequently shocking – often deliberately so – yet has an intricate connection to histories: from Perry's own personal story, his transvestism and his exploration of identity, to the history of the medium he has explored most frequently, ceramics, and those of wider civilization and the artist's role in forming culture.

Perry arrived in London in 1982 having attended art college in Portsmouth. He lived in a squat in Crowndale Road in Camden, crossing paths with various artists, including the Neo Naturists with whom he performed. Following his enrolment in evening classes and rediscovery of clay, Perry began a transition towards working with ceramics more than with any other medium. Perry's first solo show at James

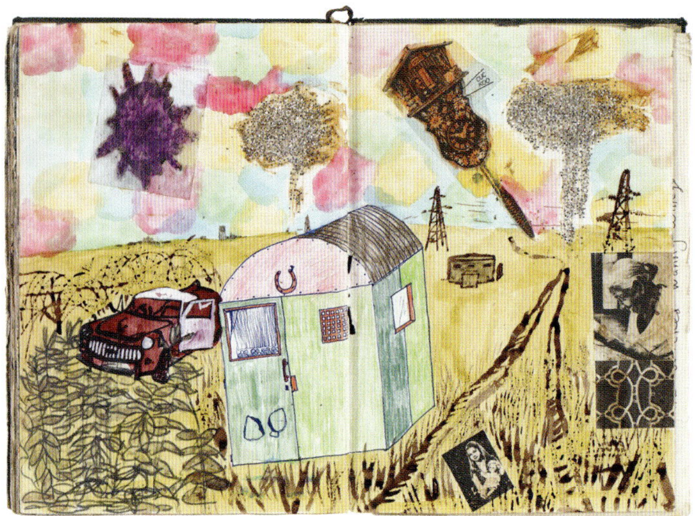

Poems for Sofas Sketchbook,
1981–82

Birch's Waterford Road gallery in 1984 reflected this, consisting as it did primarily of works in clay. Perry continued to create super-8 films, with amusing punning titles like *A Pucker-Lipped Cow* and *Rap of the Sabine Women*, which were screened at 'sardine club' film nights at Birch's gallery. In the 'cultural ghetto of awkward bohemians doing inexplicable things,' Perry saw his film work as an antidote to the serious and self-conscious trendiness of his contemporaries, Cerith Wyn Evans, Leigh Bowery and Boy George, among others.[4] The films suggest the beginnings of an ironic engagement with the medium of ceramics, from naming his production company 'Welsh Dresser Films' to the use of lettering incised in clay for the title sequence of *The Green Witch and Merry Diana* (1984), or an early scene in *The Poor Girl* (1985) (p. 94) that initially looks like an artisanal ceramic production studio and turns out to be a boil-in-the-bag ready meal being served. Very much in line with the Neo Naturists' playful make-do and mend aesthetic, here Perry uses ceramics as a shorthand for parochial Englishness with a dose of ethereal, surrealist fantasy. In contrast, the layered illustrations and collages of Perry's early sketchbooks, to which the artist continues to return for inspiration, reflect an angrier, post-Punk attitude, and 'resonate with the mixture of sexual fantasy and gritty reality that would soon become his hallmark'.[5] What marked out Perry's ceramics as something new was the unusual combination of the two.

Perry as storyteller

Perry's own personal story is by now quite familiar: Perry grew up in Essex, his childhood dramatically affected by his mother's affair with the milkman, the subsequent departure of his father and the arrival of his violent stepfather in the family home; Perry's exploration of his sexuality and realization that he was a transvestite; his creation of an imaginary world with his teddy bear Alan Measles at the helm, and his discovery of the importance of his art as a form of self-expression. Storytelling relies on collective cultural histories and shared knowledge of events. Re-examining the early works reveals how his own and others' stories became Perry's personal iconography. The themes of Essex, his loss of childhood innocence, and his sexuality are woven through the visual and textual stories he tells.

Catrin Jones

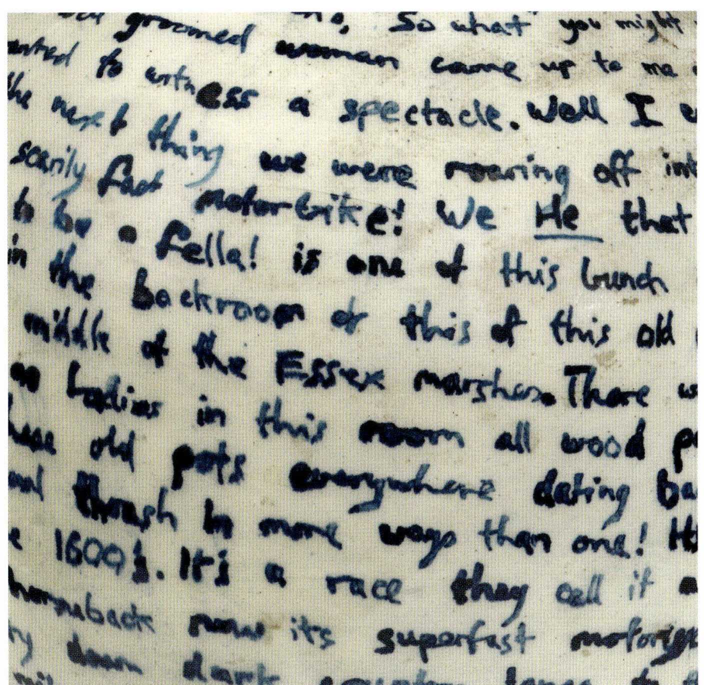

Detail of Untitled, 1987

Perry possesses that rare ability to make a specific story resonate for maximum impact and to reflect his concerns as an artist. Untitled (1987) (p. 114) is a story of two chapters; on one side a pronouncement about Essex, imagination and art, in incised lettering, the other a handwritten tale of somebody's first experience in a transvestite motorbikers' group. Is this one of Perry's own memories? The particular set of circumstances is hardly universal, yet that sense of the excitement of finding a tribe surely has a broader resonance. Untitled (1988) (pp. 124–25), which uses contrasting styles to create the effect of two entirely different pots in one, includes a narrative almost akin to a short story in its ability to conjure up a place and time:

I had a friend who was once too poor to eat for a fortnight. She traipsed through the mud all winter in her white stiletto heeled shoes. She was naturally beautiful and slim. Some days we would smile and crash a party and drink champagne, on others we would search the house for change to buy a bag of chips. Things were different then.

These often humorous and poignant tales may or may not be based on Perry's own experiences or those of people he knew. Certainly, the accounts of friends and early collectors suggest that it was a combination of both. There is a confident and distinctive commentary on class, identity and belonging in these early works. Later, more developed narratives surround such imagined figures as 'Essex everywoman' Julie Cope and Tim Rakewell, the Hogarthian antihero of *The Vanity of Small Differences* (2012) (whom Perry describes as 'my hero'). Perry's early stories are at once more and less specific than those of his later work. The growth in ambition, from short, one-off tales on a single pot to the grand narrative of a tapestry cycle, is surely a result of Perry's success and greater resources, but it also reflects a clear strategy and clearer understanding of the potential impact of imagery and narrative. The nameless protagonists of Untitled (p. 124) and other works would gradually become cyphers through which to explore the themes that interest Perry.

The world of Perry's youth, particularly the specific locations of his childhood in Essex, is closely tied to his identity. This connection is reflected through

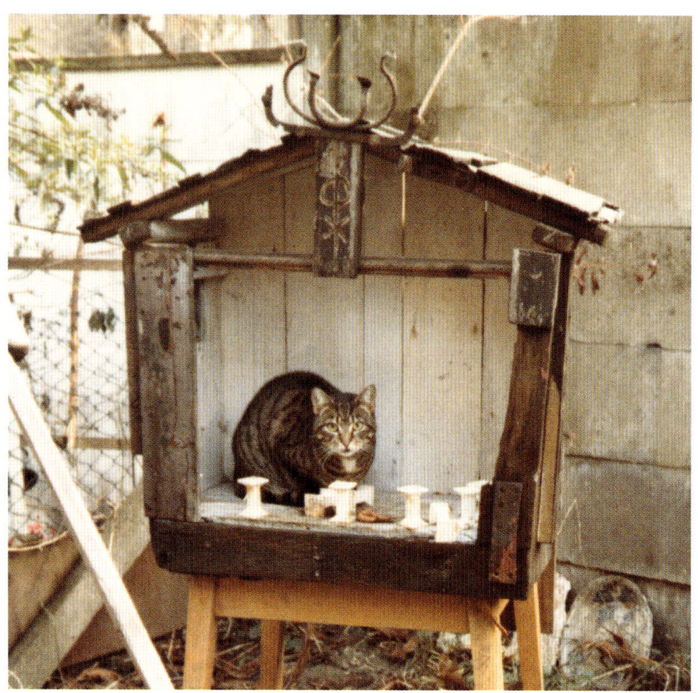

Cat called Baba Yaga in
the garden of the squat
in Crowndale Road

maps of the significant places of Perry's experience: *Map of Essex* (1990) (p. 140) records the towns of Perry's early life with drawings of each home he lived in, and motifs that he associated with the region, including petrol stations and electricity pylons. The implication of suburban sprawl is combined with the sense of a rural community. For Perry, Essex stands not only for itself, and for memories of his early experiences there, but also for its broader cultural resonances, touching on issues of class. As the art critic Louisa Buck has noted, in 'this benighted part of the UK – which is the butt of a whole subgenre of tasteless Essex Girl jokes and is much favoured by retired East End gangsters – pockets of rural picturesqueness are surrounded by desolate urban overspill, flat tracts of wasteland and unappealing out-of-town shopping centres'.[6] Perry encapsulates all the insinuated meanings of Essex in works such as *The Union of Essexmen* (1988) (p. 122). He states the case for 'those who have chosen the middle way', for average men and women, for 'oiks' like himself.[7]

A series of commemorative plates (pp. 86–87) synthesizes Perry's newly discovered technical skills with visual storytelling. 'To tap into the idea of a series, I made thirty of these press-moulded plates. I treated each one differently: some had figures, others had transfers or different textures….They were very experimental.'[8] Each plate featured an unidealized Essex scene showing a derelict house, bomb shelter and tractor, simultaneously reflecting a fascination with and desire to subvert the kitschness of display ceramics and the drab colour palettes of English vernacular pottery. This drabness and dereliction under the guise of tradition reflects Perry's uneasy yet ultimately hugely important relationship with the Essex of his past.

The stories Perry tells are often intertwined with gender. A series of television-shaped dishes in the 1980s (p. 119), complete with incised mark 'T.V.' (perhaps also for transvestite), contrast such rustic symbols of rural Essex as wheatsheaves and flowers with a faceless man on a motorbike. Each component is visible as a separate entity, alluding to Perry's archetypal 'Utility Man', who represents a past generation of men equipped with the lost skills to assemble and mend.[9] In *Honda* (1985) (p. 90), this becomes a stylized biker, an invisible man, two circles as the wheels, and a cut-out paisley motif symbolizing the helmet. *Biker Pot* (1992) (pp. 150–51) maps routes in the Essex area that form a network between tools, a motorbike overlaid by

     Catrin Jones

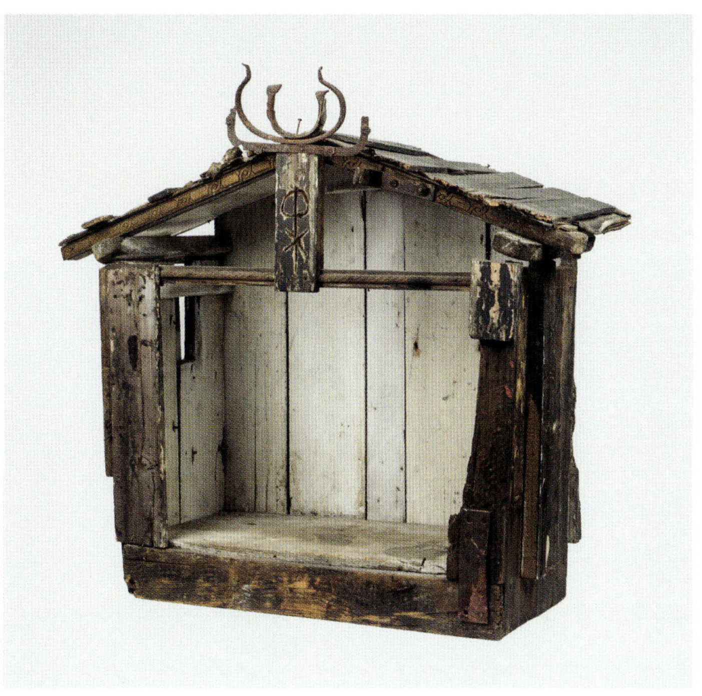

Untitled, 1985

a generic 'mother' tattoo and Nazi symbols. Together these motifs seem to suggest that masculinity and threat are inseparable. As a man and a biker himself, Perry both represents and rejects these tropes.

Motifs that are fundamental to Perry's iconography, including the shed, motor vehicles, the Essex landscape, and the depiction of women, reveal themselves to be stories about Perry himself as much as representations of a wider culture. The shed, a stereotypically male space, is a recurring motif. 'My own creativity and art practice has been a mental shed – a sanctuary as well as a place of action – where I have retreated to make things… my internal shed is always available.'[10] The shed also stands for that same 'Utility Man' who, like Perry's father, possessed a form of masculinity based on the essential ability to make and do. Perry created shed-like sculptures from found wood, such as *Baba Yaga's Hut* (1983),[11] balanced on chicken's feet in reference to a Russian fairy tale. Another shed was assembled using found wood and rusted metal, and carved to create a shrine for two vases and a bible (above and p. 84). These elements, now lost, were a tongue-in-cheek homage to the commissioner, who was an antique dealer, so Perry's shed combined the Welsh dresser (a domestic display space for ceramics) with the shed (a signal of traditional masculinity). Perry would later consider the meaning of sheds from a therapeutic standpoint. The analogy between tools, making and manhood was crystallized in psychotherapy:

> It's a form of interpreting the world in a way that I enjoy – it's as if you have a tool bag but it's too full of crap to be able to find the right tool – and then suddenly someone's shown you a shed and you can find everything: you don't throw the tools away, you just become more aware of where they are and how to use them.[12]

Just as the iconography of manhood emerges as a key theme for Perry, so too does the representation of womanhood. From his private early sexual experiences and the discovery of the arousal and freedom of wearing women's clothing, Perry began to sense that he was not alone in feeling this way. April Ashley was the first person in the UK to undergo gender reassignment surgery. Perry later recalled reading

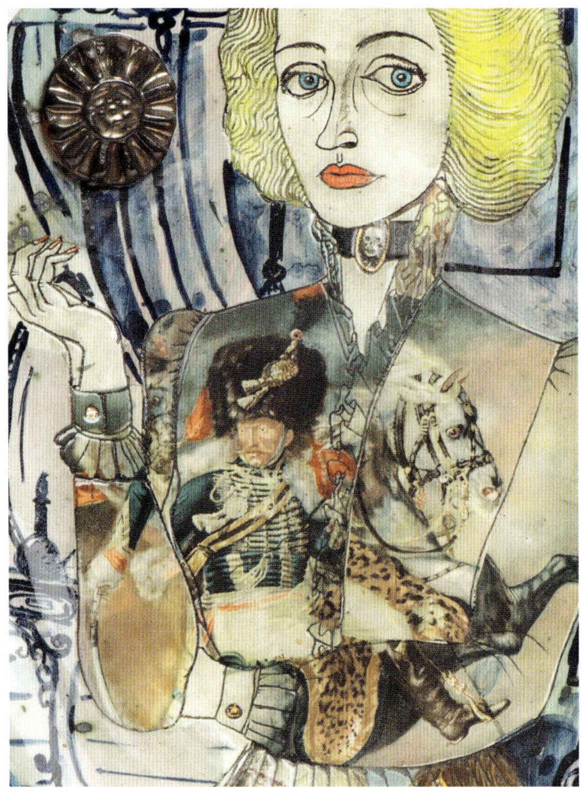

about her in the *News of the World* in 1975: 'I knew now that transvestism was a phenomenon that existed.'[13] Perry's discovery of Ashley was critical to the realization of his own transvestite alter ego. 'On 5 November 1975, which I now call Claire's birthday, I put on the full rig and stepped out of the front door.'[14] He returned to Ashley in a plate from *c.* 1984, *April Ashley in Full Sail* (p. 77), whose sgrafitto decoration of a ship at sea reflects Ashley's naval career, overlaid with her in profile with 1960s flicked out hair. Perry's representation of women cannot be separated from his own identity, and reflects the approaches and tastes of his own life as Claire.

Perry describes *Secret Woman* (1987) (pp. 106–7) as 'my acknowledgment of Claire as a central plank of my creative drive…. It's like the spirit of my femininity descending to earth and blessing me with inspiration.'[15] Early photos of Perry as Claire show her to be a stylish, of-the-moment woman, a style that Perry describes as an attempt at 'a middle-aged look'[16] but which combined something of Diana, Princess of Wales and Margaret Thatcher with a typical office girl. The white tights, padded shoulders, big glasses and big hair of well-put-together women of the period are reflected strongly in Claire's personal style. Newsreaders, impeccable with their helmet-hair, were his 'fantasy goal'.[17] In *Newsreader* (1990) (p. 141) the direct gaze, attention to styling and poise are unmistakable. Not all of Perry's women are so squeaky clean: in *Claire as a Soldier* (1987) (p. 120), she makes eye contact, and the military stylings and layered symbolism of her clothing offer a distinctive threat and appeal; in Untitled (1988) (p. 121) an unstylish, distinctly frumpy transvestite with a shopping trolley passes less successfully as a woman, conveying a sense of freedom and discovery but also unease.

Not least because of Perry's desire and ability to 'pass', his choices emphasize his physical resemblance to Princess Diana, who was 'a shorthand for idealized womanhood. The trannie in me was always interested in her deification.'[18] From the start this resulted in send-ups of 'the veneration in which she was held', such as *Saint Diana (Let Them Eat Shit)* (1984) (pp. 72–73), 'a commode-cum-coronation chair modelled on the historic throne in Westminster Abbey'.[19] Diana-like –

Catrin Jones

or is it Claire-like? – women appear in *Cocktail Party* (1989) (pp. 136–37), *A Design which Implies Significance* (1992) (p. 148), and many other works. Perry would return to this theme in the role of commentator/artist, particularly the unprecedented outpouring of grief following Diana's untimely death, which marked a sea-change for collective British culture, reflected in later works such as *Barbaric Splendour* (2003).

Beneath Every Stone is Life (1988) (pp. 128–29) presents a typical combination of humorous and graphically sexualized femininity. A female figure lifts her skirt to reveal a rabid dog, and a dismembered penis at her feet; a junky shoots up; a man-baby in a bonnet masturbates above an open coffin with a Claire/Princess Diana-like figure with a penis. Juxtaposed with these images is the inscription, 'to find beauty in all things is my mission most dear'. Are the representations of women, often shocking, grotesque and graphic, simply reflections of Perry's exploration of his own sexuality? Since Perry underwent psychotherapy it is clear that while the fascination with femininity is still a major theme of his work, he has softened his approach to the subject. Just as Claire has changed from that early moment of discovery seen in *Secret Woman*, Perry's representation of women reflects a journey towards understanding through analysis, where his understanding of himself is paramount.

Perry has described the eroticism of his first experience of wearing the 'light blue smocks for pottery…made of heavy, rubberised material…the squeaky, smooth, unyielding, restrictive plastic garment turned me on…I was being dressed like a small child, it felt *very* humiliating.'[20] The process of psychotherapy corresponded with the evolution of Claire from woman back to child. 'The sole attention a transvestite usually wants is the same attention a woman would get', Perry has said, 'whereas I search out the attention a girl would receive. Dressing up as a young girl shifts the process from authentic to symbolic because it is almost impossible for a man to look convincingly like a little girl…. People are more comfortable and a lot happier with me being dressed up as a child than as a woman because it is much less ambiguous: I am a bloke in a ridiculous frock and that's nice and clear.'[21] Perry manages to navigate the inherent contradiction in the unthreatening personification of Claire as a child, while also clearly acknowledging the fetishism and sexuality of his alter ego. He is dressed in the 'heraldry of my subconscious'.[22]

The centrality of man/woman imagery in Perry's early work is often juxtaposed with that of mythology and spirituality: the *Grotesque Devil Heads* (pp. 126–27) series, winged angels and demons, and pseudo-mythological characters. In *No God Shall Tame Me, I Am War* (1985) (p. 85), a beast with that same pointed human face and more phallic horns crouches over a bed of skulls. Perry has noted the significance of Pieter Brueghel the Elder's teeming landscapes and these fantasies also suggest Hieronymus Bosch's tortured hellscapes. Again, with applied decoration alluding to a masonic-like language of secrecy, the untamed beast with its prominent phallus

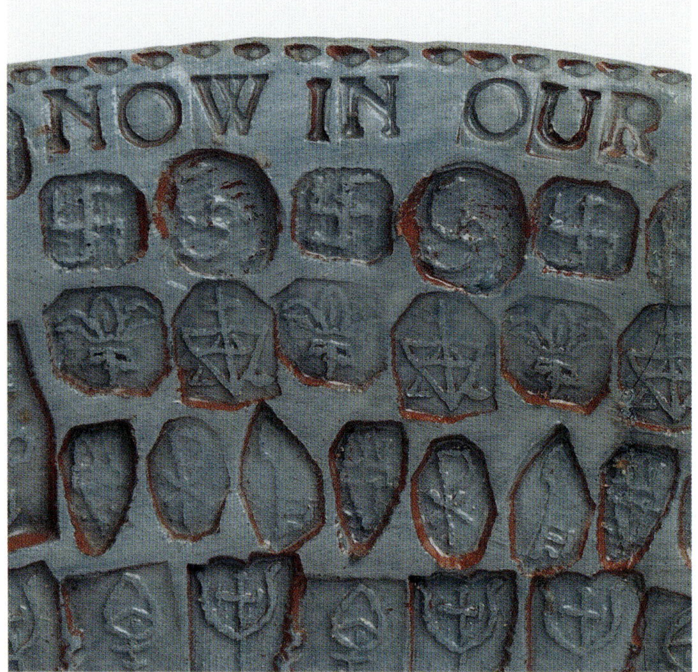

Detail of *Now in Our Green and Pleasant Land (Ye Dear Olde Bugger)*, 1984

references a singularly destructive type of masculinity. On one of the plates from Perry's first show with James Birch in 1984, *Now in Our Green and Pleasant Land (Ye Dear Olde Bugger)* (left and p. 75), the inscription reads: 'Now in our green and pleasant land we are forever in a guillotine with the red and shining blade of our mortality held above only by a thread of perverse civilization'; the image shows a winged beast poised in a generic landscape, beside the decapitated head of a woman. The rim of the dish is a network of Perry's pottery marks interspersed with incised swastikas, chains, keys and anchors. They refer to a language both packed with meaning and mysterious, inviting layered interpretations while simultaneously distancing the viewer.

Once again, a quintessential Englishness is subverted by a decorative scheme that is not as simple and pleasing as it appears. *The Devil Plate*, again from 1984 (p. 74), features the winged beast emerging like semen from an erect penis, alongside an innocent-seeming star or flower juxtaposed with a syringe. These outlines, picked out in white, lull the viewer into a false sense of security; the harder you look, the more you become aware of the artist's disturbed visions; they are 'stealth bombs'.[23] They echo the repertoire of pagan imagery employed by the Neo Naturists – indeed, the winged beast was central to Jennifer Binnie's iconography. Perry's free, swirling illustrative style is reminiscent of the body painting characteristic of Neo Naturist performances at this period, yet where those evoked a free yet ultimately unthreatening vibe, here Perry seems deliberately to contrast the aesthetic with the meaning of his works.

Reassessing meaning in the light of psychotherapy

Perry has written extensively about the centrality of Alan Measles to his real and imagined life. Measles is 'the benign dictator of my fantasy world',[24] leader of resistance to Nazi insurgents, a stand-in for his absent father, and, as God, 'my prime candidate for deification'.[25] The significance of Alan to his past emotional and imagined life and thus true understanding of his own story comes from Perry's therapeutic process, just as Perry's representation of Claire has been transformed by psychotherapy. There is a sense that it would have been problematic for an angry artist to acknowledge his teddy bear as a central

Catrin Jones

source of inspiration. With Perry's emergence as the child-like Claire, however, this exploration of childhood takes on a very different meaning. 'In the course of visiting a psychotherapist I was to discover that Alan was of course more to me than a mere cuddly toy or even a fantasy leader, he was my surrogate father.'[26]

Perry's own difficult childhood resulted in his seeking the refuge of the imagination. Long before his adoption of psychotherapy, references to strong emotion and emotional trauma are central to the imagery of Perry's work, but are also reflected in his choice of titles. *I am Angry like the Wind* (p. 143); *Patterns of Violent Behaviour* (pp. 96–97); *Childhood Trauma Manifesting in Later Life* (p. 149); *Oh God She is My Mother* (p. 87 below); *Self Portrait Cracked and Warped* (p. 98), the piece contrasting a self-portrait with the ironic manifesto that introduced this essay, a masterwork in using a technical failure to further the meaning and impact of the work itself. In *I am Angry like the Wind* (1990), Perry challenges the expectation of openness and authenticity from an artist: 'I am angry, like the wind, at everything and nothing. Why am I driven to spill my soul for you when I hate you all?'. *Patterns of Violent Behaviour* (1985) features performance artist Laurie Anderson – identifiable by the fact that she is holding a copy of her own record, *O Superman* (1981) – as a grotesque, sexualized squatting figure, while another man is prone on a bed, alongside the monarch slaughtering a deer, in reference to a medieval bestiary. The parallel between violence and sexuality is clear.

Even when the works touch on a broader sense of the world and on wider experience, Perry refocuses on the domestic and tangible: 'It's getting harder to be cynical when so many dear old mums are dying of cancer, lovers have A.I.D.S., bombs go off and cars collide, millions are poor and homeless, rainforests disappear and pet dogs get run over.' (1988) (pp. 130–31). The grandiose and remote is linked to the minutiae of actual experience, reflected in Perry's recurrent use of his own pets. In *Handsome Prince the Good Dog* (1985) (p. 91), Prince the dog appears in a matrix of profound power (faith, love, artist reincarnate, cosmic guardian). The early shed was dedicated to their cat, Baba Yaga. Later, the role that Prince or Baba Yaga played is taken on by Alan Measles, less a representation of Perry's past through autobiography, more a representation of Perry's past self. Alan Measles may be God, but he is also Perry himself.

'I am grateful to the artworld, it's been a place where my choice to live with my subconscious on my sleeve has been welcomed, even celebrated,' Perry has written.[27] Despite this, the art world – and its less trendy partner, the craft world – have often been targets of Perry's wry disdain, and sometimes ire. *Sales Pitch* (1987) (p. 115) is a playful comment on collecting, money and the art world. From the incised stamps in the centre ('100% ART'; 'MADE IN U.K.') to the tone of the treatise itself, it seeks to distance – 'if you like what you see the compliments are only accepted when accompanied by a cheque card' – while building a rapport through a sense of shared knowledge: 'With your help I can take pottery into the arena of comment

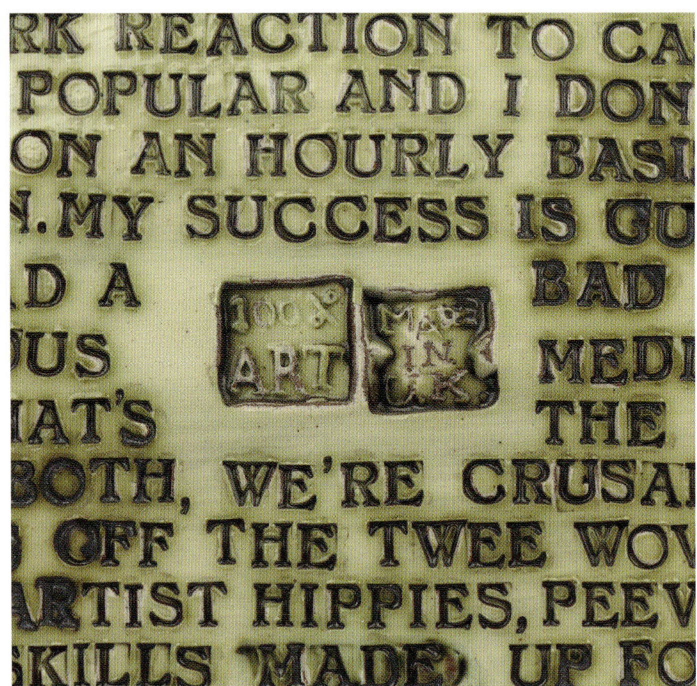

Detail of *Sales Pitch*, 1987

and ideas, dare I say it, fine art. It all sounds very pretentious but think of the money.' In contrast, later works took a more straightforward approach and aim directly at the art world, as a collective and as a group of individuals. Perry did not shy away from targeting the institutions he was a part of: *A Network of Cracks* (2003), reproduces in detail the seating plan from Tate's Turner Prize dinner at which Perry was awarded the prestigious prize; others take aim at his dealers, particularly Anthony d'Offay in works such as *As Sold by Anthony d'Offay Gallery* (1996) and *Portrait of Anthony d'Offay* (1998). There is a perverse yet undeniable pleasure in such a direct challenge to the milieu and the individuals on whose patronage Perry relied.

Perry's engagement with ceramic history

It is striking that, despite the often graphically sexual or gratuitously offensive content, Perry's 'art is…inherently accessible, in an art world where accessibility is often taken for banality'.[28] Clay is also accessible; evening classes are more popular than ever; so using pictorial motifs on decorative ceramics is a masterstroke for an artist looking for a medium in which to express real, yet identifiable, notions. 'It was precisely because ceramics was, as he put it, "an area of discomfort" for the contemporary art world that he embraced it with such vigour.'[29] For Perry, ceramics become a shorthand for Englishness, for parochialism, for familiarity; but also a conduit for challenging, deliberately provocative work that has something to say about the ways in which creativity and making are required to fit into certain narratives and the meaning of symbols to different people. Jacky Klein has argued that when Perry 'began using clay as his medium, he purposefully chose to ignore much of its 30,000-year history, its associations with everything from bricks and altarpieces to teacups and urinals'.[30] I would argue that Perry's use of the medium reflects, in fact, a thorough engagement with ceramic history, using a wealth of sources in much the same way as he did any other form of inspiration: ultimately filtering it through the lens of personal experience.

Perry has noted that an early piece made for his degree show, *The Crown of Penii* (1982) (p. 69), was:

Catrin Jones

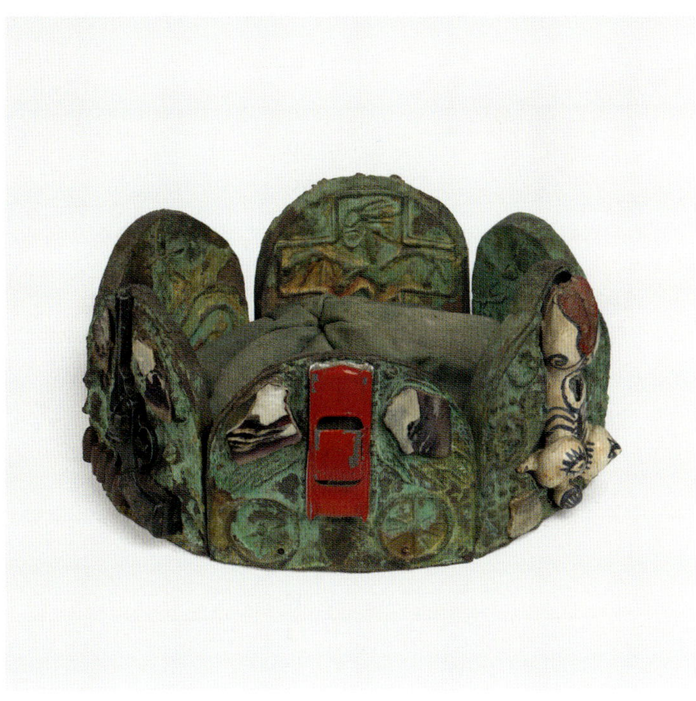

The Crown of Penii, 1982

based on a famous medieval relic, the Iron Crown in Monza Cathedral, near Milan. The iron in it was supposed to have been beaten out of one of the nails used at the Crucifixion… it combines ideas about maleness, religion and monarchy. It has lots of phallic imagery and many of the ingredients of my early work: a space shuttle; a Celtic cross; a kind of Willendorf Venus; an American car; a knife; and a pistol.'[31]

The crown introduces a methodology to which Perry would repeatedly return: taking a familiar or iconic object and creating a new version of it filtered through the artist's eye, replacing the actual decoration with the codified symbols of his own practice. They reveal a frequently careful look at the history of things and visual culture, while the viewer of Perry's 'version' is neither expected nor widely understood to engage with the original. The result is an object simultaneously with an ironic detachment from and reverential honour for the arts of the past.

Certainly, Perry has lampooned the craft world as much as the art world through his work. He characterizes the craft world as overly involved in process: 'a lot of ceramicists and potters obsess about the craft side of their work and regard the kiln as a fetishized object. Pottery exhibitions always have titles like "Gifts from the Flames" or "Fire and Earth", reinforcing the idea of some New Age goddess and celebrating the ancient danger of making pots.'[32] Yet he shows an almost reverential joy in making: he describes his methodical craftsman self, the 'Hobbit', working for 'tens of hours over the course of a fortnight' painstakingly creating an elaborate marbled pattern, only for this surface to be used as the 'mere background on which the headline imagery of the work will be overlaid – imagery usually suggested by the "Punk",' master of 'mockery and mischief-making', his other self.[33] This reminds us that the works are handcrafted by Perry himself.

Throughout ceramic history decoration has had meaning, whether political, or through positing the owner's taste. From the relaying of satirical messages to their role as valuable objects intended to impress and overpower, ceramics have often surpassed the merely decorative. For instance, the birds on a Sèvres porcelain dinner service, commissioned for Goodwood House in 1765, are taken from the naturalist George Edwards's drawings, sending a clear message about its aristocratic patron's taste, style, wealth and intellect. Just as any painting or work of art cannot be viewed in a vacuum, Perry's co-opting of decoration does not presuppose that it should not have a complex meaning, nor a genuine engagement in the arts of the past.

It is clear, however, that Perry recognizes the unusualness of his practice and the consequent difficulty he and others have had in defining his work. Reflecting on *Bad Art, Bad Pottery* (1995), he said:

> I still felt a lot of prejudice about my work, as I was being pigeonholed for using pottery and being kept out of most art establishments, yet I knew that technically I wasn't up to scratch as a craftsperson either. I've always compared my own work to historical art, which in terms of craft is usually way out of my league, because it was often made by people who had been trained in age-old techniques with strong local traditions. Someone once said to me, 'Grayson, you're trying to set yourself up against an 18th-century factory,' and I said, 'Yes, I am! And it's hard work!'[34]

Those in the art world have challenged his credentials because of the media he uses whereas the craft world recognizes Perry is not quite one of its own. Back then 'I still felt I had to cover my back, to be sure I was seen as a conceptual artist and not as a craftsman.'[35] Whether we consider his work art or craft (or indeed both) – and there are certainly arguments on both sides – Perry has positioned himself as operating in a different way like the artists he cites as his greatest influences: Joseph Beuys and the 'Outsider' Henry Darger. To return to *Sales Pitch*, Perry presumably addresses the buyer:

> true pottery is not the most glamourous media through which to become a superstar, but that's the beautiful irony of it, and so British. You and me both, we're crusaders if you like, helping this ancient art shrug off the twee woven cliché, earned by a generation of failed artist hippies, peeved because they thought their down to earth skills make up for lack of imagination and style.

Perry again tussles between defining his approach and taking a swipe at others who take their work too seriously. Or, with typical ironic humour, Perry defines his position in the art versus craft debate as 'sore from sitting on that fence'.[36]

From the small vase surmounted with glass teeth that formed part of the *Transvestite Jet Pilots* dressing table, Perry's earliest experiments with ceramics were either sculptural works in bronze and occasionally clay, or flat dishes, treating clay like a canvas. Perry defines the first piece as *Kinky Sex* (1983) (p. 70). It owes a clear debt in form, style and decoration to the simplicity and graphic clarity of the

Catrin Jones

17th-century slipware dishes of Thomas Toft that Perry had seen on an early trip to the V&A. Toft's work has been seen as embodying an essential 'Englishness'. It is visually striking, graphically clear and was simple to make, but perhaps the most important aspect in the context of Perry's work was that Toft was one of the few makers of the period to sign his works. Slipware techniques are among the first that Perry would adopt in decorative terms. Sgraffito, where a design is scratched into the wet slip surface when a piece has been dipped in glaze, would enable Perry to make best use of his distinctive drawing style, while riffing on highly recognizable ceramic traditions.

Although the majority of Perry's work in ceramics consists of plates and vases, his earliest work was more varied. The range of forms reveals an experimental bent: there are cups and saucers (p. 105), toby jugs (p. 104) and porringers (p. 112), perfume bottles (p. 102), sculptural beasts (p. 85) and gargoyles' heads (pp. 126–27). They reveal a playful reflection of a much broader range of influences. What becomes apparent is that many of these early experimental forms were less well executed, and less successful as conduits for the stories that would become increasingly important in Perry's work, or as surfaces on which to convey a message. From the start, Perry was drawn to creating works quickly, and often this meant making plates. Writing later, Perry observed how he was able to use the form almost as a sketchbook.

> I was put off making plates for a while because they seemed too easy, like
> a ceramic equivalent of drawing. But as my work has become more elaborate,
> my pots are taking months to do and many man-hours to put together.
> I have an idea for a pot and I'm then wedded to it for the next three months.
> A plate takes a matter of hours. I find that the speedy ones work the best.[37]

As his technique improved, he began to collage, combining cut-out images (in this early period ready-made transfer-prints) with hand-drawn decoration, incised marks and bright colour washes in the same object. *Cocktail Party* (1989) (pp. 136–37) takes a swipe at the 'scene' while capturing a detailed representation of experience: angular women who don't look like they're really enjoying themselves stand in a frieze-like row, awkwardly eating or listening. Perry uses transfers of chintzy fabric designs for their array of different versions of late eighties outfits in a way that suggests close analysis and admiration; a Laura Ashley-style dress is juxtaposed with a slick Chanel suit, while another woman wears a variation on Madonna's famous Jean-Paul Gaultier bustier. A creative re-use of ready-made transfers is apparent: a delightfully seventies paisley pattern appears on one woman's dress on *Cocktail Party* but, cut out and applied as a separate motif in *Meaningless Symbols* (1993) (pp. 152–53), it becomes pseudo-traditional decoration; in *Honda* it represents a figure's cycle helmet. Again, the title *Meaningless Symbols* reflects a deliberate and

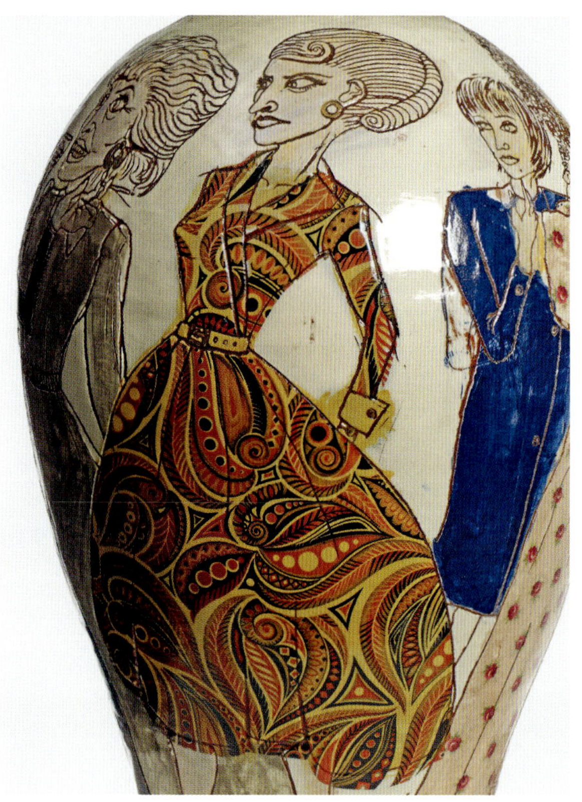

ironic distancing of the visual appeal of the piece, laying a challenge to the viewer to unpack the meaning of the work, and its status as a desirable object.

The form that has become most clearly associated with Perry is that of the vase. Historically, vases have had decorative and functional purposes, but Perry is certainly not the first to understand the visual symbolism and technical ambition the vase could represent: 18th-century potter and entrepreneur Josiah Wedgwood described his own mission as becoming 'Vase Maker General to the Universe'.[38] Once again, Perry's knowledge of historic ceramics both links and distances his work from the art of the past. He recognized that the essential element of the vase was the shape: 'For me the shape has to be classical invisible: then you've got a base that people can understand.'[39] The simplicity of its outline and grand scale means vases can be sculptural presences, and anthropomorphic ones at that; the large surface area creates scope for the complex and layered imagery of Perry's practice. Despite recognizing the power of the vase and its meaning, Perry's methods are a complete rejection of the technical advancements of the past. He uses coiling, a basic and time-consuming technique never used in industrial production and rarely in artisanal practice, which favour casting and throwing for any work of scale.

Most of his vases are marked with Perry's various incised marks, a nod to the many factories associated with British pottery industries, once a stalwart of British trade and industrialism. It is almost comical to see Perry's marks in the *Dictionary of Pottery Marks* alongside those of Wedgwood and Chelsea. Again, heavy with irony, Perry's marks reveal their subversiveness: 'W' above an anchor creates a visual pun and spells 'wanker'. Similarly, a closer look at the applied decoration of coloured clays, which is central to Perry's early style, reveals a network of designs intended to shock and surprise. 'I was fascinated at the time, as I still am, by the Masons, shamanism and the occult. I always liked the mystery of secret societies...Timothy Prus gave me a load of masonic regalia – aprons, medals and heavy brass badges – which I made into sprig moulds.'[40]

Perry's engagement with ceramics is primarily a visual one, rather than technical. By returning again and again to the plate and the vase, Perry is not ignoring ceramic

Catrin Jones

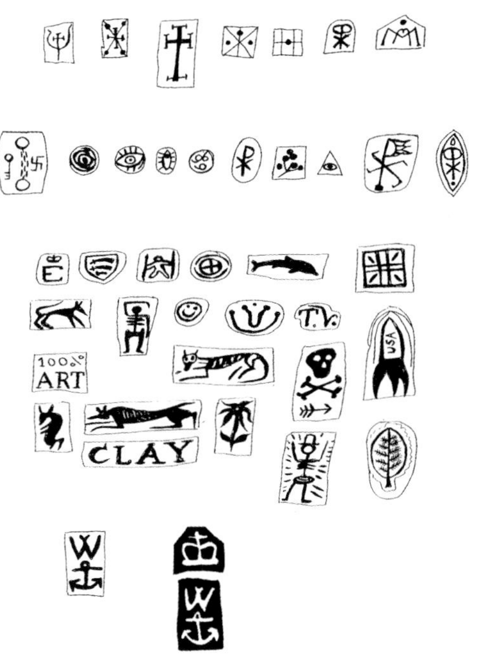

Grayson Perry's pottery marks, from *British Studio Potters' Marks*, 2015

history but using the two forms that serve his work best: plates are akin to sketchbooks, space for experimentation and direct expression; vases are the grander, more permanent sculptural expressions. Perry has said that 'ceramics aren't used for public art' but I would argue that historically vases although dismissed as decorative are in fact private, public art.[41] Coming from a tradition of display does not mean that the vase is purely decorative. As modern viewers, we have forgotten or no longer understand the didactic properties of these pieces. Perry is therefore able to use our own failure to understand the artefacts of the past to create (or rather, re-create) a new genre where the decorative object has a strong message to share. The closer you look, the more the object rewards viewing and reveals its position. This links back to Perry's interest in taste. He has studied history; he is well aware of the fact that different classes have different tastes and within that context objects have more meaning than simply being decorative. 'A childhood spent marinading in the material culture of one's class means taste is soaked right through you.' For Perry, this comes directly back to the legacies of his own tastes: 'cut me, and beneath the thick crust of Islington, it still says "Essex" all the way through.'[42]

Perry's own journey of discovery through therapy has made him more aware of his own practice: 'people often have difficulty reading a message that fights too much with the medium.'[43] The pictorial possibilities of the flat dish and the dominating, sculptural presence of the vase clearly emerged as the forms with the most potential for Perry's message. This is also echoed in his later adoption of digital jacquard weavings inspired by tapestry traditions. 'As I gain more confidence, I'm tiptoeing towards crafting decorative art – while trying to drag the definition of contemporary art with me.'[44] By tackling another 'craft' form, that of textile art, he secured his ability to engage with and subvert the histories of these practices. As an artist, Perry's tendency and prerogative is to select the forms that offer the most creative potential while nodding to traditions that are taken for granted by viewers. The forms instead become inviting fora in which to discuss the ideas that preoccupy him: identity, culture, society.

Perry's public persona has afforded him more space, time and media than many artists with which to explore and explain his work. Popularity and its place in culture is a topic Perry has investigated in his work and through his writing. His selection for the RA summer exhibition was one of the most successful exhibitions of 2018, and followed 2017's *The Most Popular Art Exhibition Ever!*, which directly tackled the cultural sector's symbiotic yet problematic relationship with popularity.[45] Perry doesn't shy away from the power that accessibility provides, a charge that could be laid at the door of both craft and art world discourse. If the idea is interesting, you don't need to over-complicate it: people will engage if they can understand it. That his television series and exhibitions have such popular reach speaks to the fact that audiences love his work as much as hearing his views. This very popularity allows him to present ideas – including some that from another commentator might cause outrage – as innocuous commentary on contemporary culture. As Louisa Buck has put it, the great appeal of Perry's work lies in his ability to 'breathe new and incisively relevant life into another unfashionable notion which has always been a hallmark of his work: that of the personal as political'.[46] Therapy means Perry himself is, or presents himself as, more comfortable than ever in his own identity. In his written work, such as *The Descent of Man* (2016), or the television series *All in the Best Possible Taste* (2012), he is, therefore, able to use his identity in his approach: 'as a practitioner, and not necessarily an expert in the wider sense, I can use autobiography as analysis.'[47]

How, then, can we reconcile this new popularity with the searing work of his early years? Perry himself and others have argued that his later work is more accomplished, more refined, more technically skilled.[48] There might be imagery in these early pieces that is deliberately shocking, or, as Perry puts it, revealing his 'punk' (the challenger) rather than his 'hobbit' (the craftsman). The artist's own status has clearly changed since those early years. He has won the Turner Prize, he is a Royal Academician (for printmaking, not ceramics!), he has a CBE for services to contemporary art. The target in the past was in some ways himself. He presented himself as an outsider, neither a straight contemporary conceptual artist nor a craftsperson. His early strategies reflect a certain nihilism: they are provocative, and often deliberately inflammatory.

Perry's targets today are very different: the shallowness of contemporary art and the elevation of his own understanding of and interest in craftsmanship. His 2013 Reith Lectures and book, *Playing to the Gallery*, reveal not only a genuine interest in examining the art world and concepts of museums' ambitions for 'inclusion' but also a serious and earnest engagement with the idea of art as a vehicle for changing people's perspectives. It's much easier to lampoon once you're on the inside. Perry is an observer, a commentator, looking both from inside and outside the groups of which he is a part. It is clear that everything he presents is filtered through his imagination, whether direct takes on historic

Catrin Jones

ceramics and the history of art or biting social commentary. The commentary, however, does not dilute the impact of the stories, which might ultimately be why the works are so popular.

Yet this poses a question in terms of the content of this early work: do we accept the undeniably brutal sexuality, misogyny and racist symbolism as part of Perry's personal journey to a more enlightened place? Perry's recognition that these are the 'pre-therapy years' certainly allows him to create some distance from the views he once presented as part self-expression, part deliberate challenge to the establishment. Yet they also reveal a controlled reassessment of the past: much of the iconography of Perry's early years, as I have argued, has a deeply personal resonance. His movement towards representing his past not as it was felt and expressed at the time, but by using what Adrian Searle refers to as the 'Graysonabilia',[49] particularly Alan Measles and Claire, is surely a reflection not only of an adult who has engaged with the therapeutic process, but also of a perceptive, engaged and intellectual artist carving out a space to discuss wider issues that are clearly of great importance to him.

'My job is to make meaning. To make meaning in a meaningless world.'[50] Grayson Perry's early works reflect this search for meaning. Therapy might have elucidated this meaning, providing a new perspective on his work, but the elements, the visual language and the ambition were surprisingly well formed from the outset. Perry's personal story is both more and less prominent in his work and his public persona. Where the early imagery was more inadvertently personal, this new iconography is constructed through archetypes. The raw explosiveness of the early works presents an unedited Grayson Perry. The discovery of archetype as narrative has enabled Perry to master the use of autobiography as analysis, and to explore the personal through his persona rather than through his personality.

PAGES 54 AND 55: Birch & Conran private view, 1987

PAGE 56, FRONT: Birch & Conran private view, 1987, Robin Dutt (centre)

PAGES 56–57, BEHIND: Andrew Logan and Grayson Perry at Birch & Conran private view, 1987

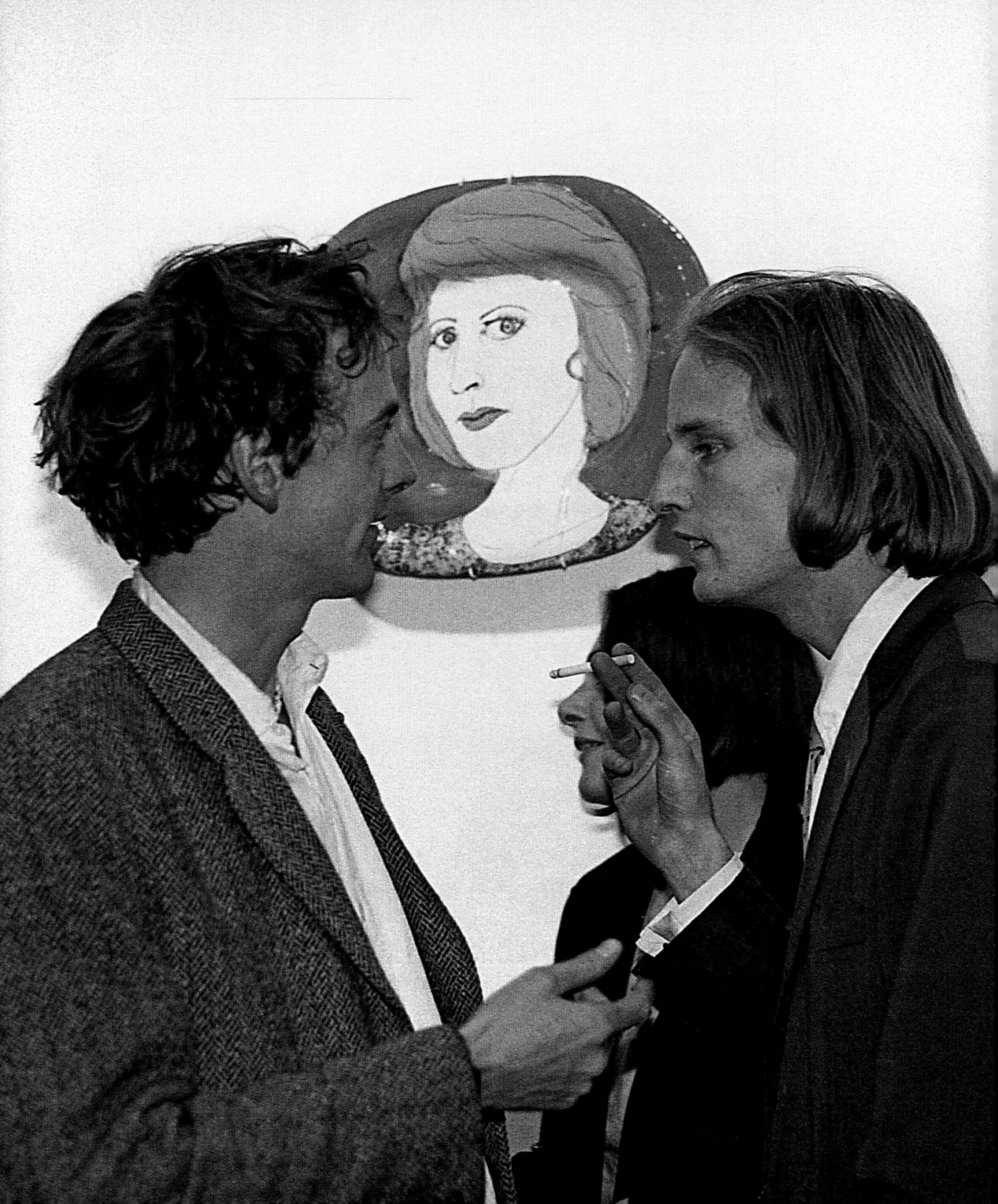

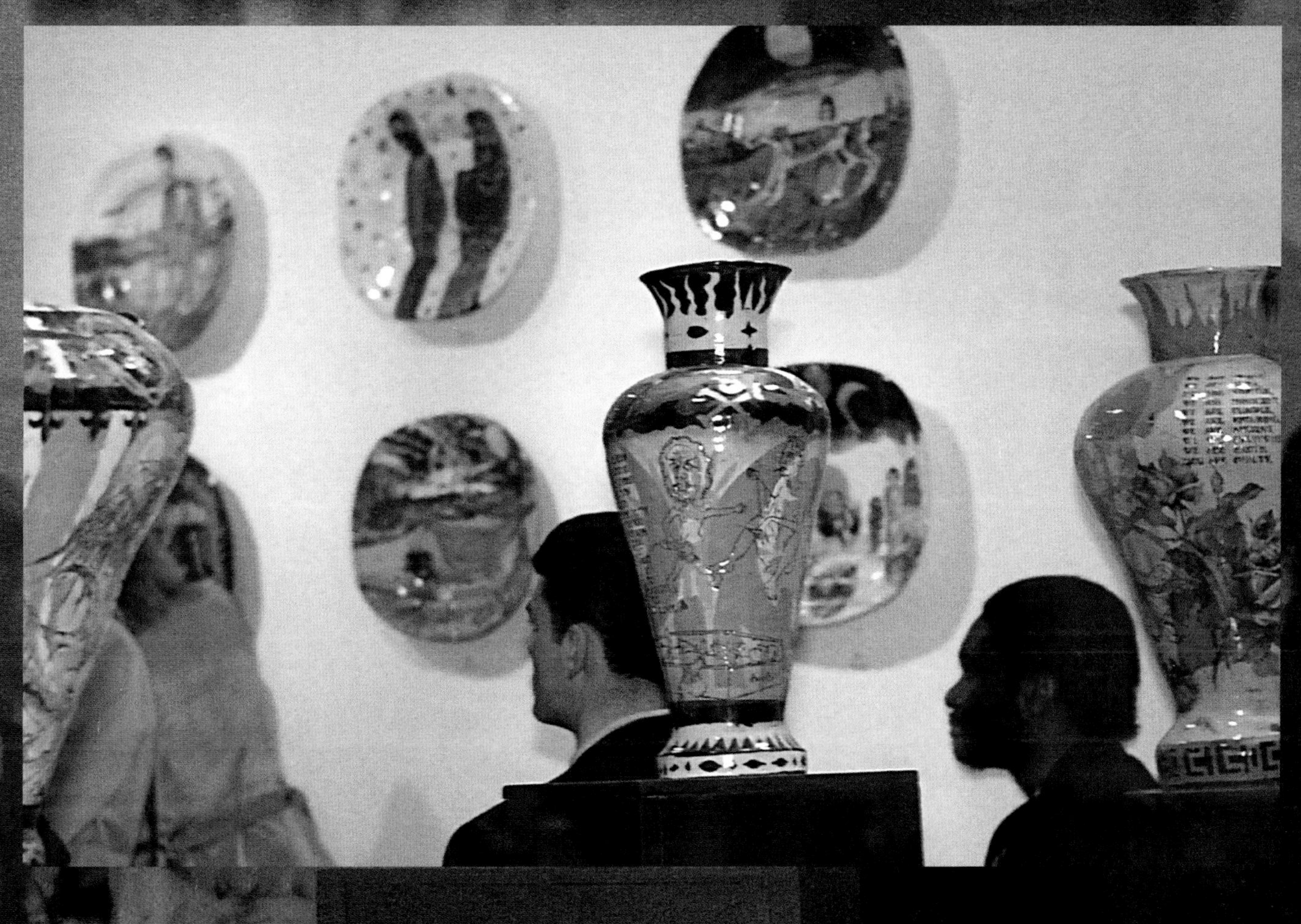

GRAYSON PERRY

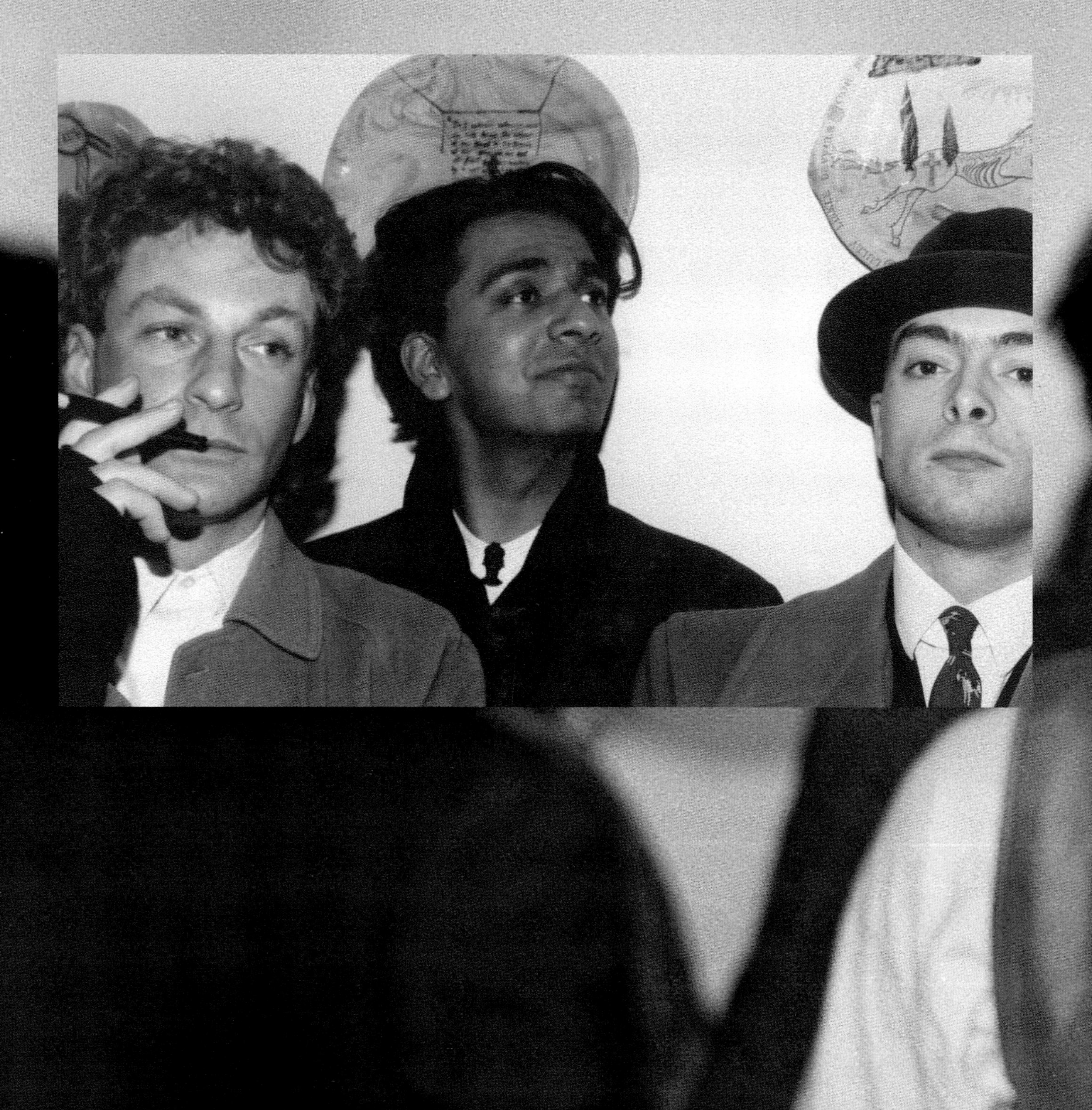

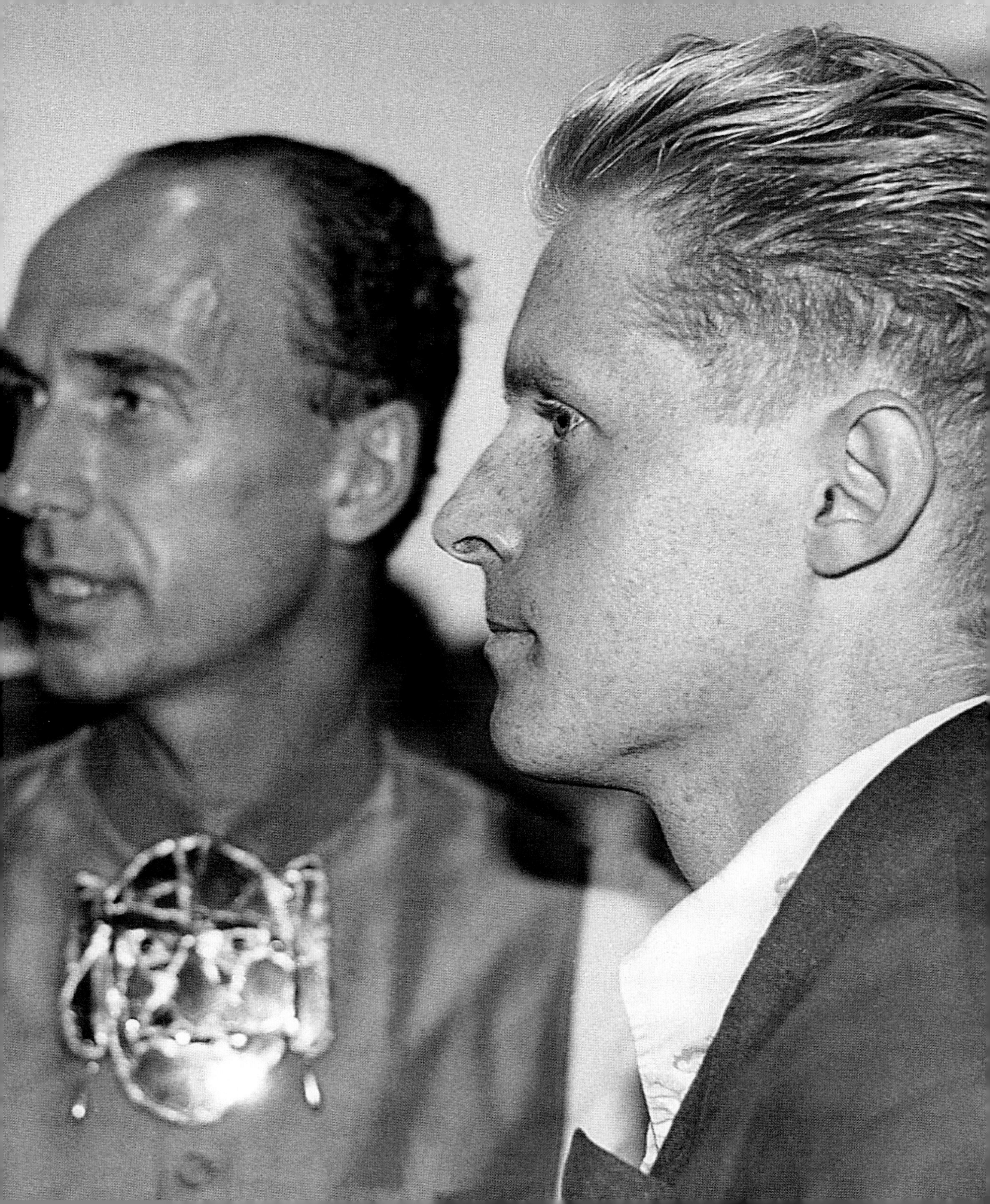

CLIMBING EVEREST WITHOUT OXYGEN

Grayson Perry

I have a strong brand, I am the Transvestite Potter, but I wasn't born this way. Many people still seem to hold onto the fantasy that artists somehow pop out fully formed. They believe that artists are born complete with a unique take on the world and an innate skill in the art form they were destined to master. Bollocks. Like everyone else I was formed by my environment growing up, a chance set of encounters. It's a lottery. Looking back at my own career it is tempting to see the controlling hand of fate guiding me to take up the pottery tools that would forge my reputation but it would be a mistake, post-rationalization at best. The truth is, like a lot of artists I stumbled into my version of a career and somehow justified my choices to form a coherent narrative. At any point, especially in those early years, if you had asked me where I was heading I wouldn't have had a clue; I was living in the moment, just enjoying making stuff and having a laugh with friends. This exhibition covering the years 1982–94 shows me fumbling towards becoming the artist that I am today.

It is now over thirty-seven years since I graduated in fine art from Portsmouth Polytechnic and there has been one central constant in my working life. When I start something I usually don't have much of a clue where I am heading. I grasp at the thinnest, most indulgent or silly of motivations. These starting points might be, Oh, I fancy doing something red today, or a landscape or something angry or fiddly or a piece of furniture or a picture of me in my new dress. The important thing is that I make a start, I make a first mark, lay down a blob of clay, google a glimmer of a thought. From these fuzzy early imaginings I build and negotiate within the constraints of the craft and my skill. Most of the time I don't really know what the work is about until it is at least half finished. Often I have only understood what a piece is about when I have seen it complete, away from the clutter of the studio, installed ready for exhibition.

A big part of my haphazard career strategy is that I have always learnt techniques and skills on the job. My art is a dialogue with tools and materials: I imagine what I want to make and the reply comes back, 'no way!' or 'maybe, but like this'. When I started designing tapestries I had not a clue how to use Photoshop, I only used its most basic functions. After a couple of projects I had a little training, but I still ask more experienced friends for advice and in this way I've learnt to do what I need to. Sometimes what I learn are the limitations but often a new technique opens up a whole field of artistic inspiration to me.

As the Transvestite Potter I am now known as much for my wardrobe as for my artworks. In those early years I was still a shy fetishist and my psychosexual passions played more of a part in my work than they did in my public persona. In my pre-therapy days you were more likely to see evidence of my taste in clothes on the pots than on my body. I look back and feel a bit sad that despite having the youth, the figure and the looks I did not have the confidence, the skill or the budget to pull off the carefully crafted array that I present on the red carpet these days.

Which brings me to pottery. At art college I had made many things in clay. Several of the tutors who were an influence on me, Richard Mackness, Ed Allington and particularly Larry Knee, had a background in ceramics but they were all determinedly contemporary artists first and the ancient traditions of the medium played little part. One tutor told me 'craft is dead'. The hotshots of the art world at the time, Julian Schnabel or Georg Baselitz, bore this out. So the clay objects I made at college were ostentatiously crude, often stuck with found objects and pieces of glass and metal. I approached clay like the well-behaved contemporary art student that I was, with an innocent expressiveness and a regulation disregard for tradition and craftsmanship.

That spirit of the art school was still very much within me when I started pottery evening classes in 1983, the year after I graduated. My girlfriend's sister, Christine Binnie, had trained as a potter. We were all sharing a squat together in Camden and she had found an evening class nearby at the Central Institute where she could keep her hand in. She suggested I attend as well. We were on the dole so the classes were practically free and the teachers, Caroline Whyman and Kate Wickham, were nice, she said. I went along. For the first week or two I carried on where I had left off on graduating, making crude sculptures, but I could not help overhearing the advice and short introductory talks on technique. I also attended a class visit to the Victoria and Albert Museum's ceramics department. Maybe I was genuinely inspired – or maybe just filling time while one of my sculptures dried enough to continue working on, whatever the motivation I made my first recognizably traditional ceramic: a circular earthenware plate with a crudely incised drawing of a crucified man with a melted coin over his genitals, bordered by traditional old English latticed slip-trailed decoration and the legend 'Kinky Sex'. In a way, in that moment, I had laid out the ingredients for my entire career: tradition, subversion, decoration. The main thing about my work that changed over the next decade or so was that I gradually became better at making pots.

I made crude vessels covered in crude drawings of crude acts. Sado-masochism, bondage, ritual humiliation, cross-dressing and infantilism formed my core subject matter, accompanied by sprinklings of swastikas, crucifixes and many references to my home county of Essex, witchcraft and digs at what I saw as the pretensions of the art world. I was an angry young man and I liked the fact that no matter how offensive the images I used the fact they were on pots somehow neutered my provocations. Well not quite. Unbeknownst to me a delegation of fellow students had complained to the head of the institute about the nature of my 'controversial' imagery. Kate Wickham, god bless her, had defended me vehemently and I worked on in blissful ignorance that she had risked losing her job for me.

I continued with the evening classes for a couple of years. I learned the basics of the craft but I studiously avoided even sitting at a potter's wheel. One reason being that I was in a hurry and learning to throw well was a protracted business.

Grayson Perry

I could learn to coil build a substantial (if wobbly) vessel pretty quickly. But the main reason for not taking up throwing was that I wanted to avoid the signature ceramicist's skill because it would mark me too easily as a potter and I was clinging onto my newly minted identity as a contemporary artist. I cannot remember how aware of it I was at the time, but retrospectively I characterize the first decade of my career as a clomping dance around the disputed border between art and craft. I had trained as a fine artist; I hung out in central London with performance artists and arty filmmakers; pottery in my view was steeped in associations with wholemeal lentil-chomping rural hippies throwing lumpen salt pigs decorated with runes.

Whether I knew it or not, these unfashionable vibes had an upside. The low status of pottery somehow acted as a semi-permeable membrane to keep me at an intellectual and aesthetic distance from the orthodoxies of the fine art world. However inept and insubordinate I was, pottery *was* craft, not art, pottery was the business of skilled tradesman not gentleman academics, pottery was humble, small and domestic and seen as feminine. All these associations, I felt, disqualified my work from a 1980s art world that seemed to me to be in thrall to either dry academic conceptualism bolstered by intellectual gobbledegook – what sociologist Alix Rule and artist David Levine dubbed 'International Art English' – or huge, often macho, paintings by supplicants to the cult of the expressive brushstroke.

I look back at my early pieces now and I find them delightful and hilarious. I enjoy their frenetic energy and humour but I wince at some of the texts stamped into the surface. One thing that has changed a lot about my art in the intervening thirty-five years or so is that I have a lot less fear around clear communication. Like many young people, I think I hid behind the idea that I was a 'misunderstood individual'. I was right, but not because I was an undiscovered genius or unusually sensitive. I was misunderstood because I was sometimes a pretentious obscurantist.

I also wince a bit at how angry and bitter I was. I was carrying a lot of unexamined baggage from my childhood. These fermenting emotions were at once powering the work, but also, I am sure, making me a tricky character to deal with.

This show is called 'the Pre-Therapy Years' because I sometimes joke that Victoria Miro was fortunate to take me on as one of her artists in 2003, after I had been through psychotherapy for six years. The relationship between artist and art dealer is often fraught and in the previous twenty years I had loaded a lot of shit onto a few of them. Dealers were ripe for becoming substitute parents, particularly for this refugee from childhood. I looked to them for approval, validation and cash. I look back and realize I was an innocent in some ways, but as I stated previously, I did not have a clue where I was headed. But I did, as I often say to young artists, 'take advantage of every opportunity, for you never know what it might lead on to'.

In 1982, I didn't know it but spending a week in the nude in an art gallery led to my first solo exhibition. I had participated in a five-day Neo Naturist performance at the B2 gallery in Wapping. The Neo Naturists were a loose group centred around Christine Binnie, her sister Jennifer and Wilma Johnson. Fourteen of us lived in the gallery wearing only body paint, which changed each day to fit the themes: Art, Fashion, Macbeth, Black Rapport and Punk. Timothy Prus, a young art dealer, had bought some of my girlfriend Jennifer's paintings that had been on display at the B2. Later he brought another young dealer called James Birch round to our squat. Seeing my early plates lined up on the mantelshelf James offered me an exhibition there and then at his space on Waterford Road in Fulham.

The show opened in December 1984. It consisted of about sixty ceramic pieces made at evening classes plus a few sculptures constructed on the kitchen table using detritus found around our squat, on the street or on the beach. The opening was thronged with friends and James's Chelsea/Soho set all plastered on cheap wine and to my great delight the exhibition nearly sold out. This may well have been due to the timing and the low prices as much as anything. It was just before Christmas and most of the works were plates priced £35–50. Top price of the show was £85 for a pair of vases. Coming from a working-class background, and then struggling financially as a young artist, I have always been acutely aware of the need to sell my work, but somehow I have not let sales dictate my agenda. From the beginning I have resisted the temptation of churning out near copies of works that were in high demand. This flush of integrity may just have been avoidance of boredom. It was 1998 before I earned what I would regard as a living wage from my art.

After that initial whiff of success I gradually committed myself more to ceramics. I was offered use of a kiln and workshop in the basement of Battersea Arts Centre, which I took advantage of for a year or two. The squat in Camden came to an end; I moved to an ACME studio house in Leytonstone and bought a lightweight top-loading kiln. James Birch teamed up with another dealer, Paul Conran, and they opened a gallery in Dean Street, Soho, where I was to have three more solo shows.

Looking back at the 1980s, I realize I was living in a very different London from the super expensive, professional hipster city of today. Though I was unaware of it at the time, the cultural scene around me, fuelled by an energy of joyful amateurism, was about to be turbocharged. Soho still reeked of postwar bohemia, the Birch & Conran gallery was bang next door to the Colony Room, the epicentre of the alcohol-steeped scene that included Francis Bacon, Jeffrey Bernard and John Deakin. Next door to the Colony though, a younger, smarter, richer culture had announced its arrival in the form of the Groucho Club. By the end of the decade soaring rents were driving out the sleaze or, as some called it, old school charm. In the eighties, art critics were reluctant to stray east of Regent Street into Soho, let alone take a cab to Hoxton, but the art world was about to get fed through a very well-funded advertising agency, and a young man called Damien and his friends were graduating.

Grayson Perry

It was a great time to be an artist but my relationship with clay was still uneasy. Technically, I still had many failures. I joked that I charged extra for cracked works that needed Araldite, and the pile of sherds in the back garden grew. Conceptually, I hesitated on the margins of the art and craft territories. When asked, I sometimes exhibited in shows with other ceramicists but I was acutely aware of a class divide. I did not want to settle down on the craft side of the fuzzy boundary; I did not want to be defined by my medium. I learned that defining myself as an artist was important, it framed the work for me and for my audience. Anxiety around this issue did not leave me until after I won the Turner Prize in 2003 and after I had gained a reputation in other media such as tapestry and printmaking.

Birch & Conran had to close in 1990 owing to the rent trebling overnight. For the remainder of the period covered by this exhibition I was supported by gallerist David Gill until I was taken on by the Anthony d'Offay gallery in 1994.

During the 1990s, while the YBAs rocketed to international stardom, my art career only inched forwards. I think someone described me at the time as an 'artist's artist'. Though I was popular with collectors and a growing audience, and despite being shown by the most powerful gallery in London, acceptance by the gatekeepers of fine art institutions was still several years away. By the time I won the Turner Prize I was boasting that I had never been featured in an art magazine, calling it 'climbing Everest without oxygen'. Not that I was bitter, no way, not at all, definitely not.

Over the decade 1984–94 I gradually became more technically proficient, inching closer to my goal of having the relaxed fluency to use clay, slip, glaze and enamel in the same way that I used paper, pen, paint and collage in my sketchbooks. This gain in skill prompted me to attempt works that were more ambitious both in scale and complexity, this in turn resulted in fewer and fewer works made. Each piece was taking longer. In the mid-eighties I was making 80–100 pieces a year, a decade later maybe half that, this year I might manage a dozen. I look back on my pre-therapy years as a period of prelapsarian spate when the river of my unconscious ran steep and fast.

I am grateful to Chris Stephens and the Holburne Museum for proposing this exhibition. Putting together this show has been a delight. Many of the works I have not seen since they were exhibited and sold three decades ago. I was a poor photographer and kept scant records so it has been wonderful to be reacquainted with the outpourings of a different me. Immediately I notice I am more forgiving of them now as I have more compassion for my young self. In my early career I was very hard on myself. I had a low opinion of my talents, smashed a lot of pieces, or gave them away. More than once I could not be bothered to pick up work after a show so just left it with the gallery, where somebody must have claimed it.

Psychotherapy helped me deal with my low self-esteem and other unhelpful influences of my upbringing and was also useful in handling the benefits and success of being the Transvestite Potter.

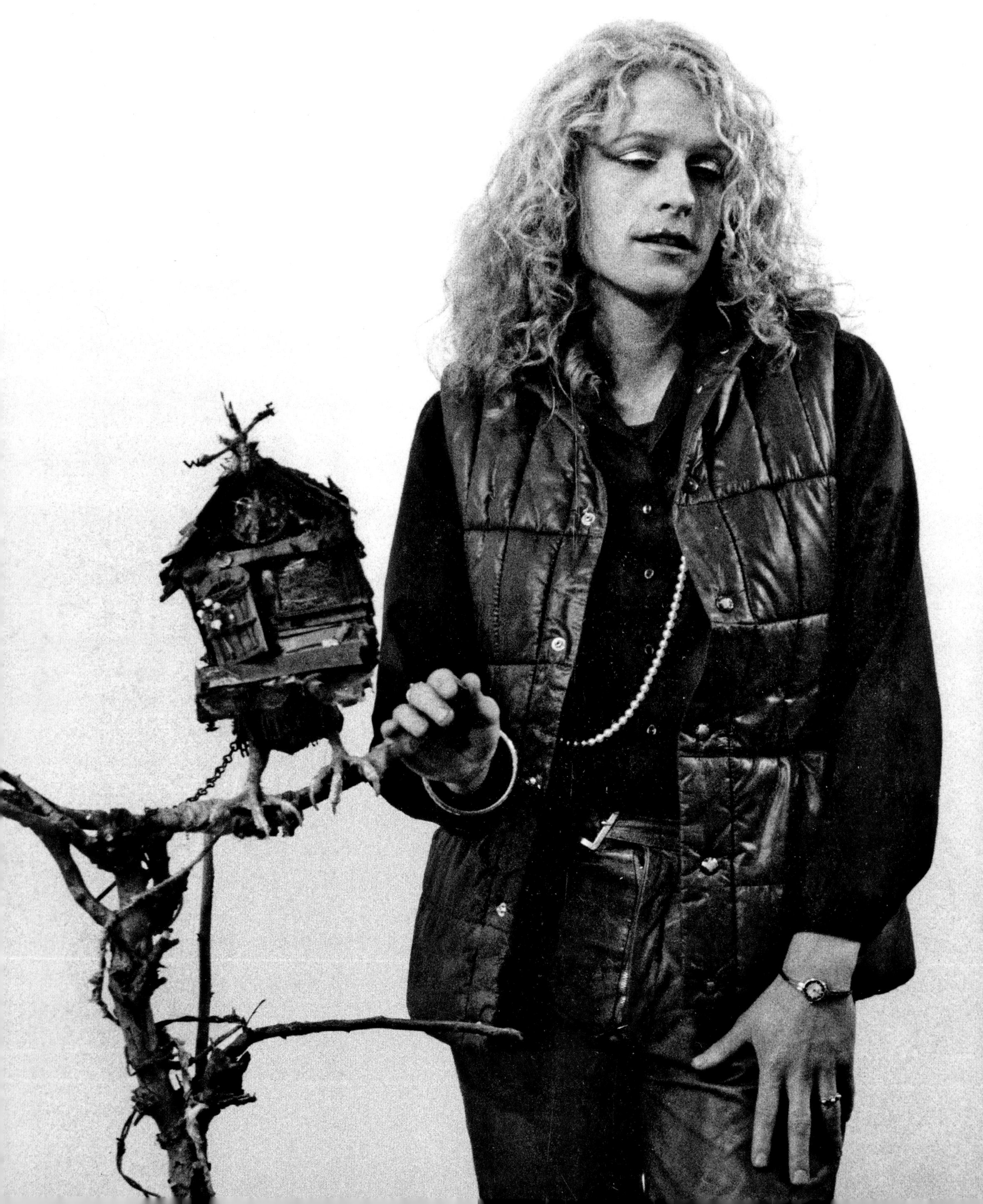

PRE-THERAPY
ARTWORKS

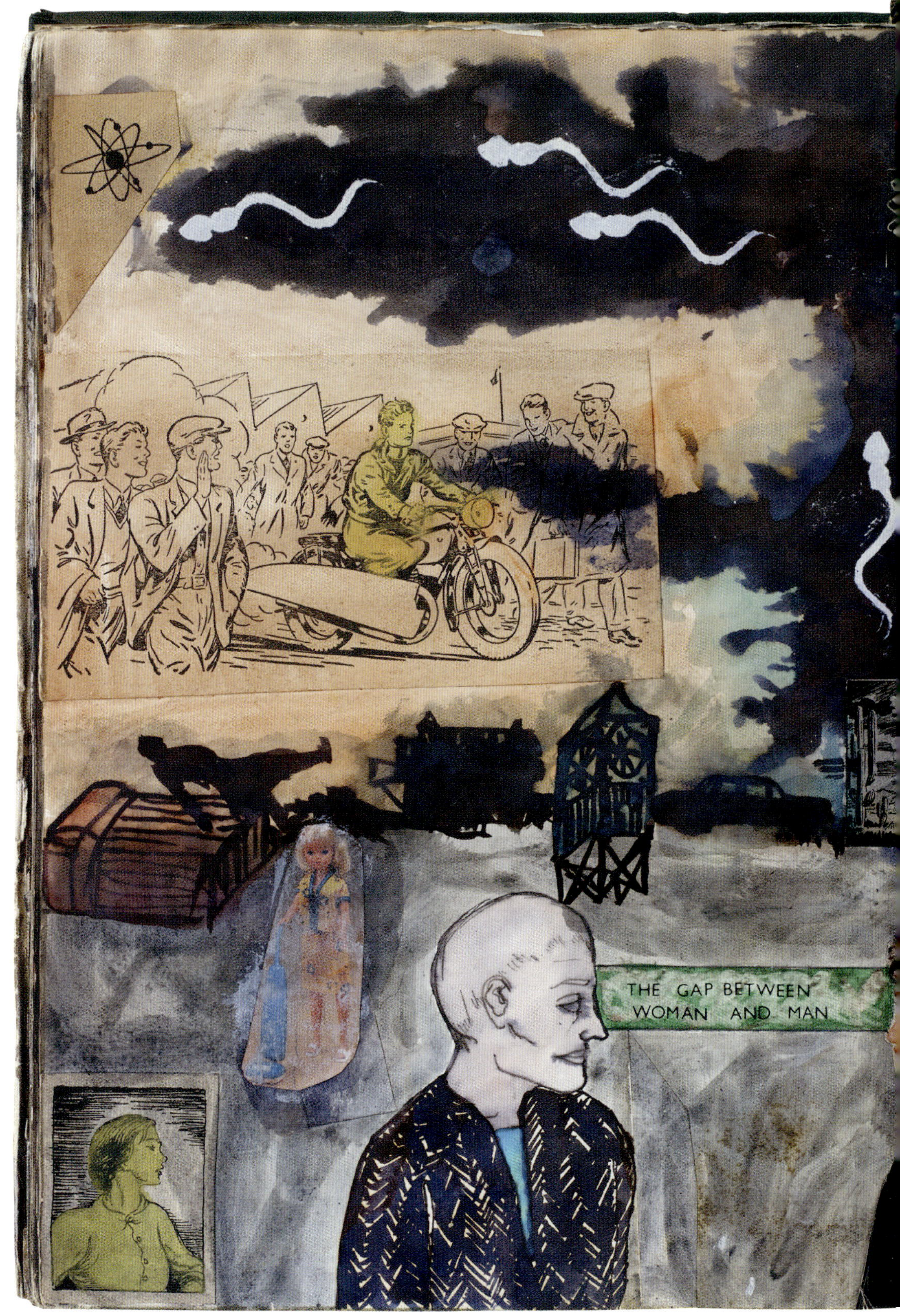
THE GAP BETWEEN
WOMAN AND MAN

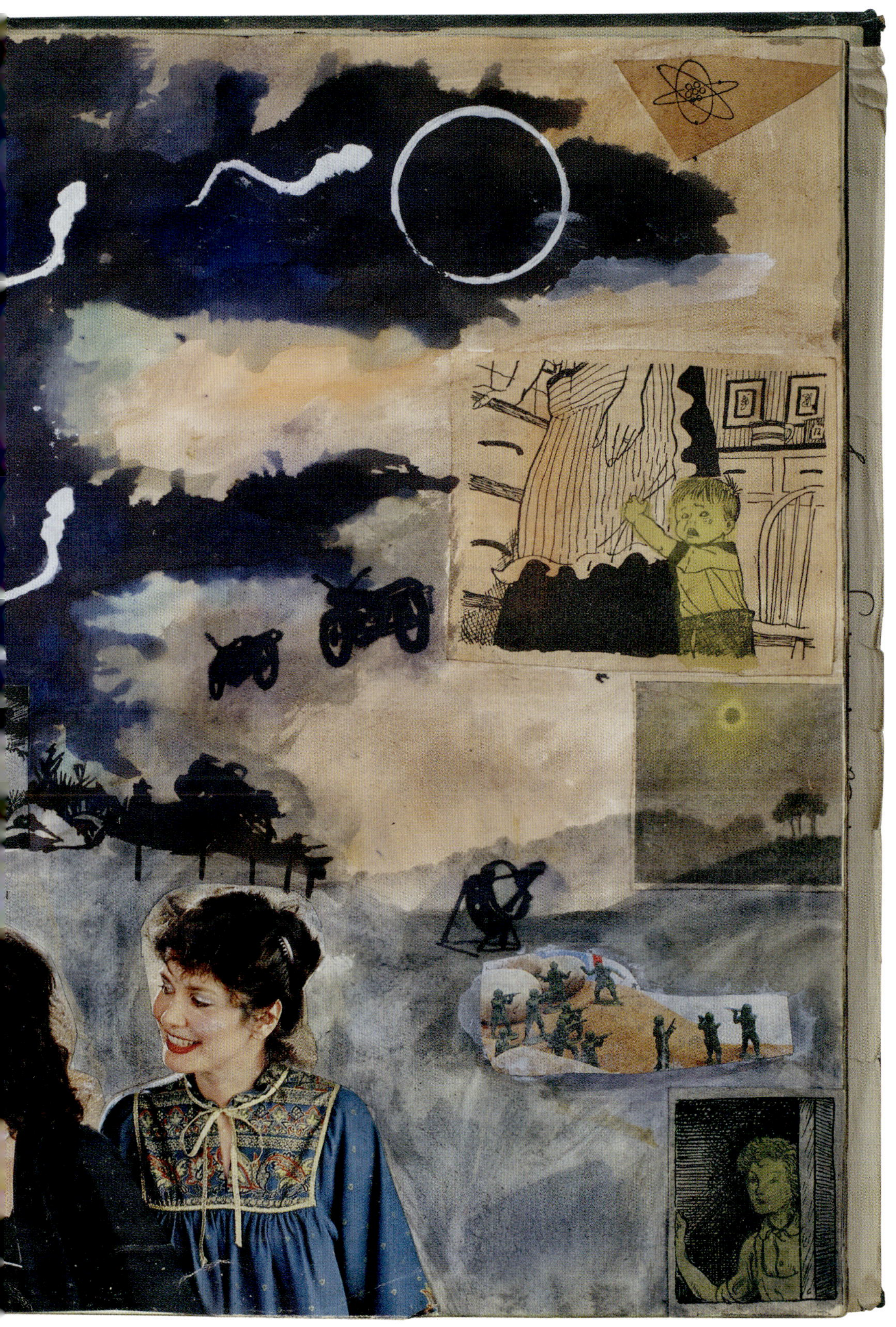

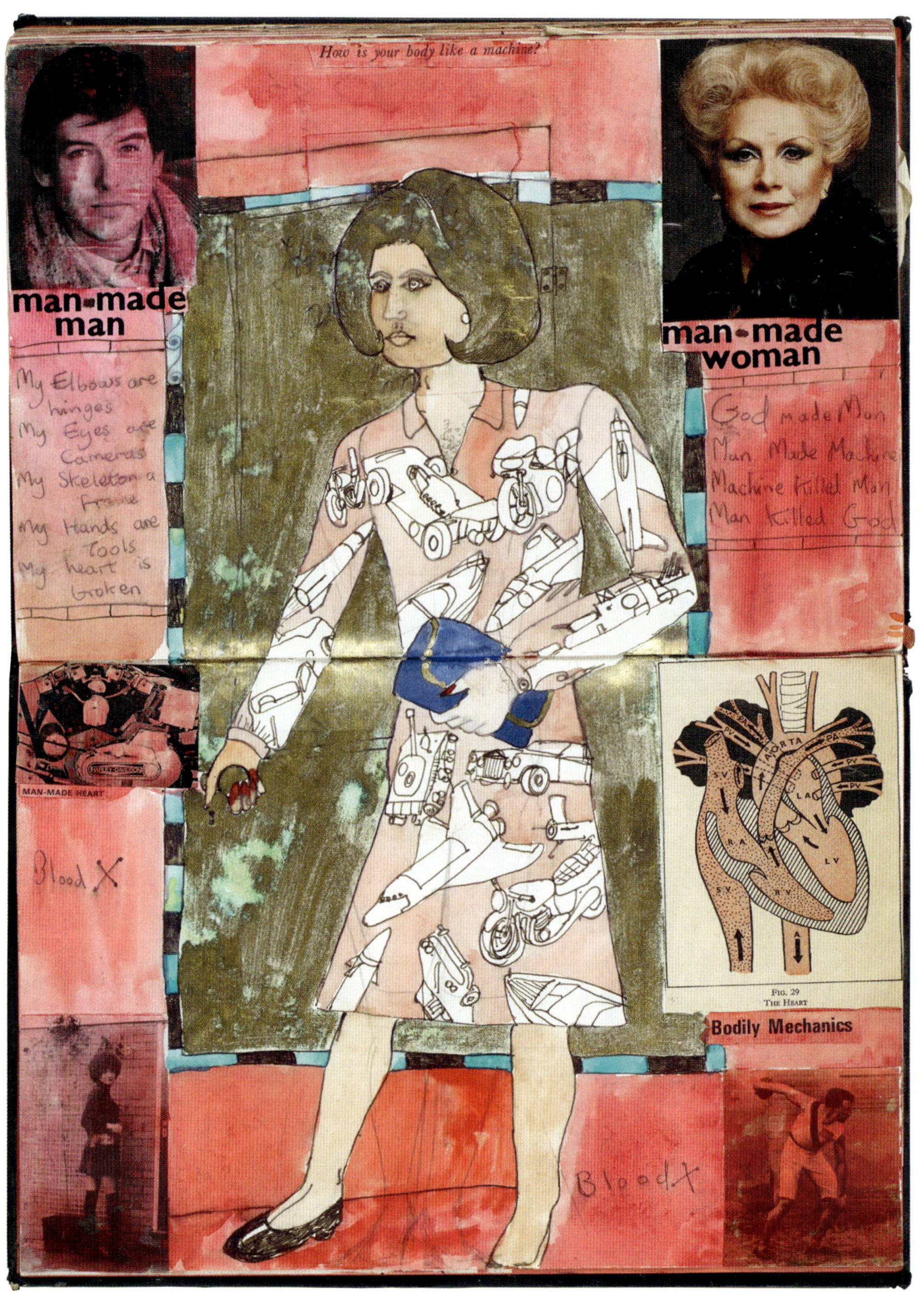

PRECEDING PAGE: *Poems for Sofas Sketchbook*, 1981–82
A4 Sketchbook, 30 × 21 cm

ABOVE: *The Blue Guitar Sketchbook*, 1981–82
A4 Sketchbook, 30 × 21 cm

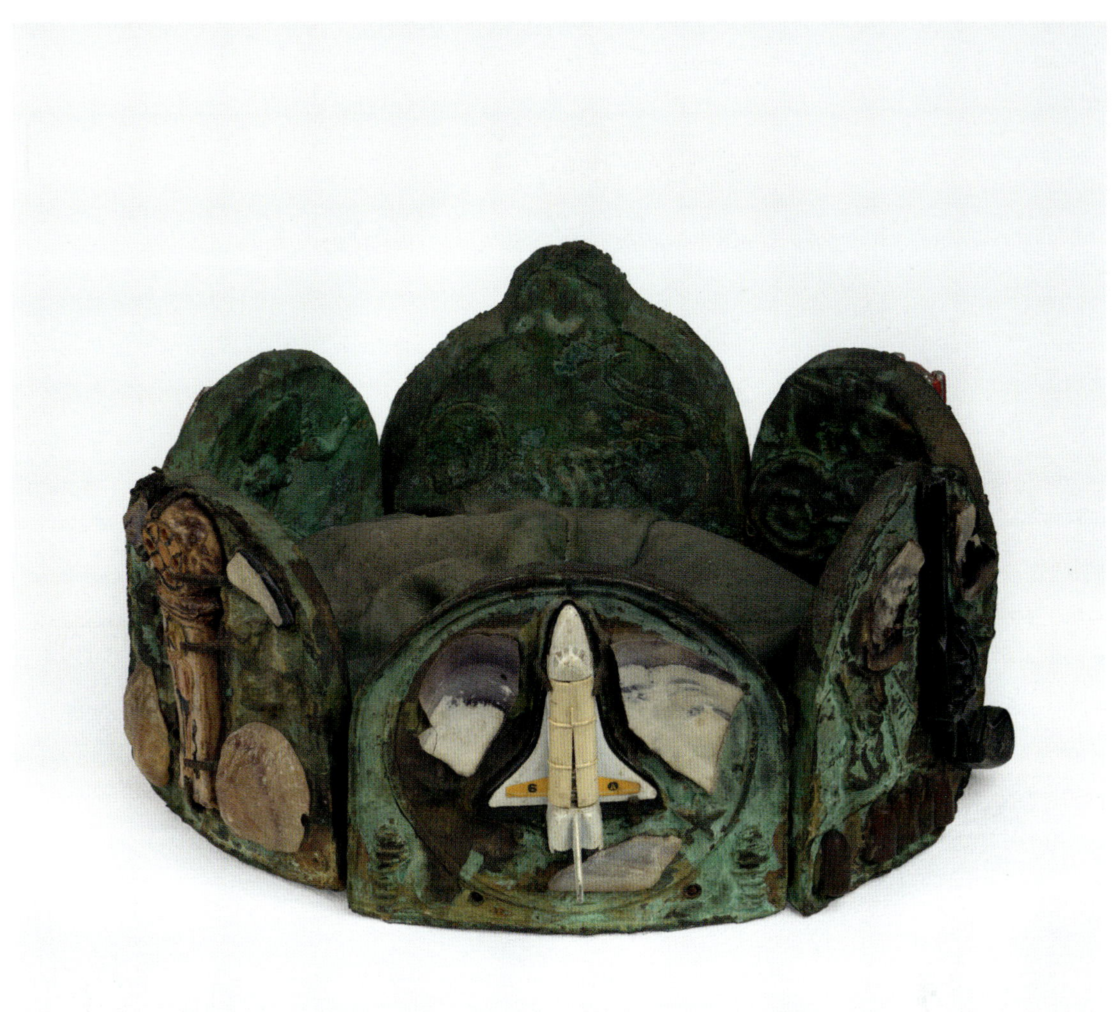

The Crown of Penii, 1982
Bronze, steel, leather, ceramic and found objects, 12 × 24 cm

This work is based on a famous medieval relic, the Iron Crown
in Monza Cathedral, near Milan. The iron in it was supposed to
have been beaten out of one of the nails used at the Crucifixion.
This was my version, made while I was at college. The pieces
are all set into little bronze plaques with bits of seashell as
decoration. The band is steel and it has a leather centre; the
little attachments are either ceramic or found objects like toys.

I called it the *Crown of Penii*: it combines ideas about
maleness, religion and monarchy. It has lots of phallic imagery
and many of the ingredients of my early work: a space shuttle;
a Celtic cross; a kind of Willendorf Venus; an American car; a
knife; and a pistol. The first space shuttle mission had been
launched in 1981 and I'd taken a great interest in it; we all thought
it would blow itself into smithereens.

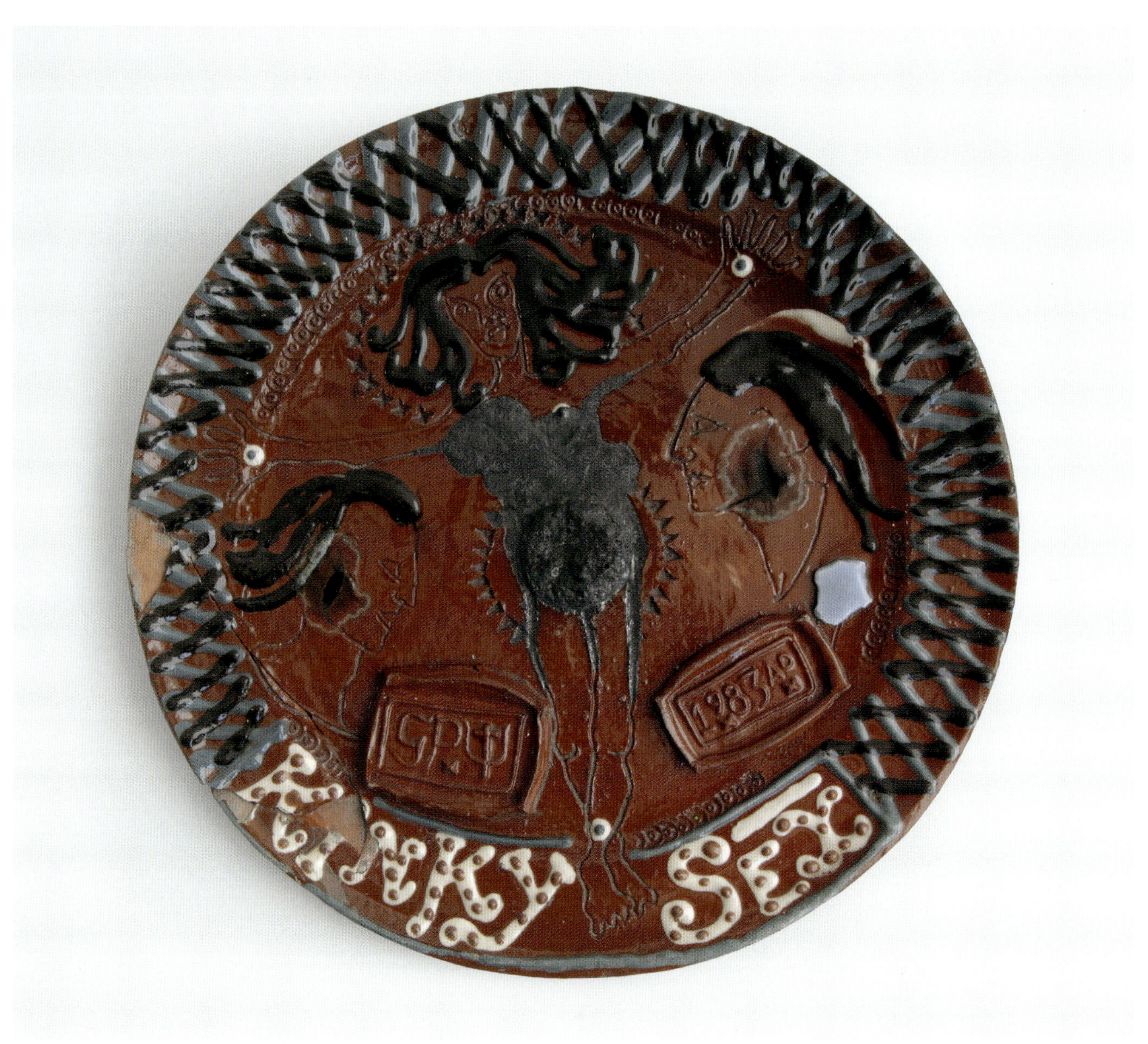

ABOVE: *Kinky Sex*, 1983
Glazed ceramic, diameter 24.5 cm

OPPOSITE: *Animal Love*, 1984
Glazed ceramic, 23 × 26 cm

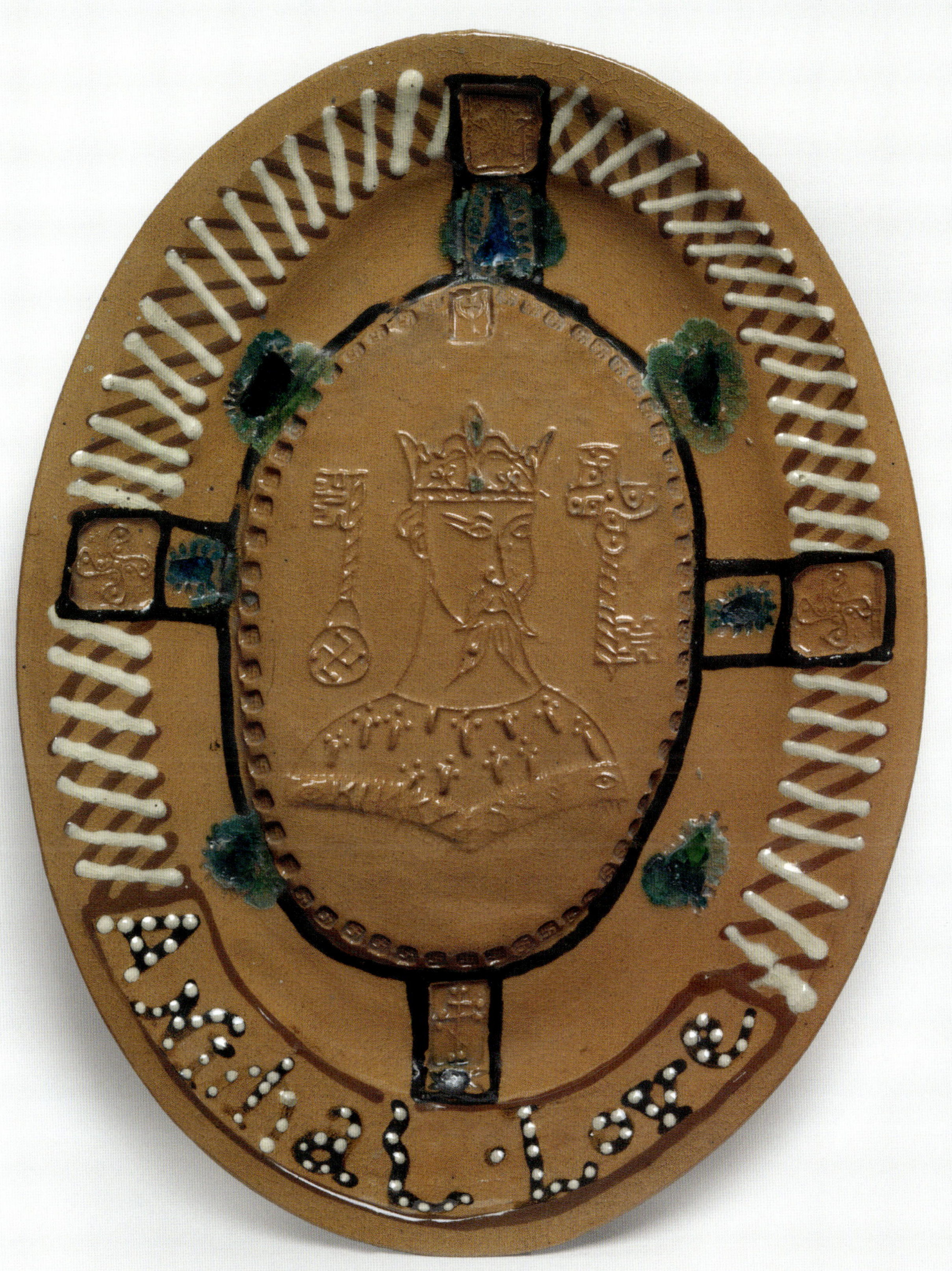
AKMAL LORE

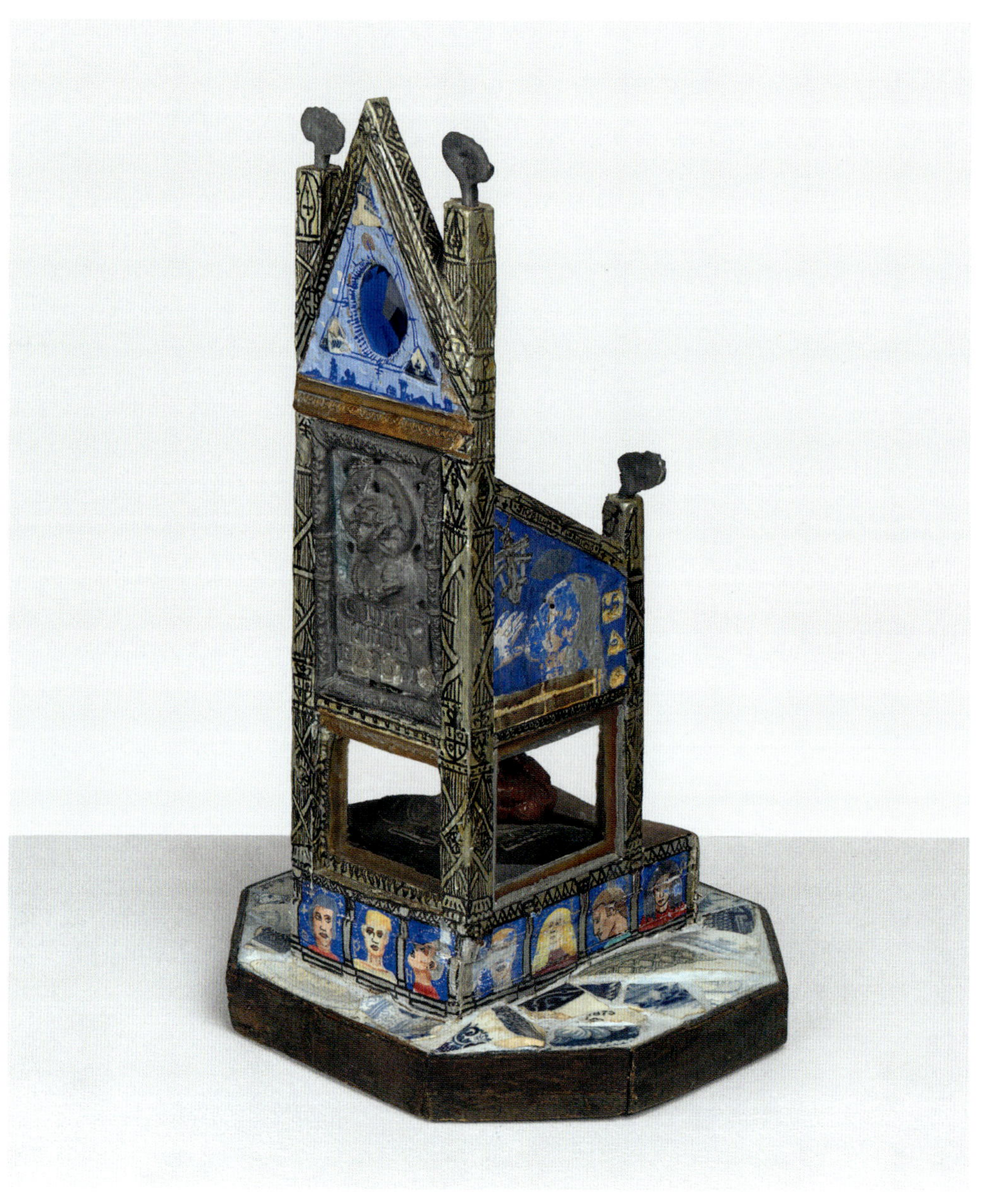

Saint Diana (Let Them Eat Shit), 1984
Mixed media, 38 × 23 × 19.5 cm

I was at once fascinated and repulsed by the cult of Princess Diana
that flowered in the years after her marriage to Prince Charles. This
reliquary is crafted from detritus scavenged from round our squat
and pottery sherds found mudlarking on the Thames foreshore.
It is in the form of a miniature coronation chair. The original in
Westminster Abbey was made in 1300 to house the sacred Stone
of Scone. My miniature throne come commode houses a sacred
turd. Perhaps inspired by Piero Manzoni's *Artist's Shit* (1961), I had
tried to encase one of my own faeces in a block of resin, which
ended in a smelly mess, so I made a fake one out of ceramic.

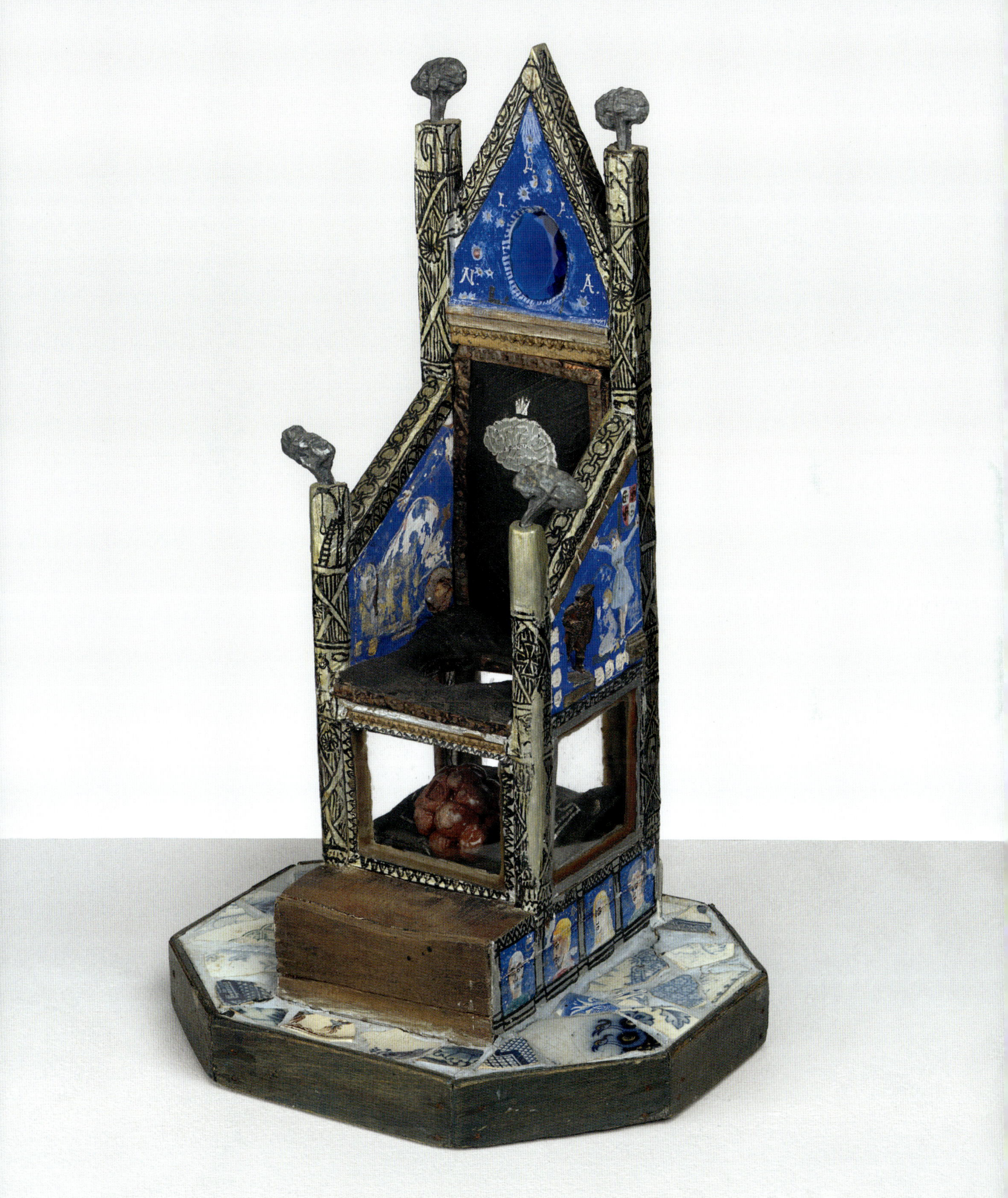

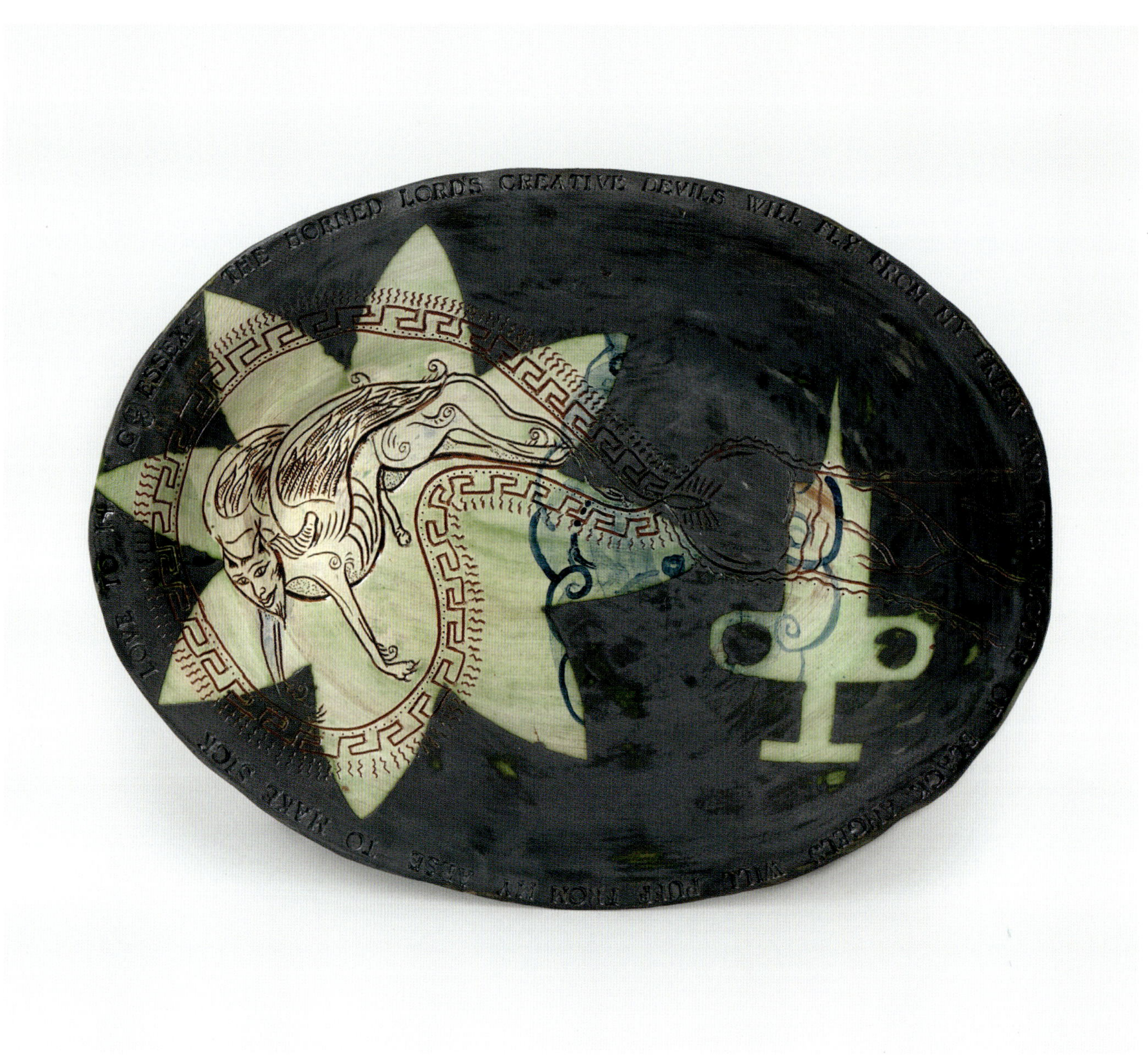

The Devil Plate, 1984
Glazed ceramic, 27.9 × 35.6 cm

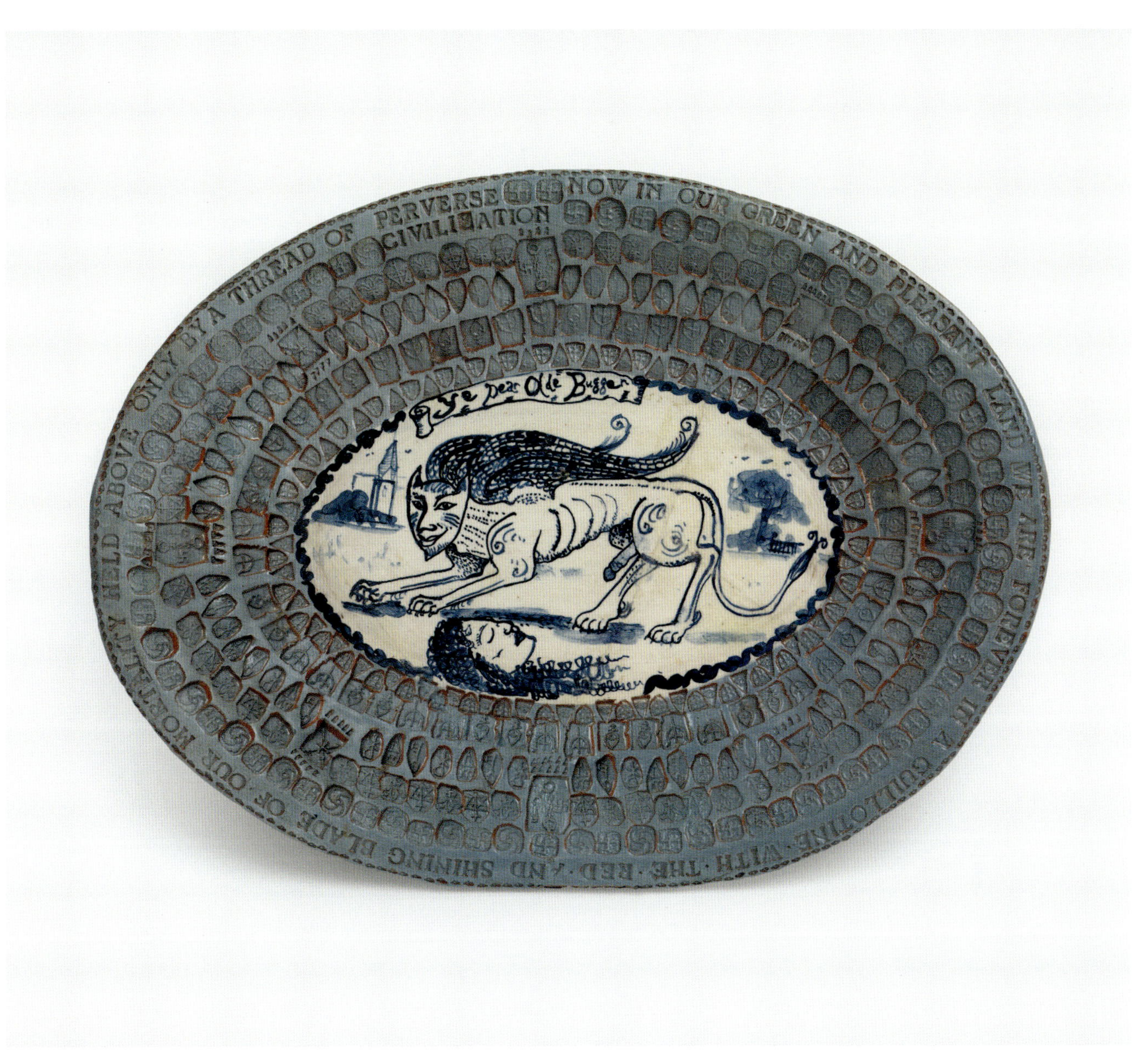

*Now in Our Green and Pleasant Land
(Ye Dear Olde Bugger)*, 1984
Glazed ceramic, 27.9 × 37.5 cm

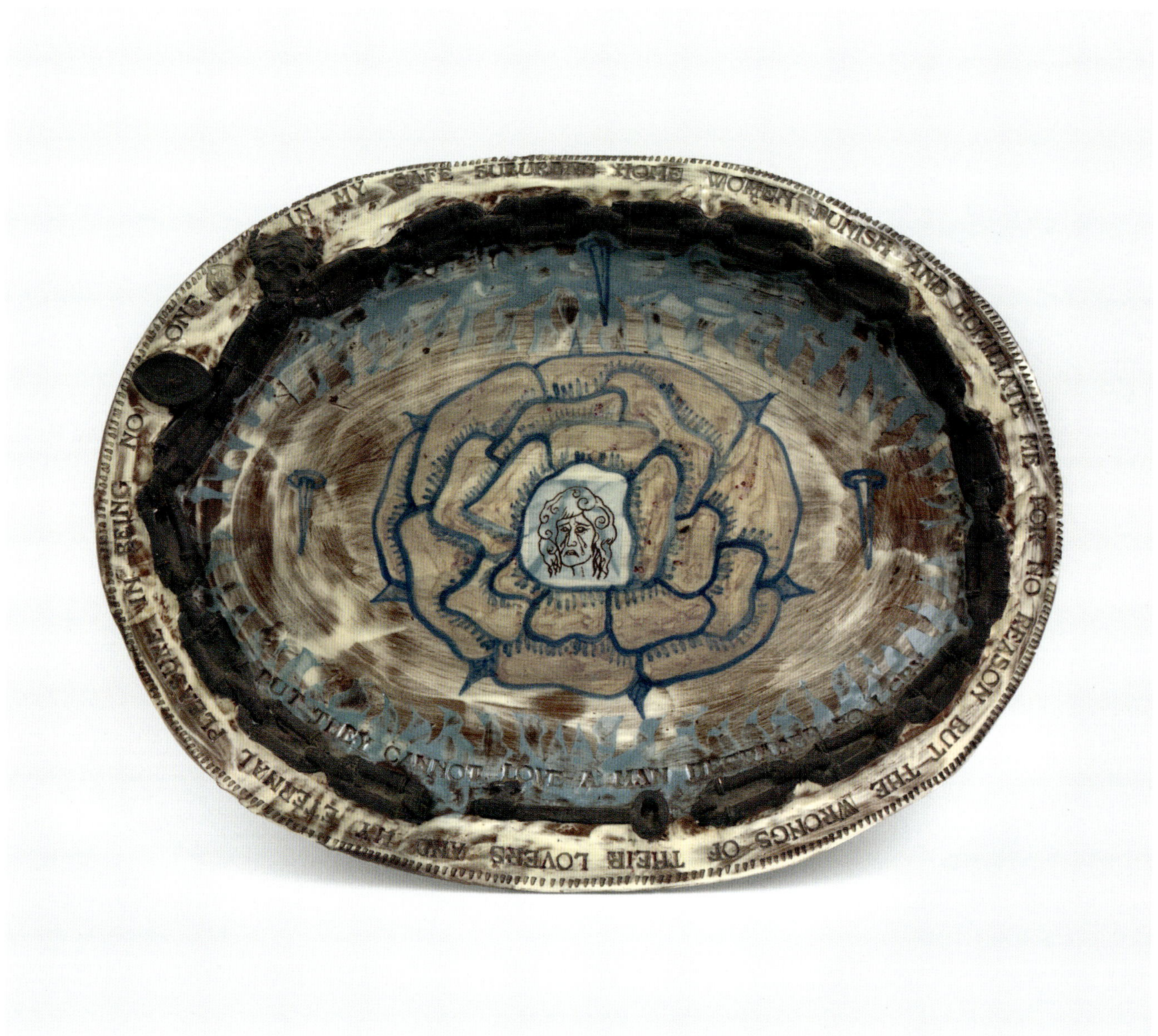

Untitled, 1984
Glazed ceramic, 26.5 × 34 cm

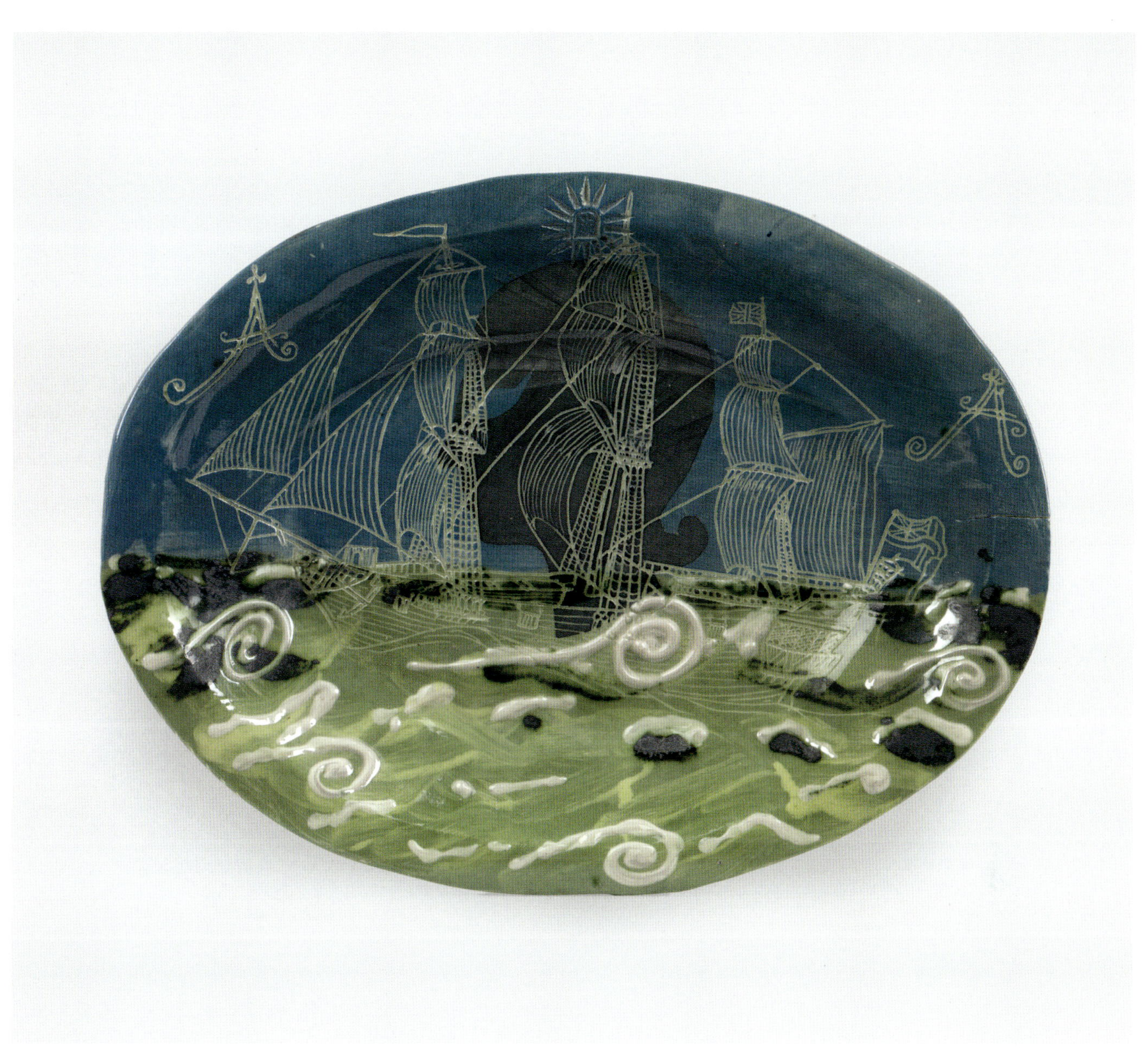

April Ashley in Full Sail, c. 1984
Glazed ceramic, 26 × 34 cm

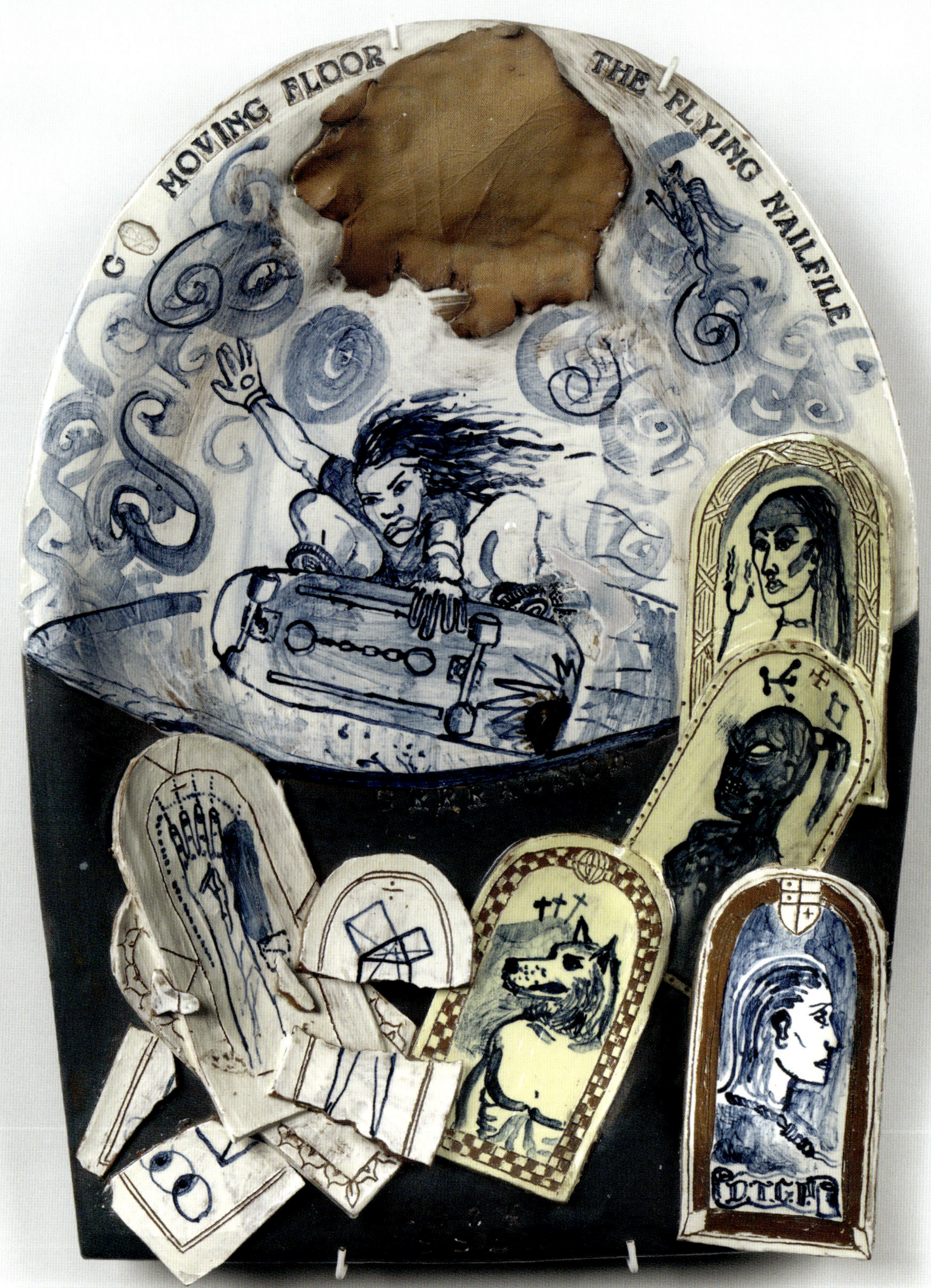
MOVING FLOOR
THE FLYING NAILFILE

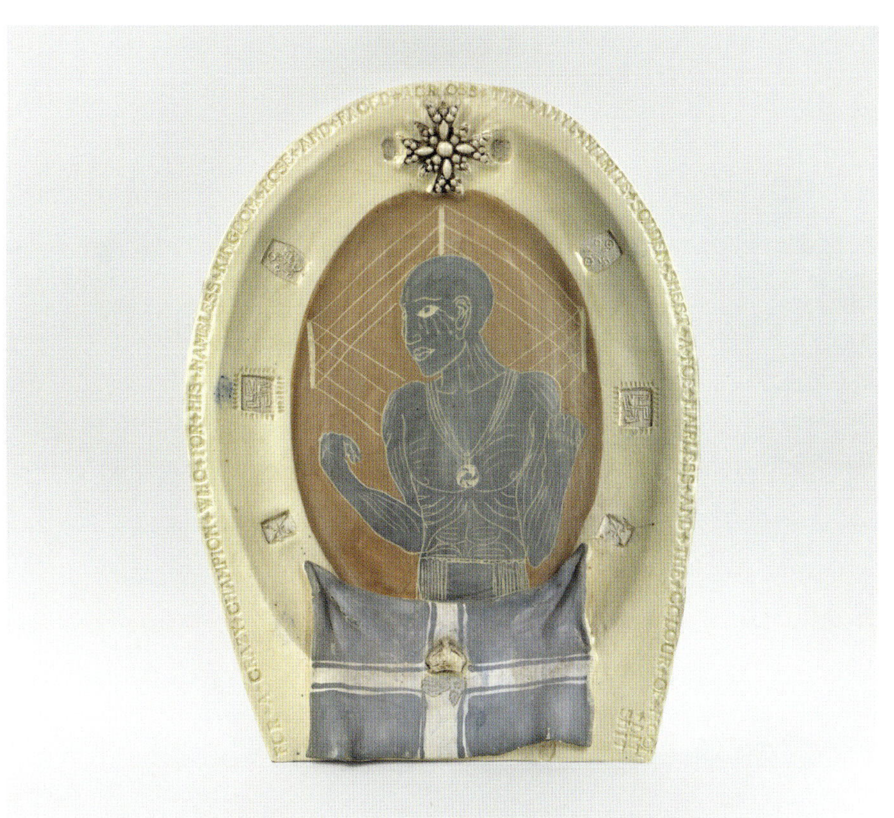

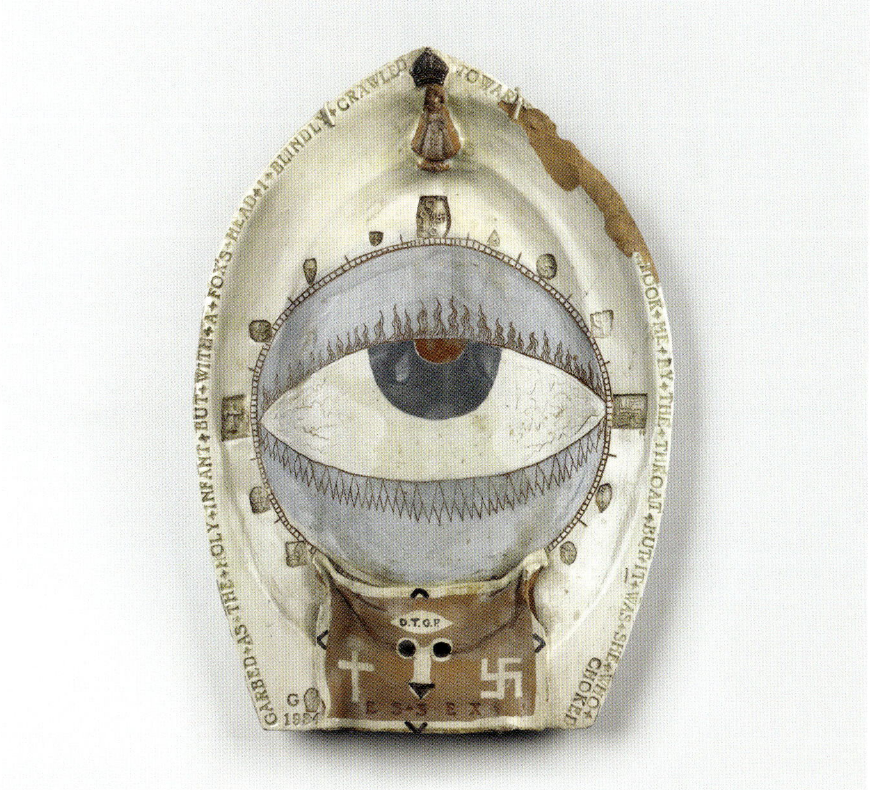

OPPOSITE: *The Flying Nailfile*, 1984
Glazed ceramic, 36.5 × 26.5 cm

ABOVE: *For a Crazy Champion*, 1984
Glazed ceramic, 38.5 × 29 cm

BELOW: *Eye Plate*, 1984
Glazed ceramic, 37.5 × 26.5 cm

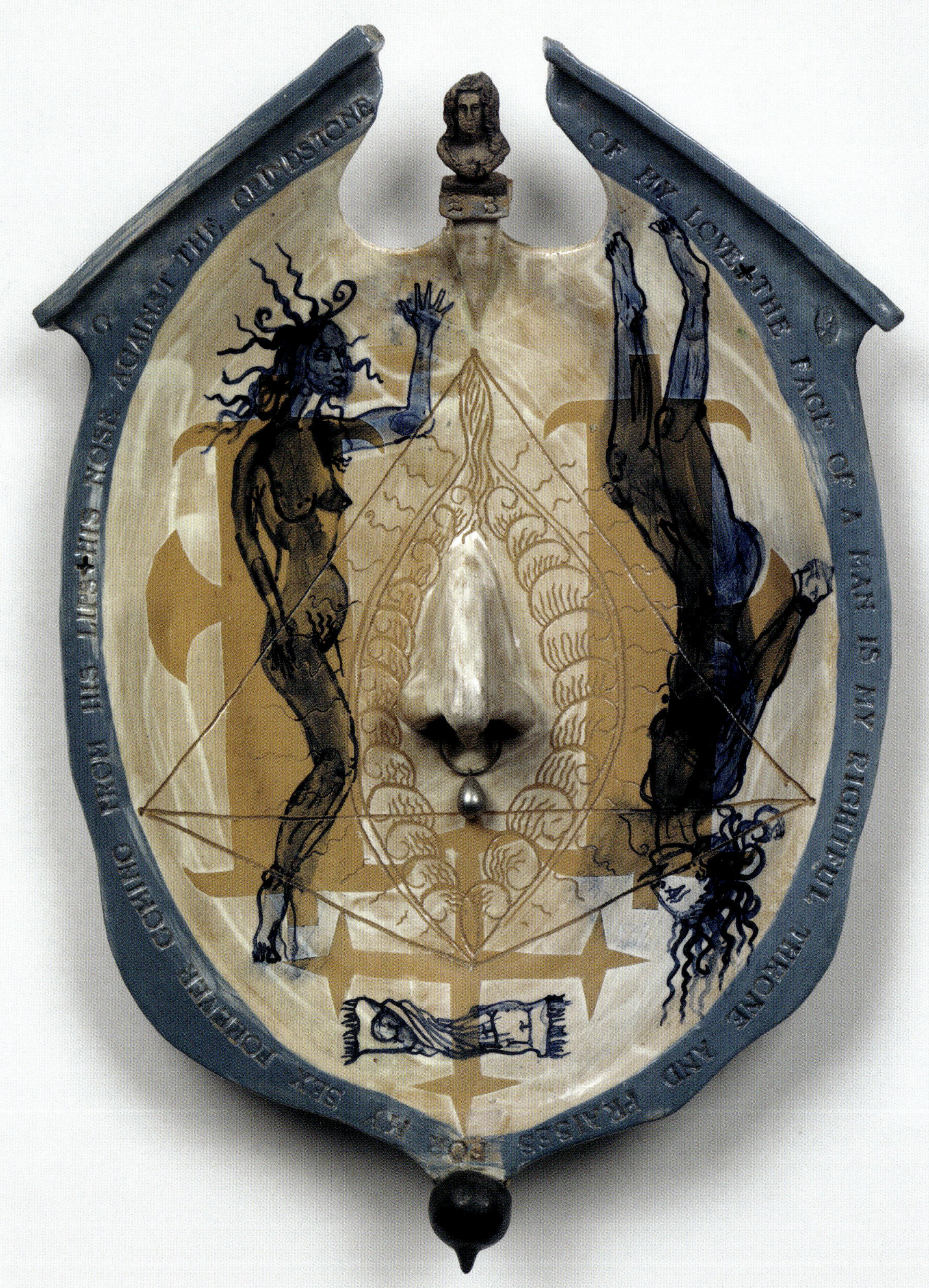
AGAINST THIS GRINDSTONE
OF MY LOVE THE FACE OF A MAN IS MY RIGHTFUL THRONE AND PRAISES FOR MY SELF FOREVER COMING FROM HIS LIPS

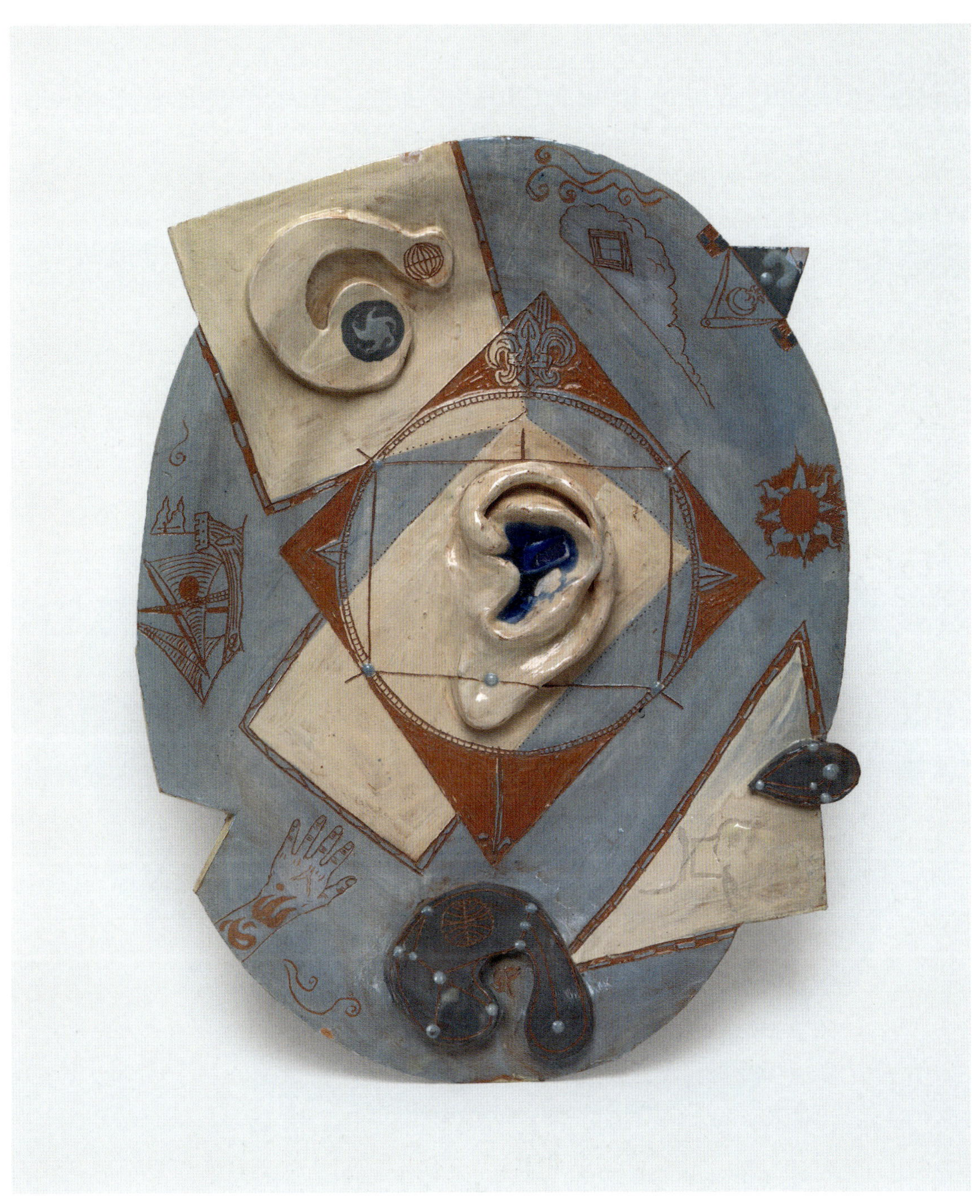

OPPOSITE: *Nose Plate*, 1985
Glazed ceramic, 41.5 × 29 cm

ABOVE: *Ear Dish*, 1985
Glazed ceramic, 37 × 28 cm

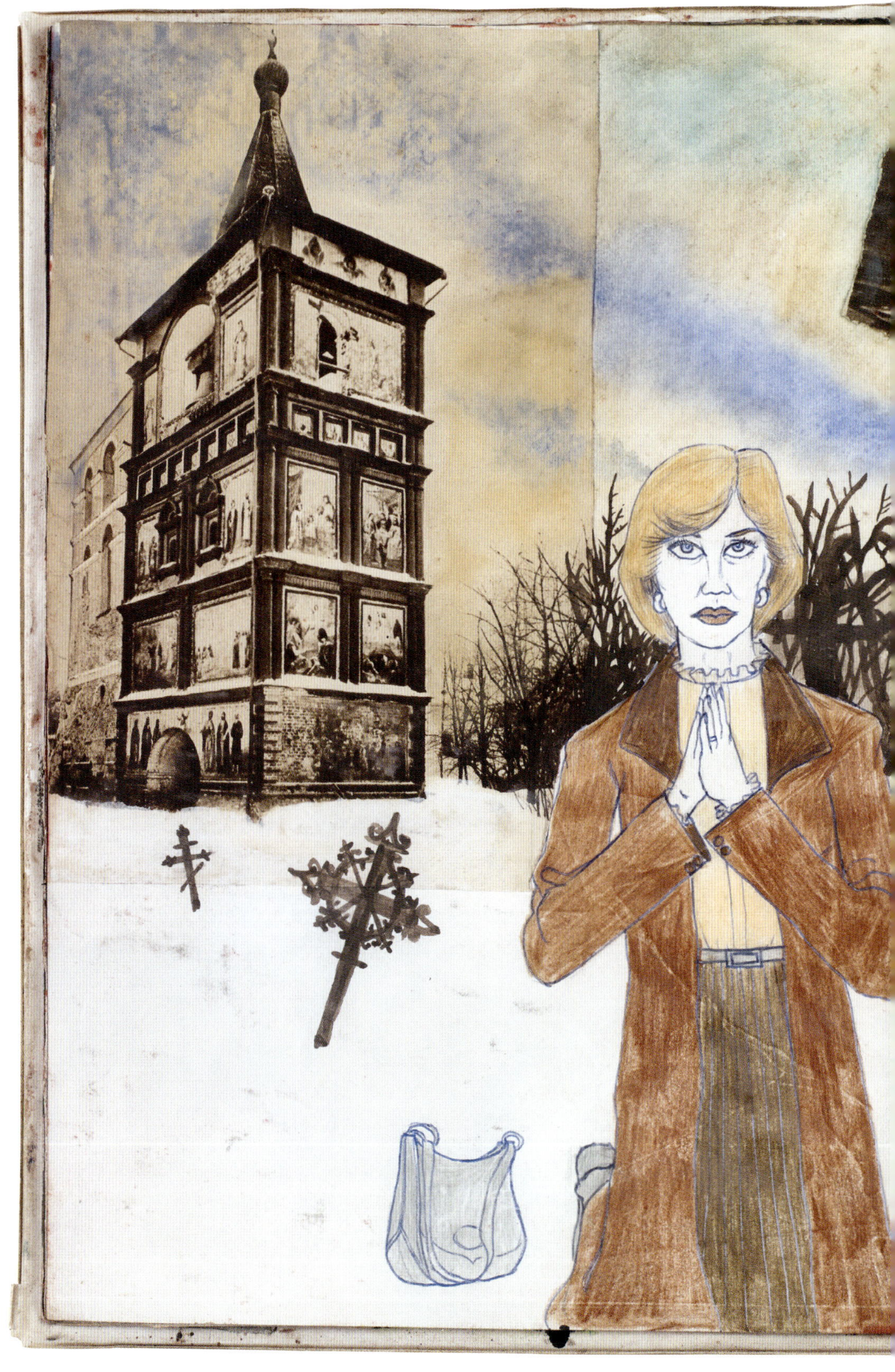

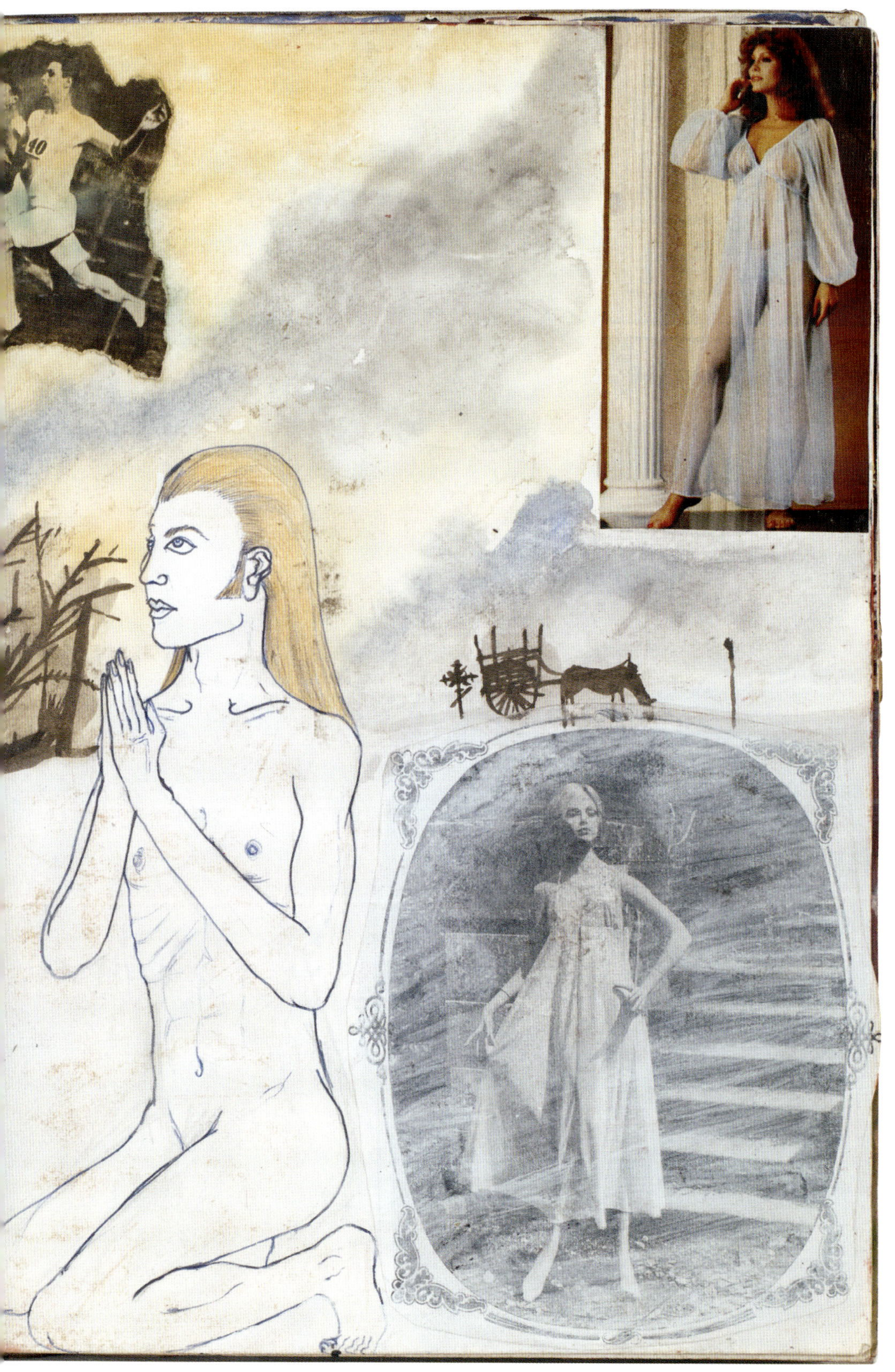

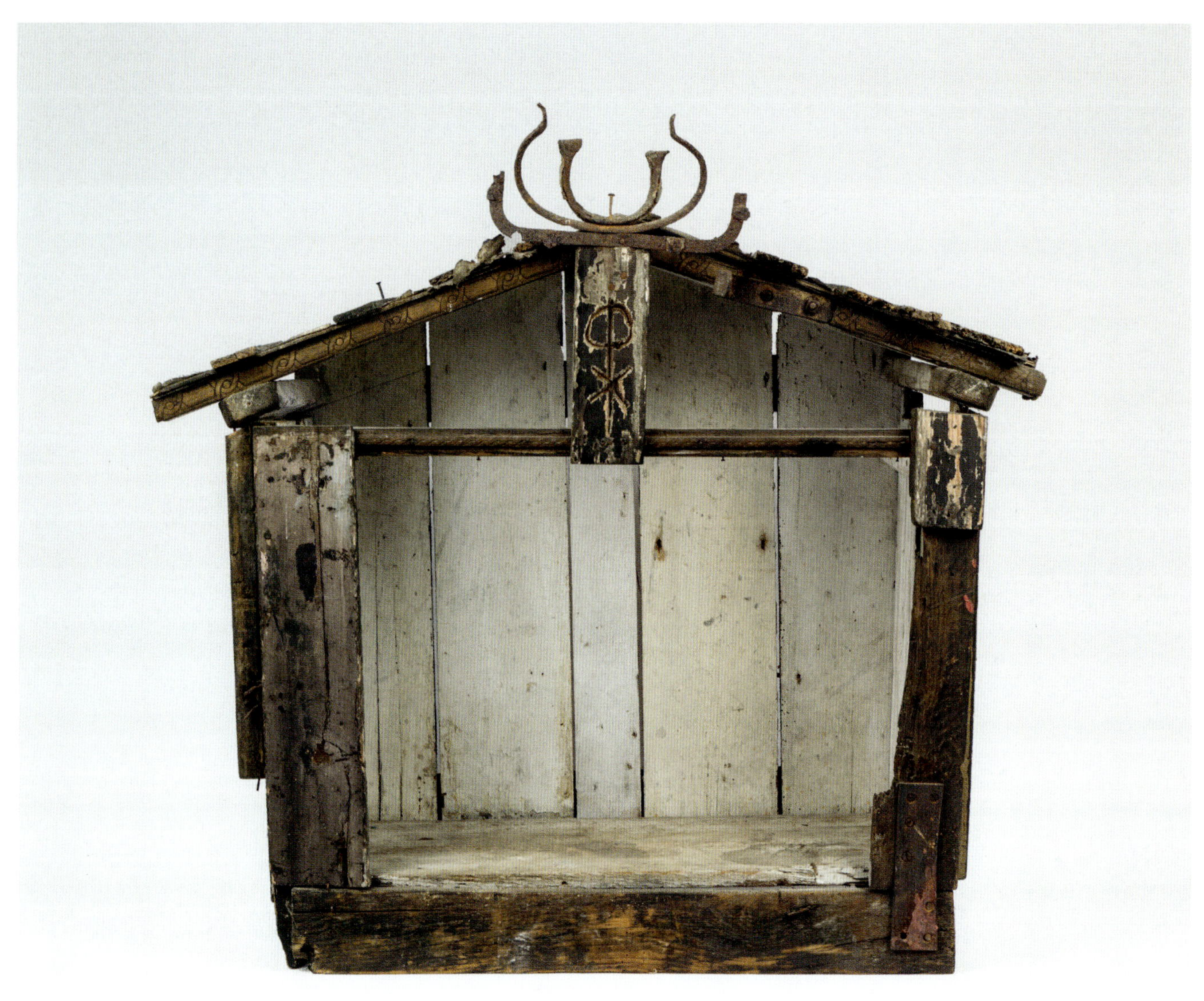

PRECEDING PAGE: *The Orange Sketchbook*, 1984–85
A4 Sketchbook, 30 × 21 cm

ABOVE: Untitled, 1985
Wood, 85.1 × 86.4 × 35.6 cm

OPPOSITE: *No God Shall Tame Me, I Am War*, 1985
Glazed ceramic, 19.1 × 27.9 × 12 cm

84

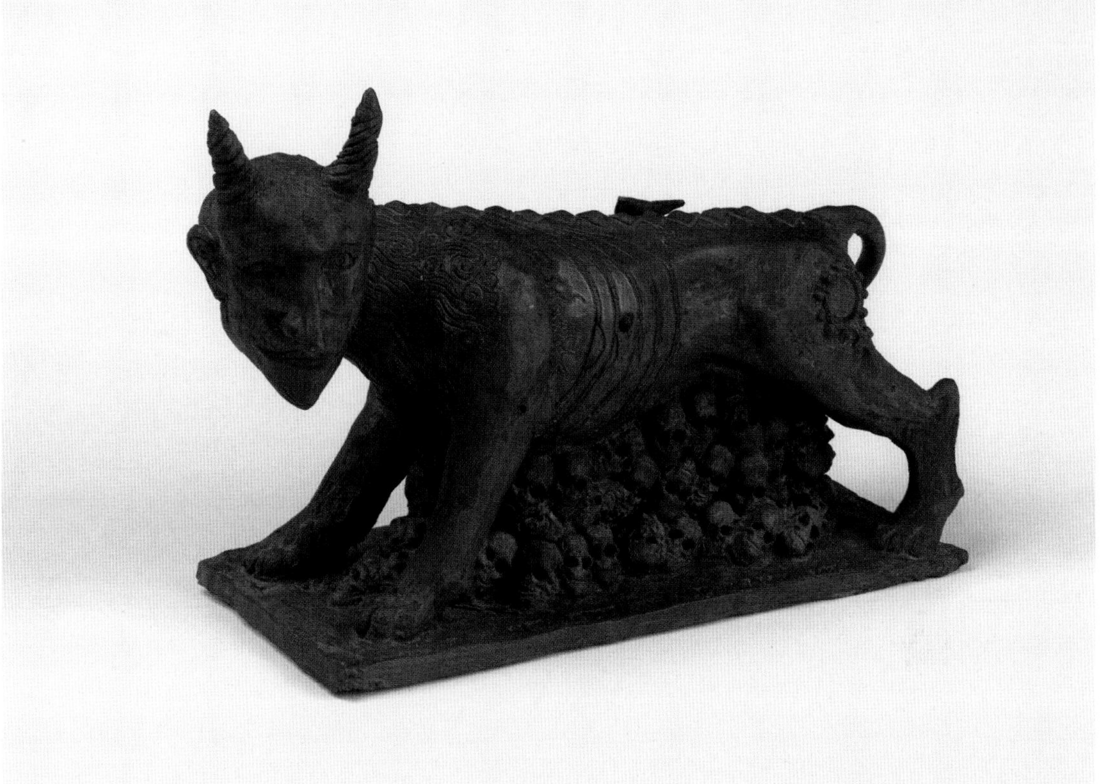

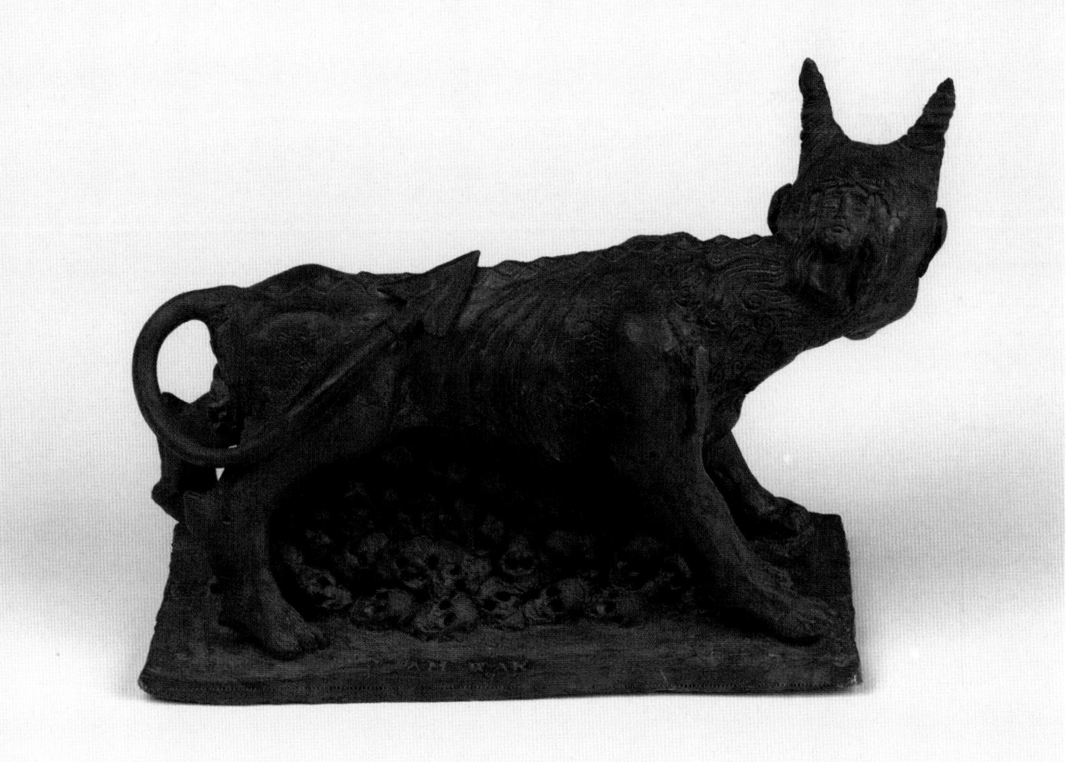

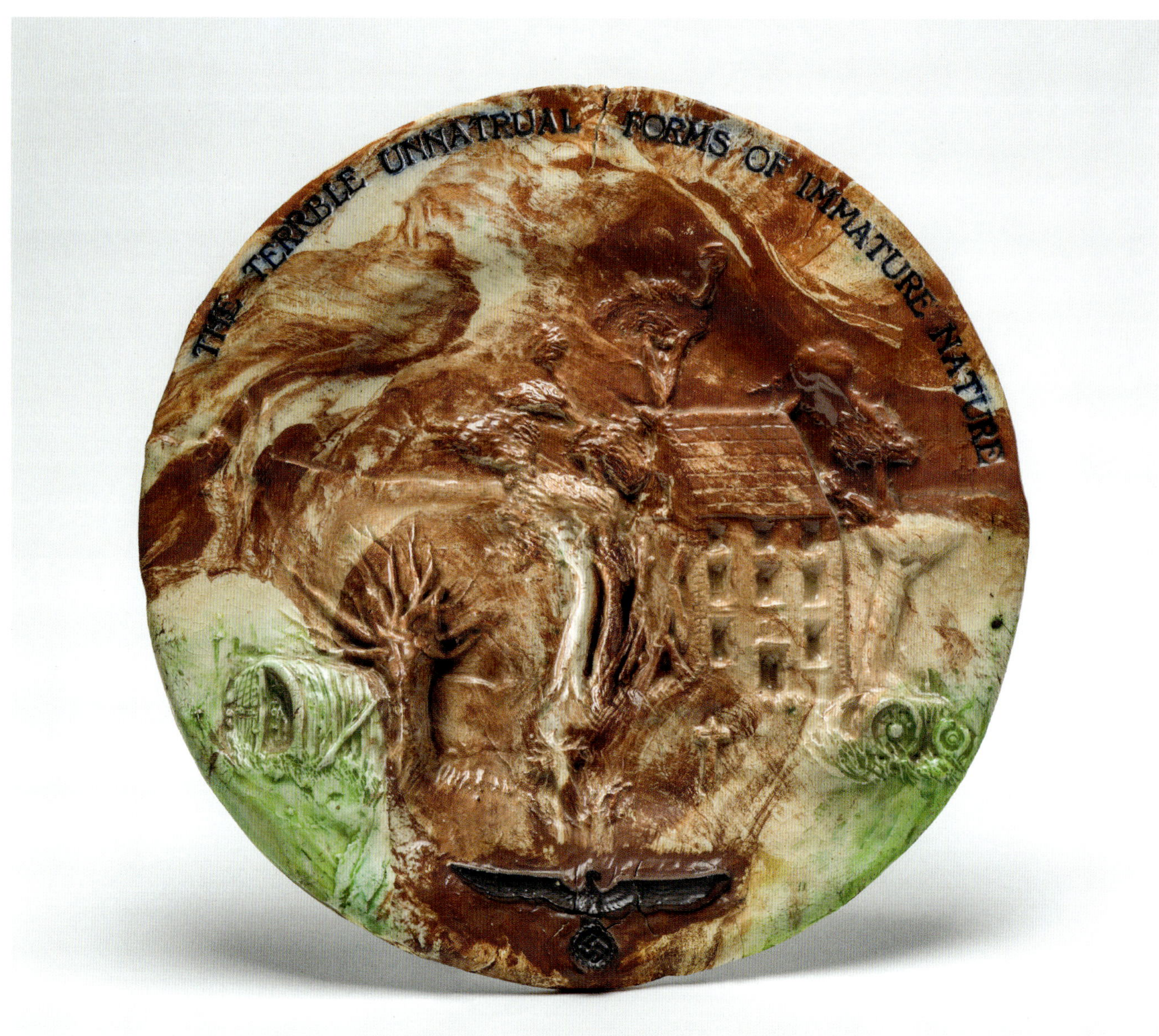

The Terrible Unnatural Forms of Immature Nature, 1985
Glazed ceramic, diameter 25 cm

This press-moulded plate is number eight in a series of about thirty, all made from the same mould. I was fascinated by 'collectors plates': kitsch commemorative wares made in huge 'limited' editions and sold through full-page advertisements in the back of women's magazines and tabloid newspapers. The bas-relief depicts an abandoned house, a rusting tractor, a grave, a pollarded tree and a Nissen hut; in short, a typical Essex country scene. To tell you the truth, I am mystified as to what I meant by the text and how it relates to the Nazi insignia. Perhaps it was a dark premonition of Brexit!

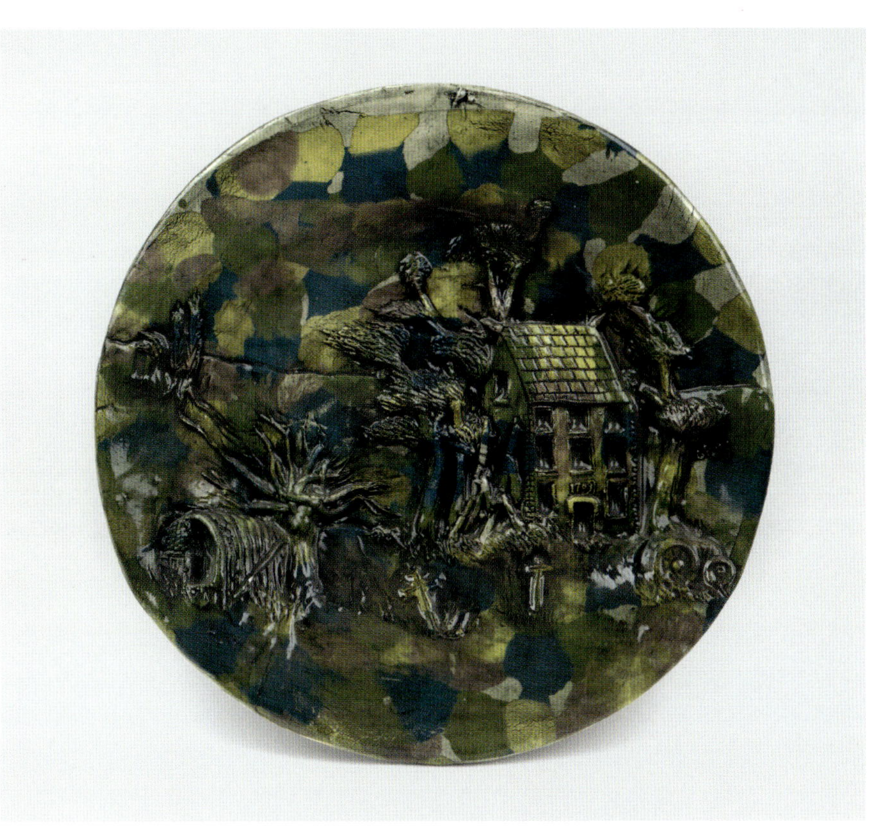

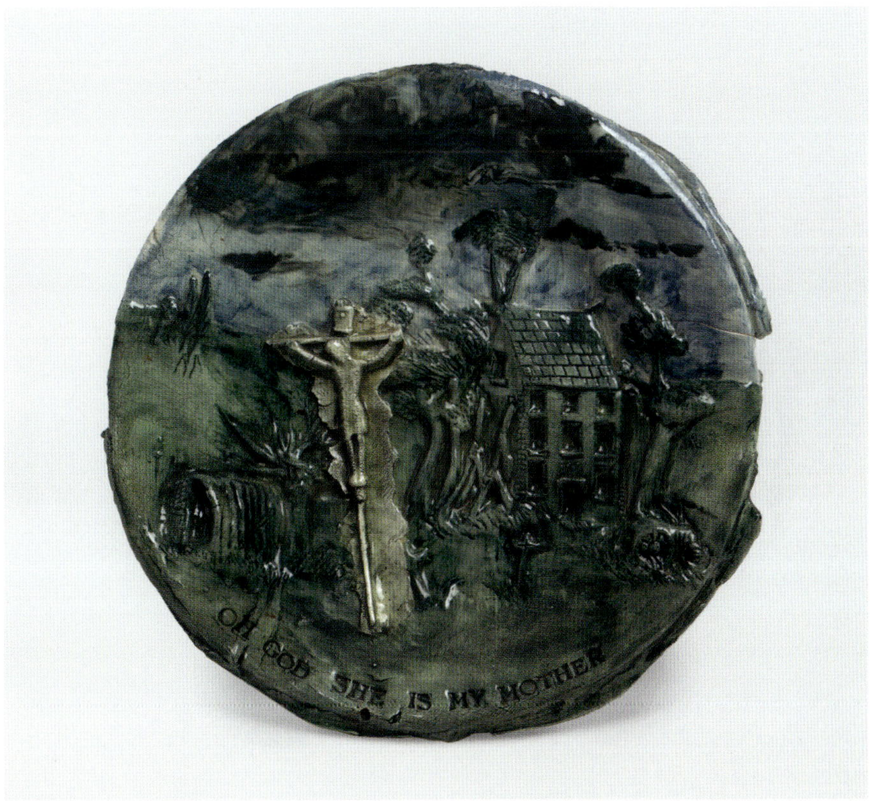

ABOVE: *Commemorative Plate No. 17*, 1985
Glazed ceramic, diameter 25 cm

BELOW: *Oh God She is My Mother*, 1985
Glazed ceramic, diameter 25 cm

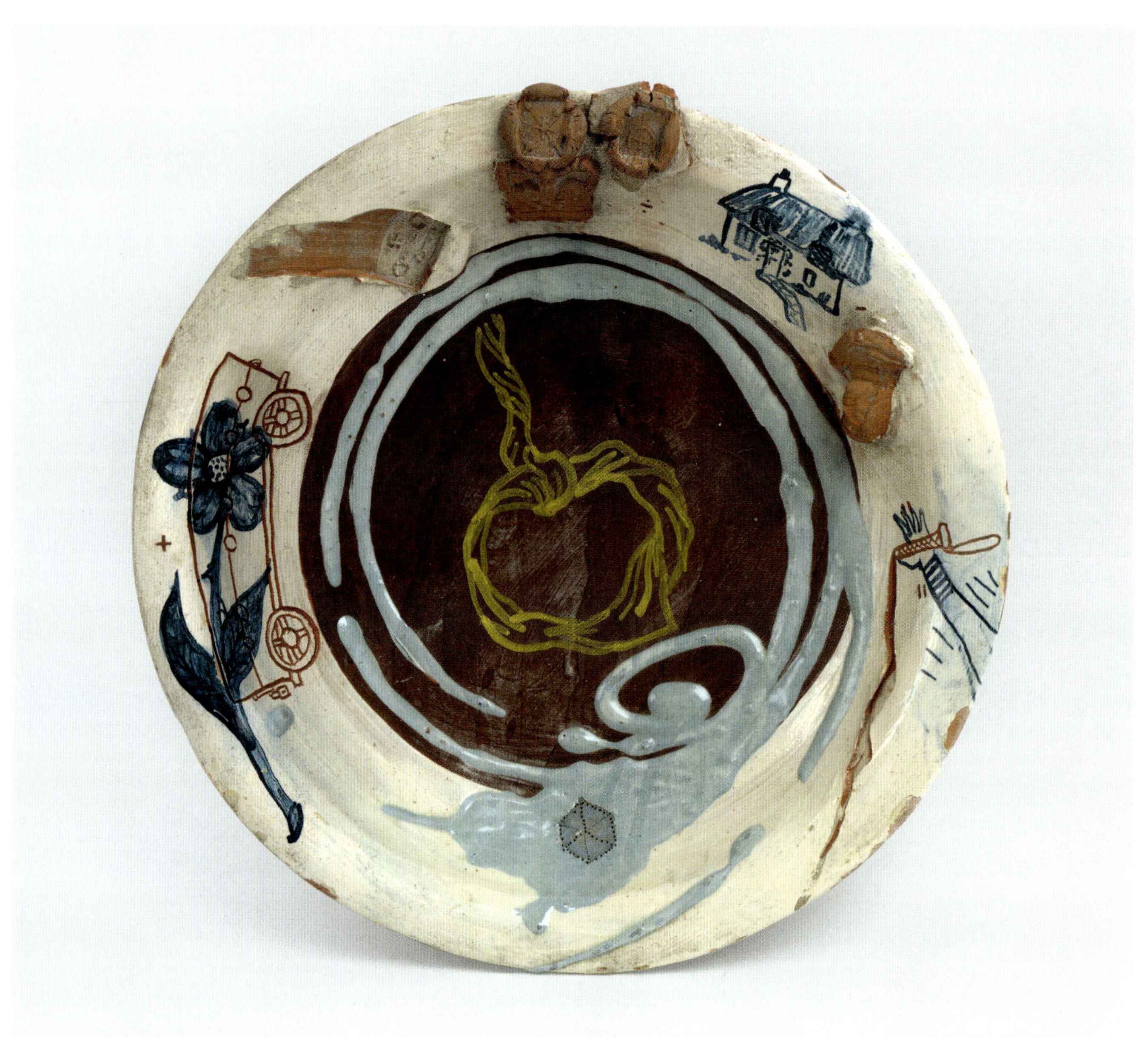

ABOVE: Untitled, 1985
Glazed ceramic, diameter 26 cm

OPPOSITE: Untitled, 1985
Glazed ceramic, 30 × 39 cm

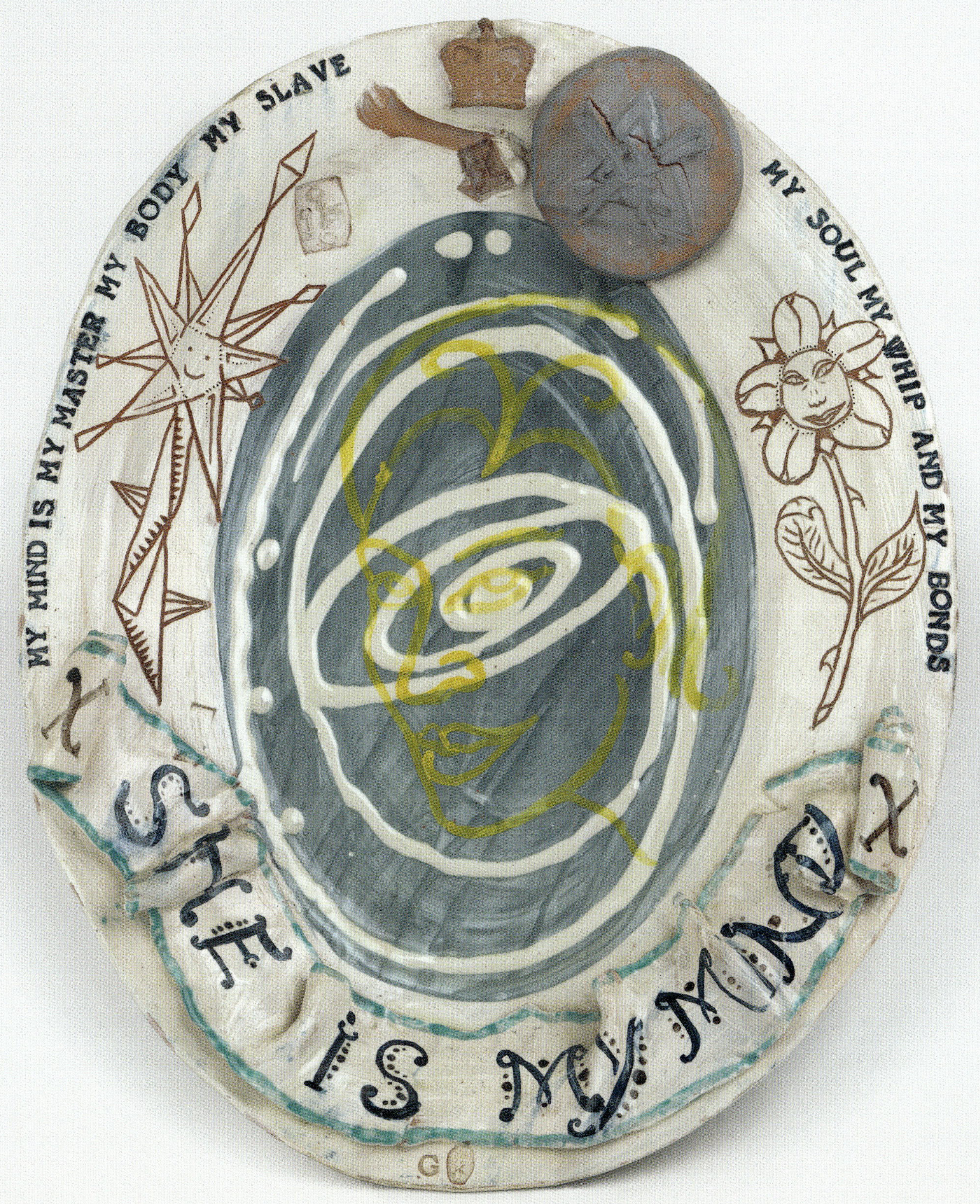

MY MIND IS MY MASTER MY BODY MY SLAVE
MY SOUL MY WHIP AND MY BONDS
SHE IS MY MIND

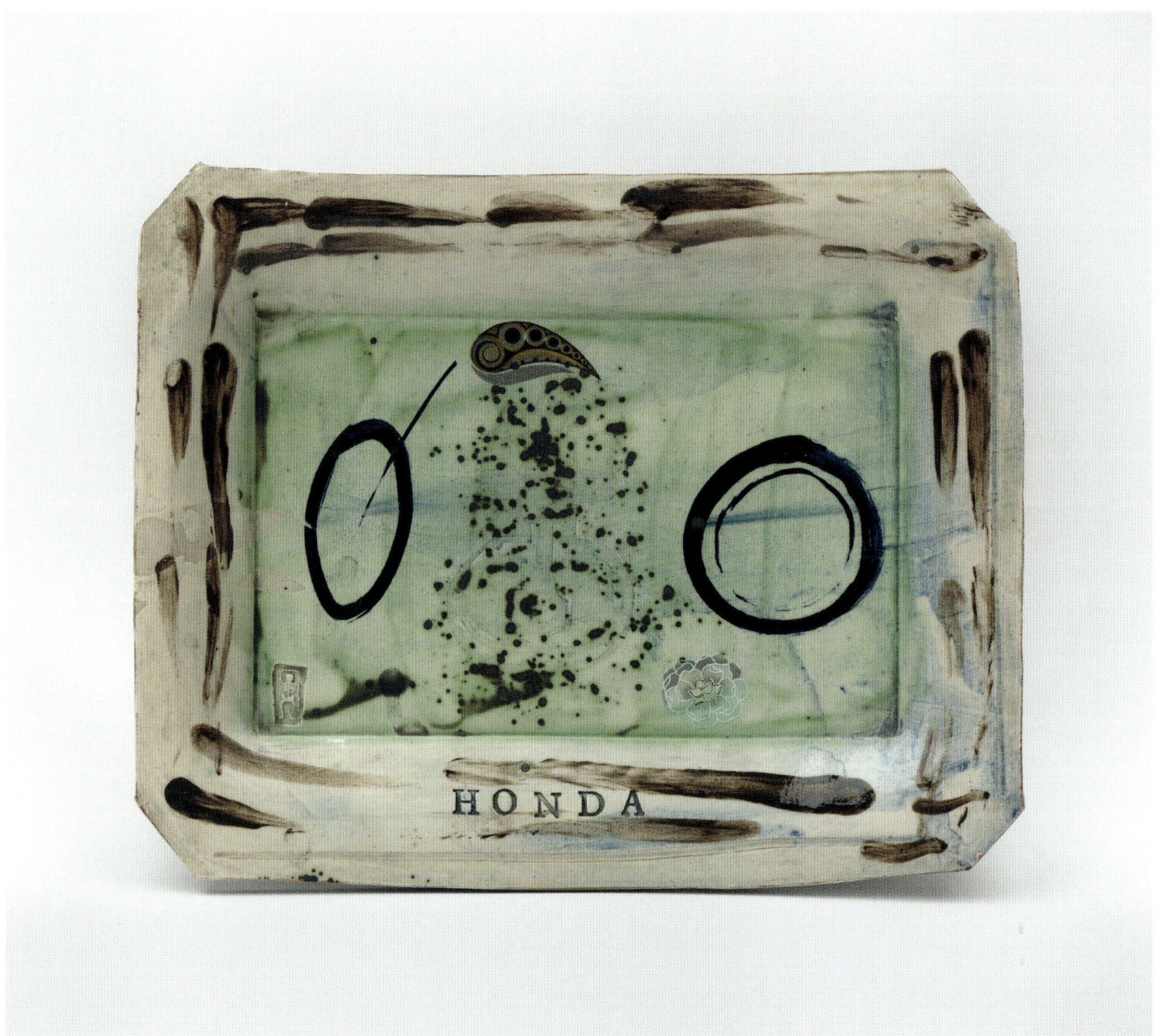

Honda, 1985
Glazed ceramic, 25 × 31.5 cm

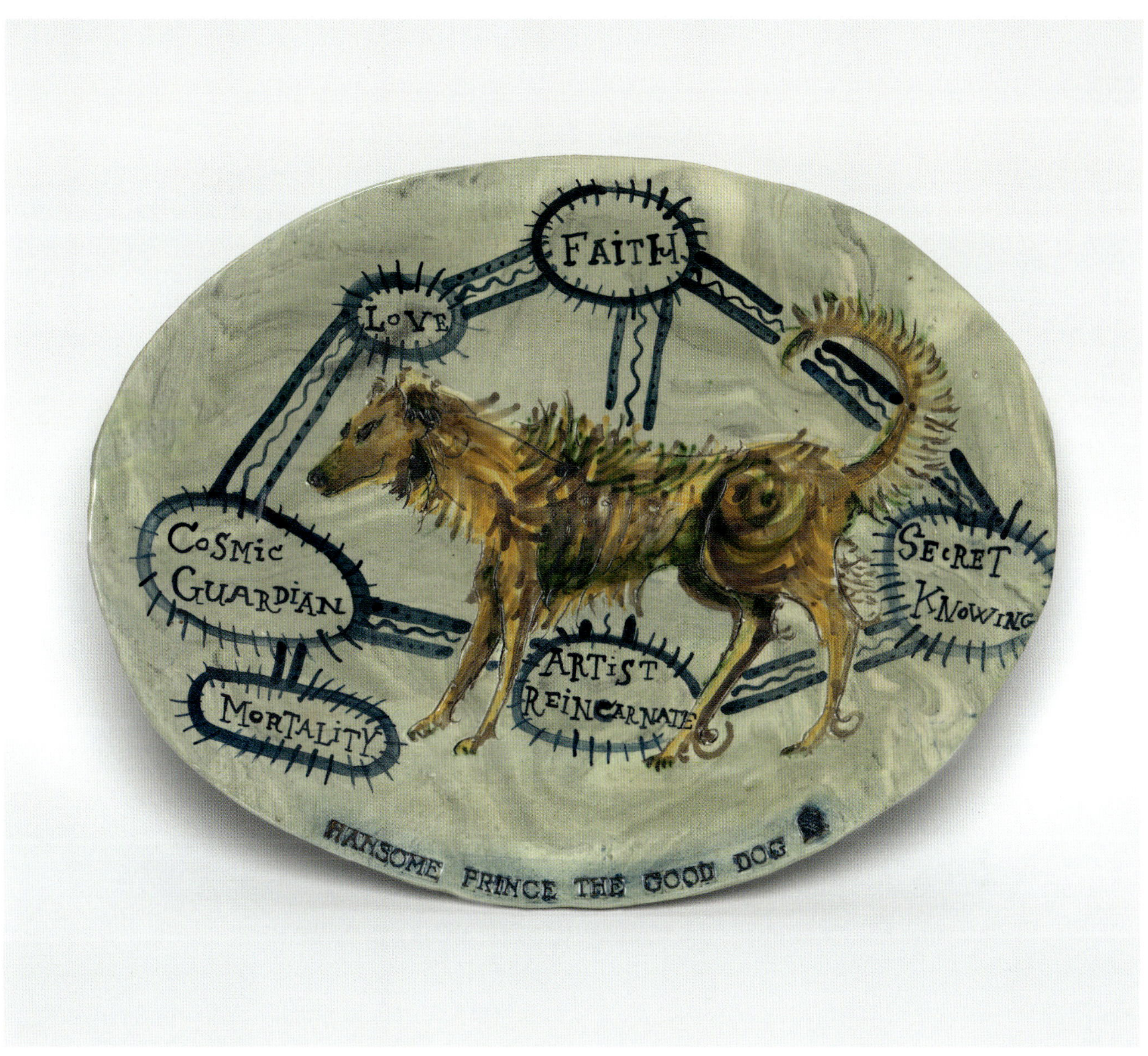

Handsome Prince the Good Dog, 1985
Glazed ceramic, 38 × 30 cm

Soon after we moved into our squat in Camden my girlfriend
Jennifer bought a puppy. He grew into a red haired collie who
we loved dearly. We project all sorts of things onto our pets.
I'm not sure how satirical this plate is; there was a lot of mystical
nonsense floating about the squat in a haze of illicit smoke. *Prince*
turned out to be an urban rogue. Jennifer moved to the country
where he savaged some sheep and he had to move back to
London with her sister.

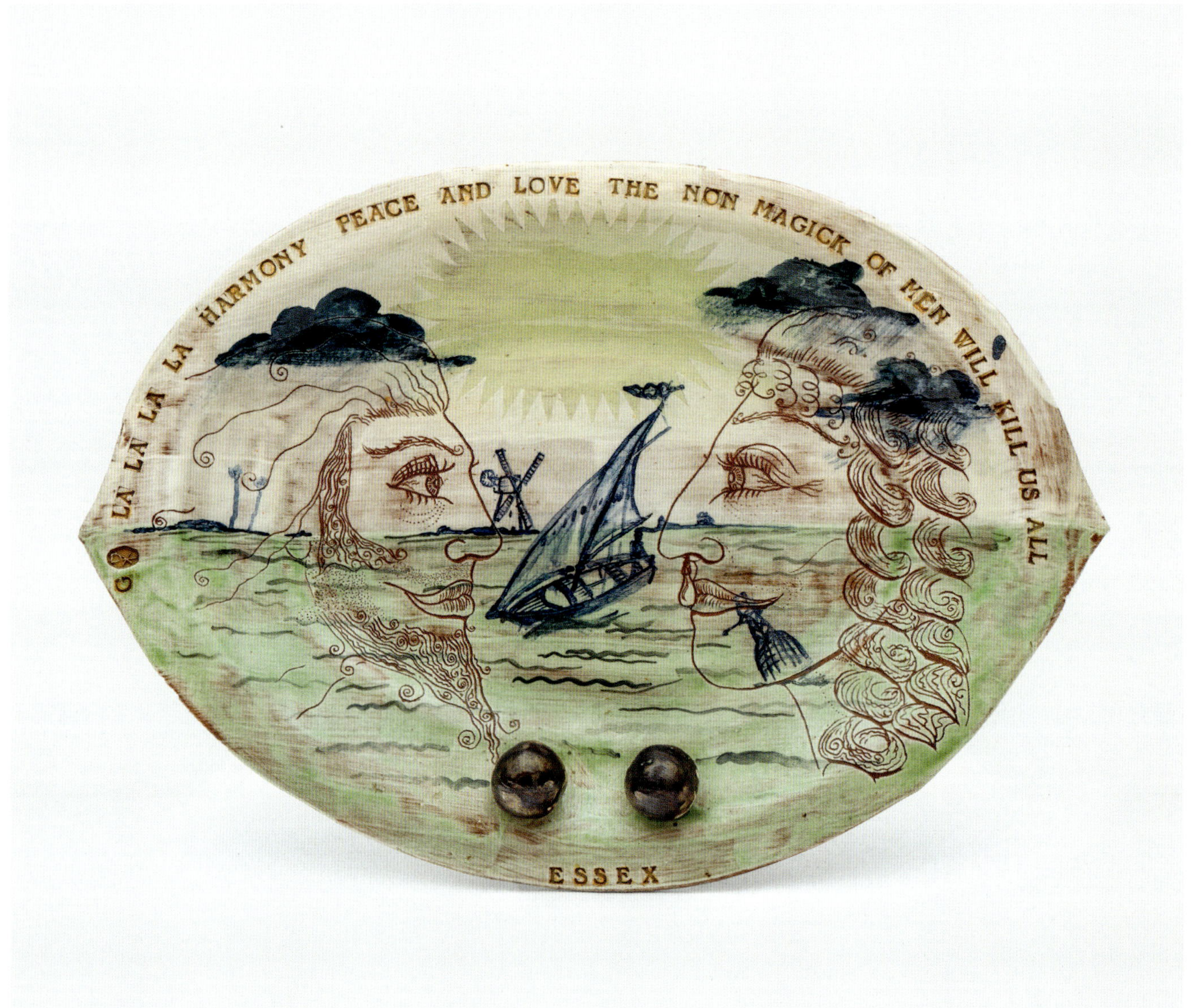

ABOVE: *Essex Plate*, 1985
Glazed ceramic, 28 × 40 cm

OPPOSITE ABOVE: *Essex Landscape Plus Stocks*, 1985
Glazed ceramic, 29 × 36 cm

OPPOSITE BELOW: Untitled, 1985
Glazed ceramic, 26.5 × 34 cm

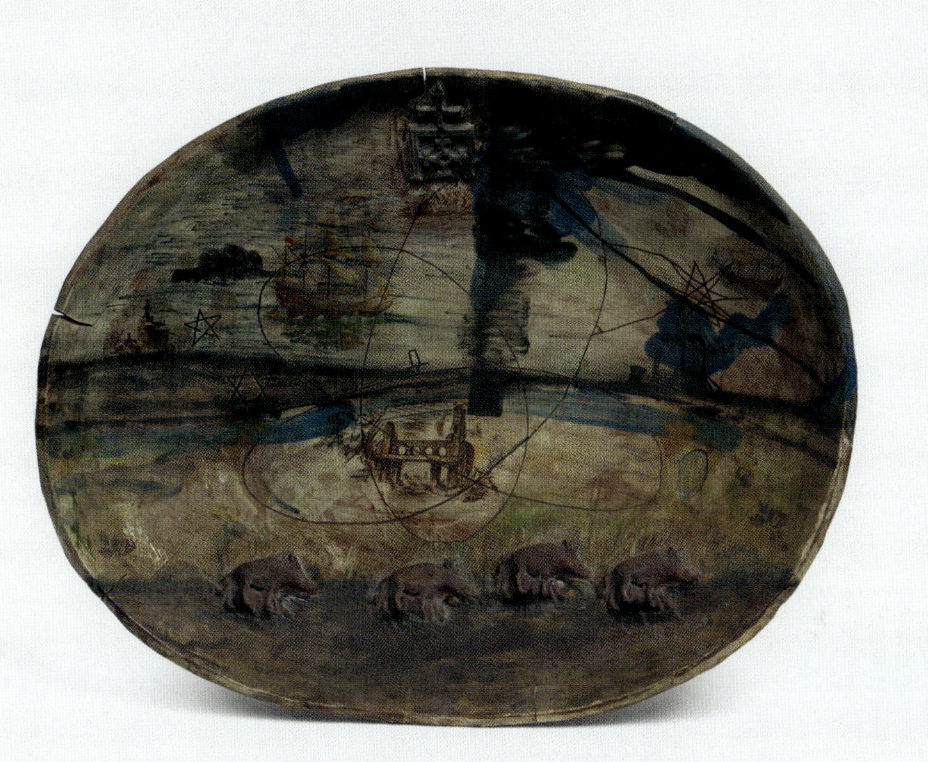

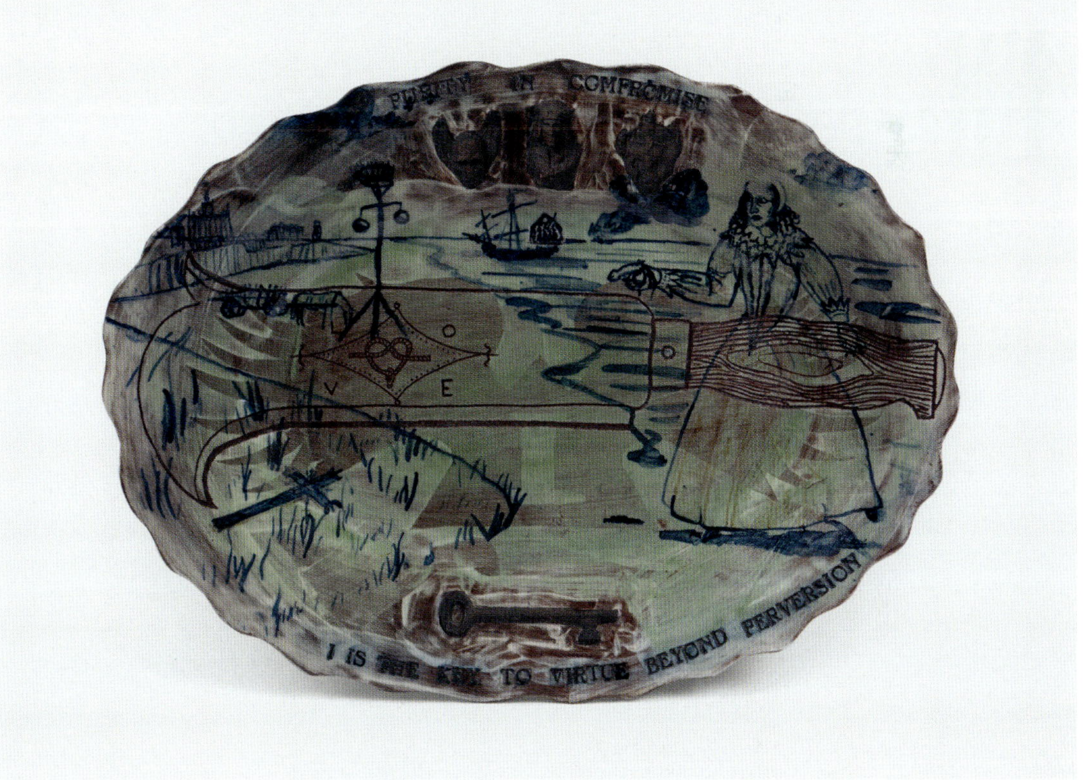
PURITY IN COMPROMISE
V
E
I IS THE KEY TO VIRTUE BEYOND PERVERSION

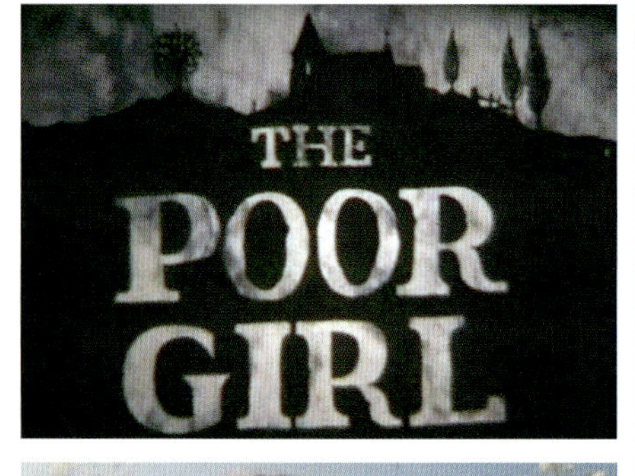

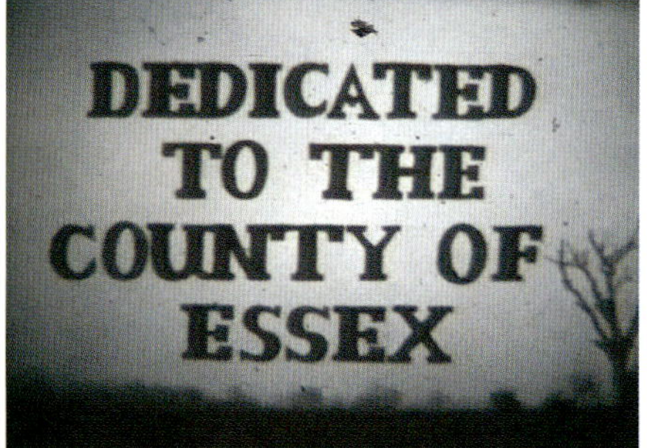

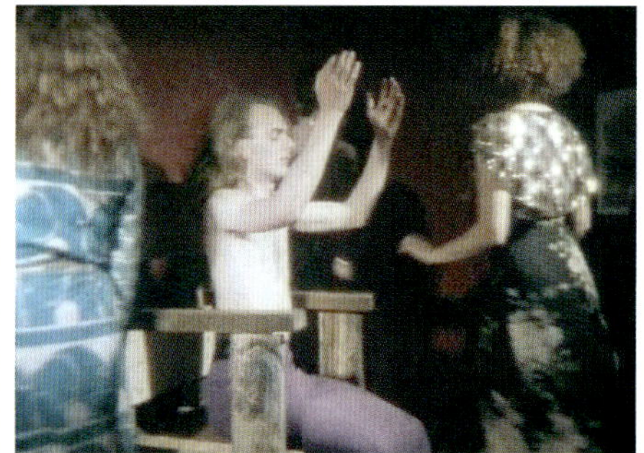

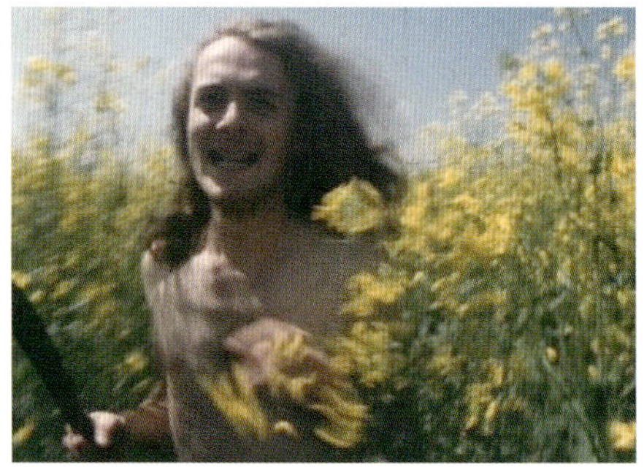
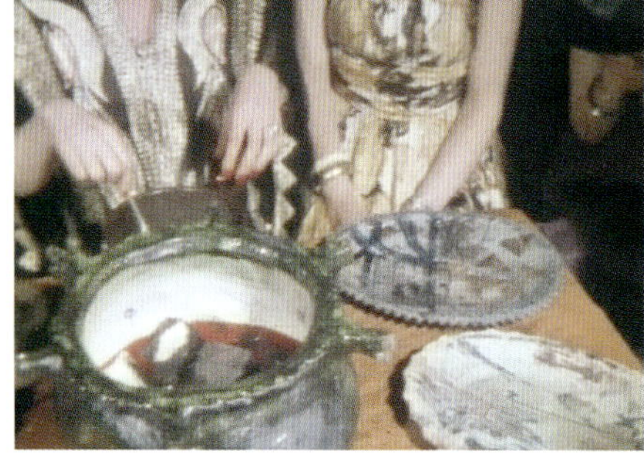
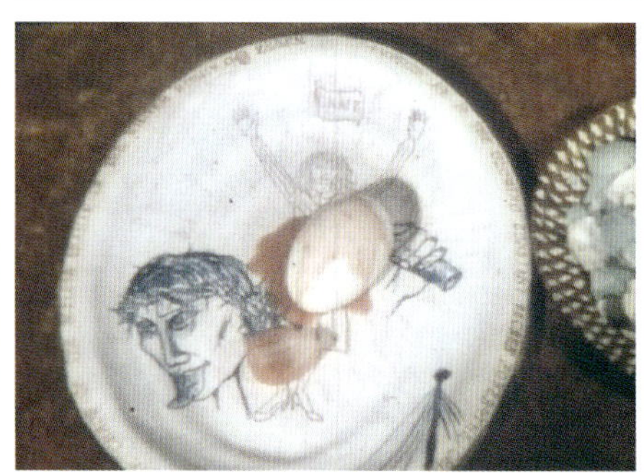

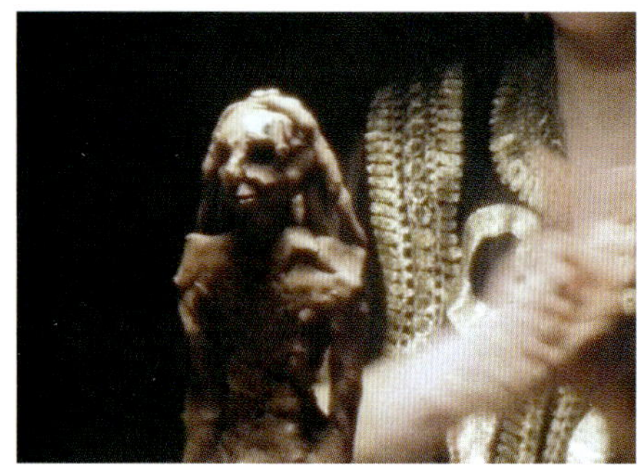
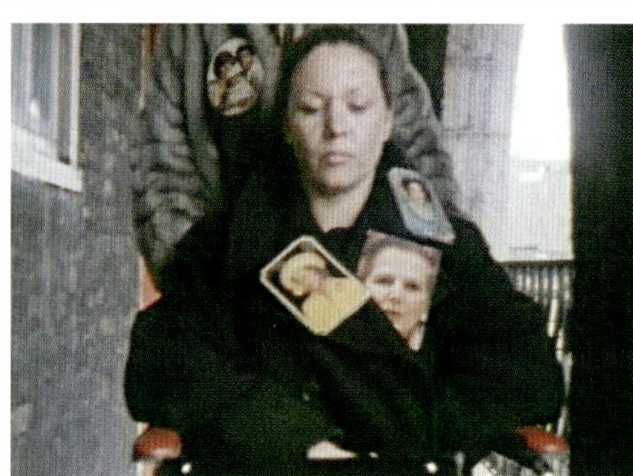
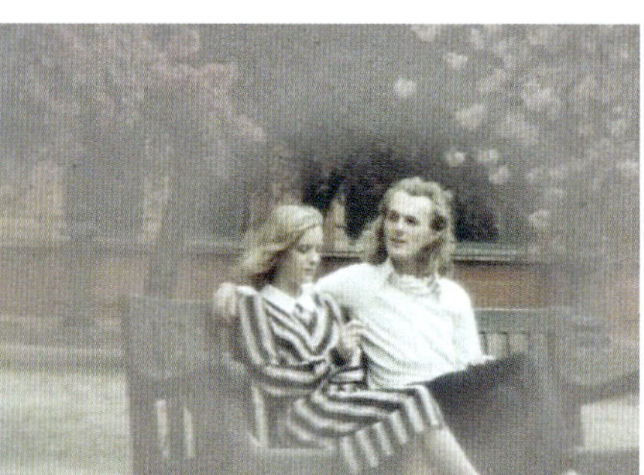

ABOVE: *The Poor Girl*, 1985
Super-8 film transferred to DVD
47 minutes 13 seconds

OPPOSITE: Untitled, 1985
Glazed ceramic, 34 × 26.5 cm

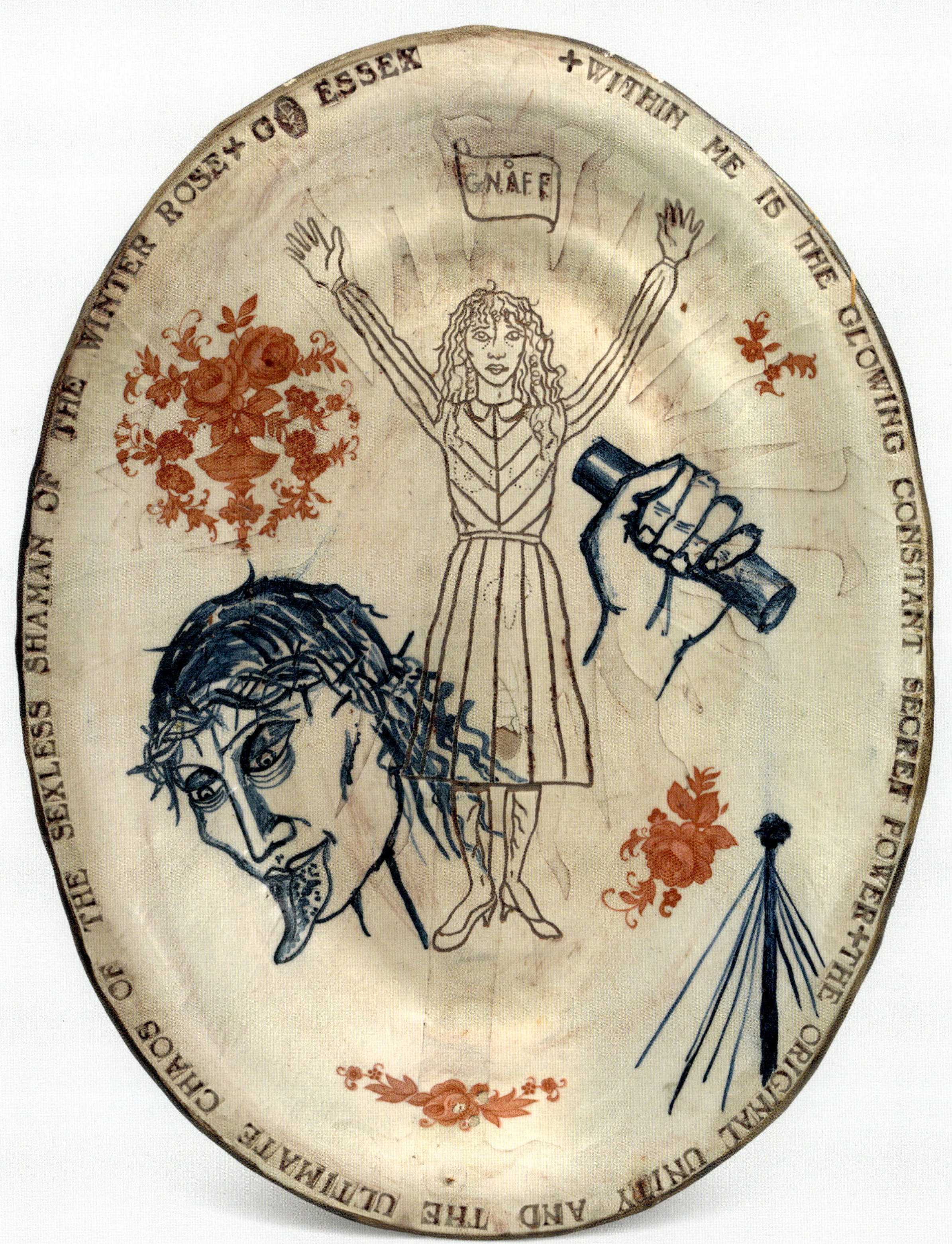
WINTER ROSE+ GOD ESSEX
+WITHIN ME IS THE GLOWING CONSTANT SECRET POWER+THE ORIGINAL UNITY AND THE ULTIMATE CHAOS OF THE SEXLESS SHAMAN OF THE
G.N.A.F.F.

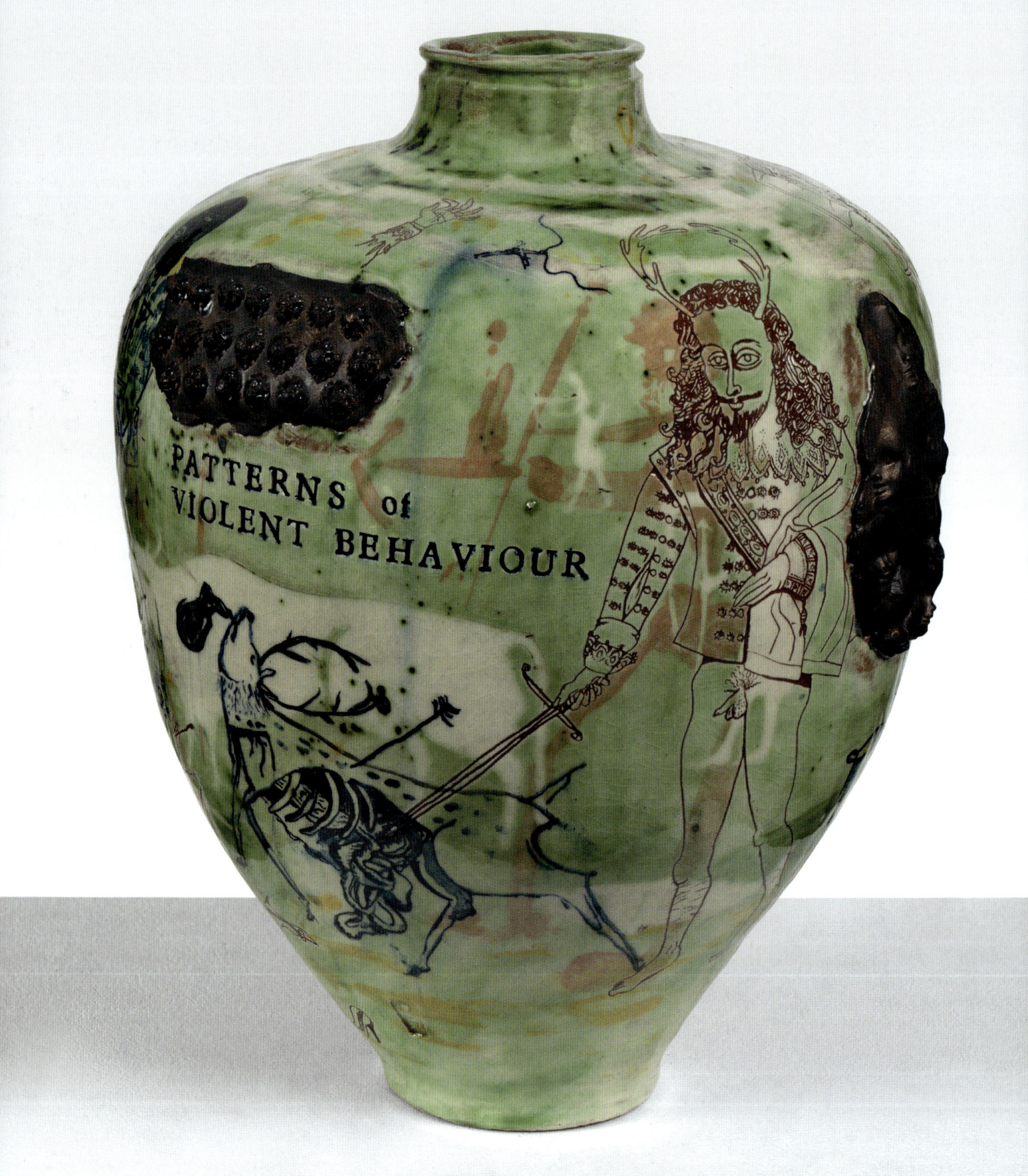
PATTERNS of
VIOLENT BEHAVIOUR

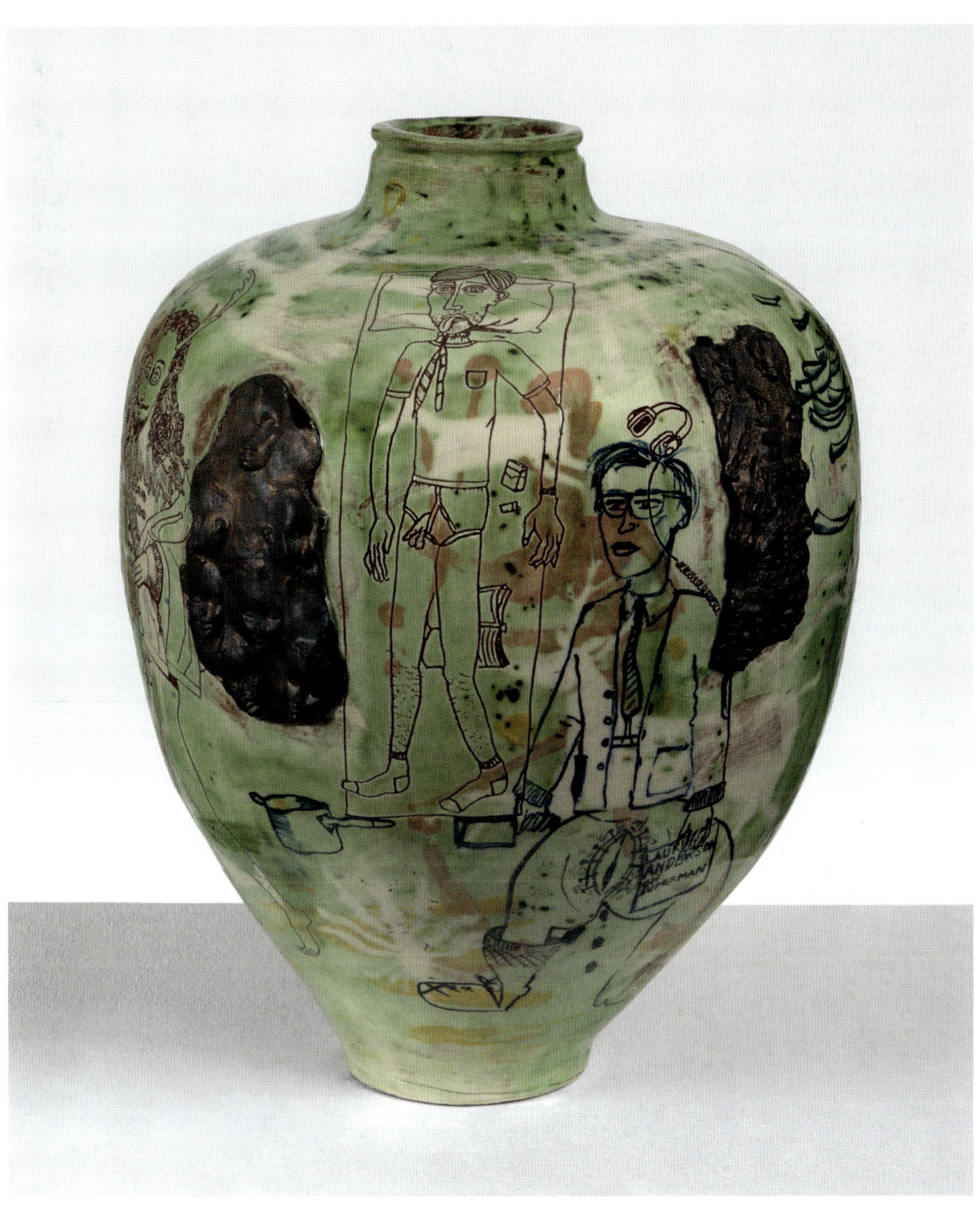

Patterns of Violent Behaviour, 1985
Glazed ceramic, 41.3 × 33.7 cm

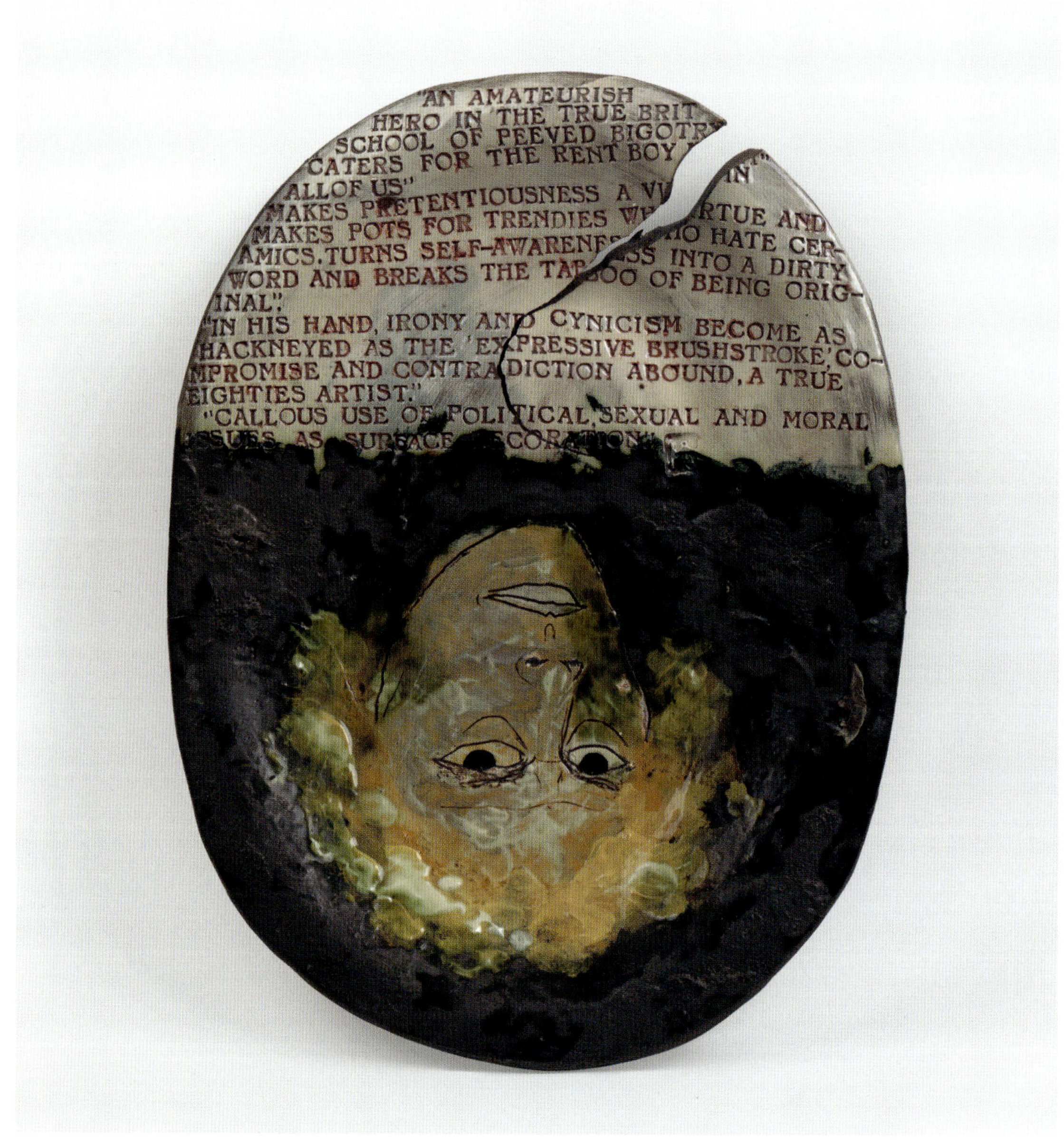

Self Portrait Cracked and Warped, 1985
Glazed ceramic, 35.6 × 25.4 cm

I remember being very pleased with this work when I made it even
though it had gone disastrously 'wrong'. The split and subsequent
warping are genuine, in that I did not contrive for them to happen;
it was just poor handling of the piece while it was drying. The
fault of course adds greatly to the idea, as if the gods of the kiln
had passed judgment on me and my work. The portrait image
being upside down is a reference to the work of the hot painter
of the 'expressive brushstroke' at the time: Georg Baselitz.

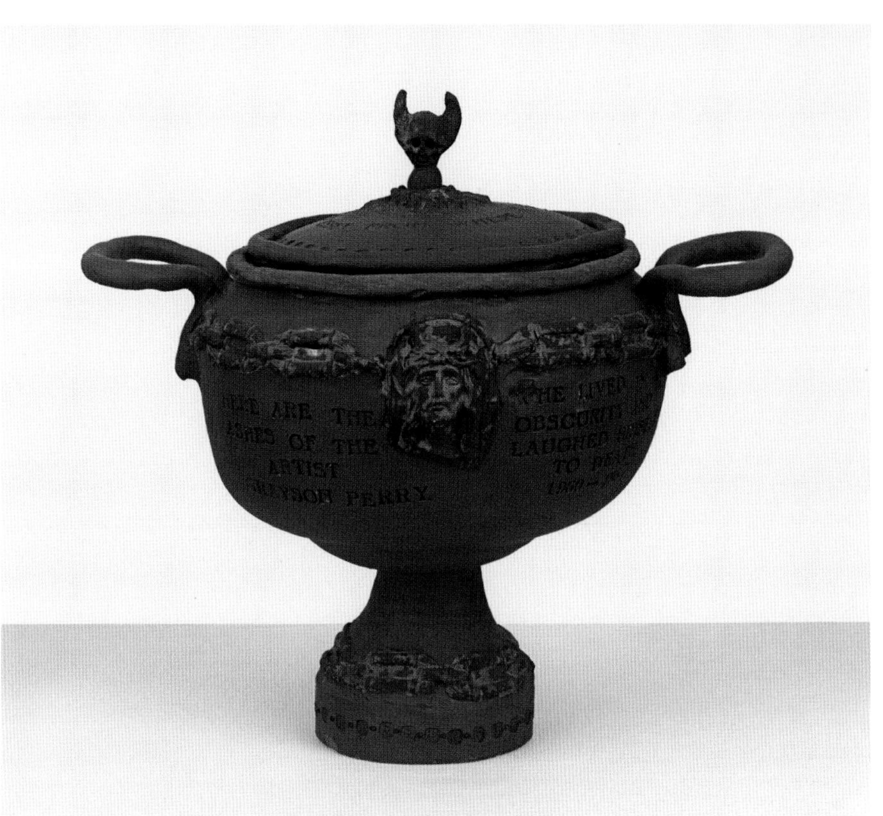

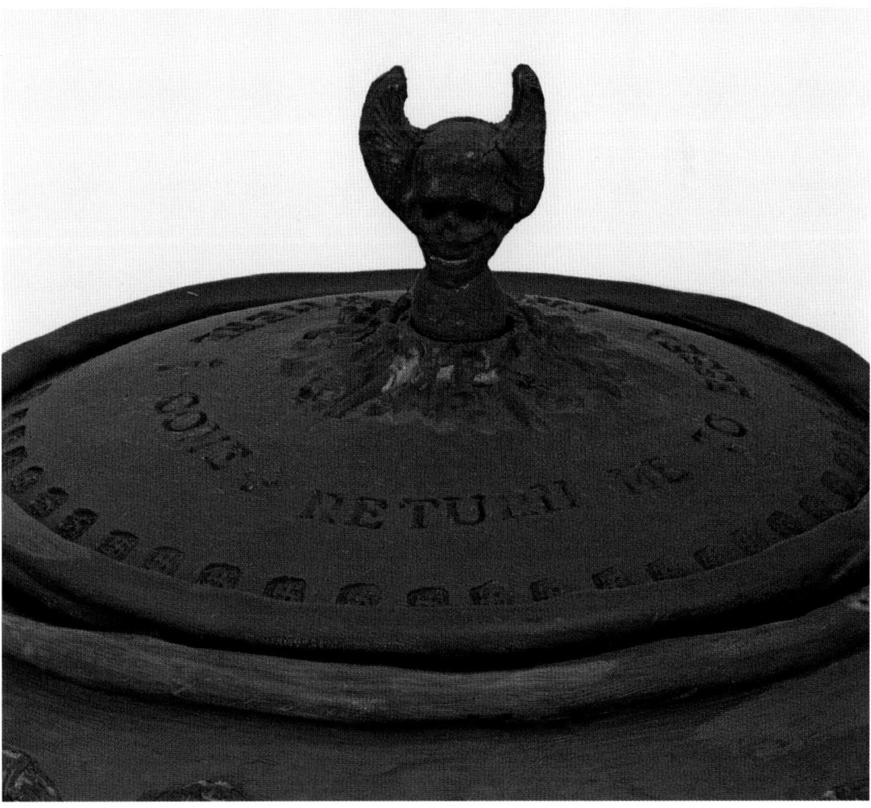

Return Me to Essex
from Where I Come, 1985
Glazed ceramic, 25.4 × 30 cm

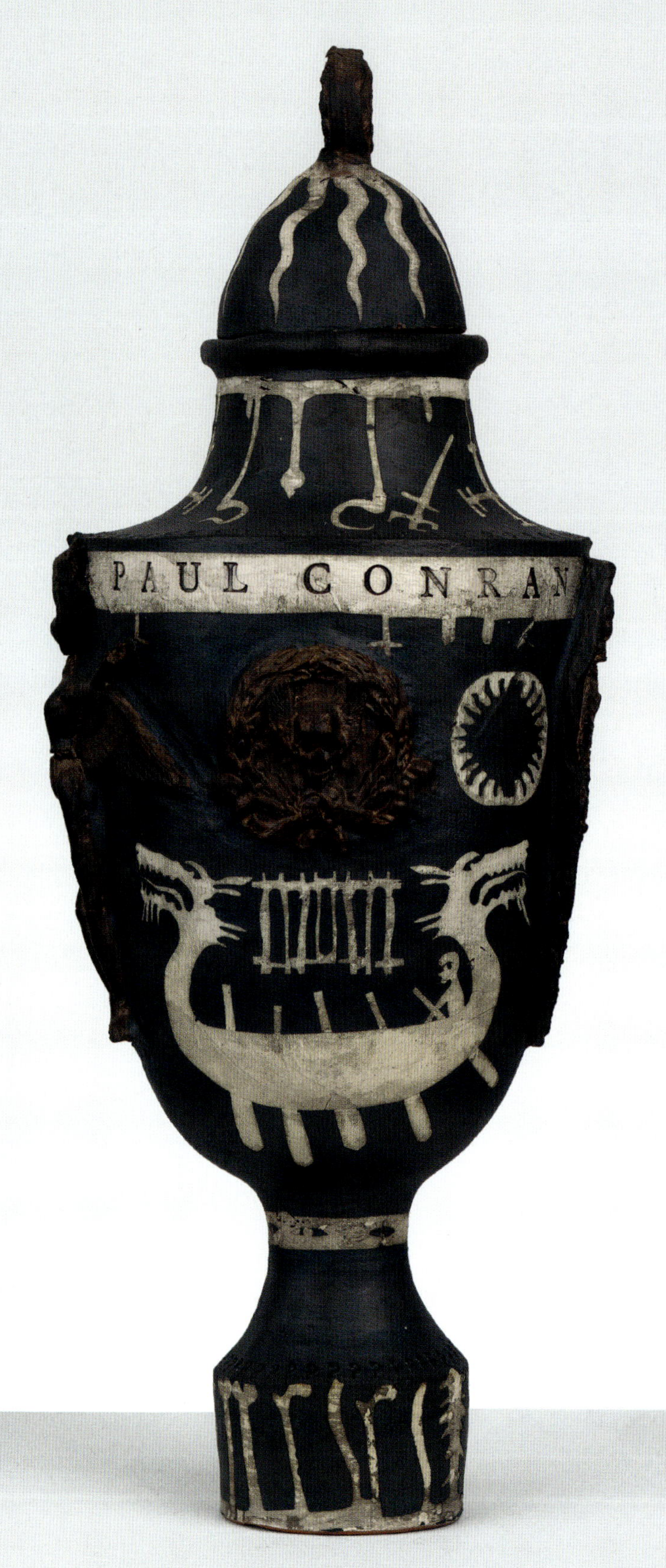

PAUL CONRAN

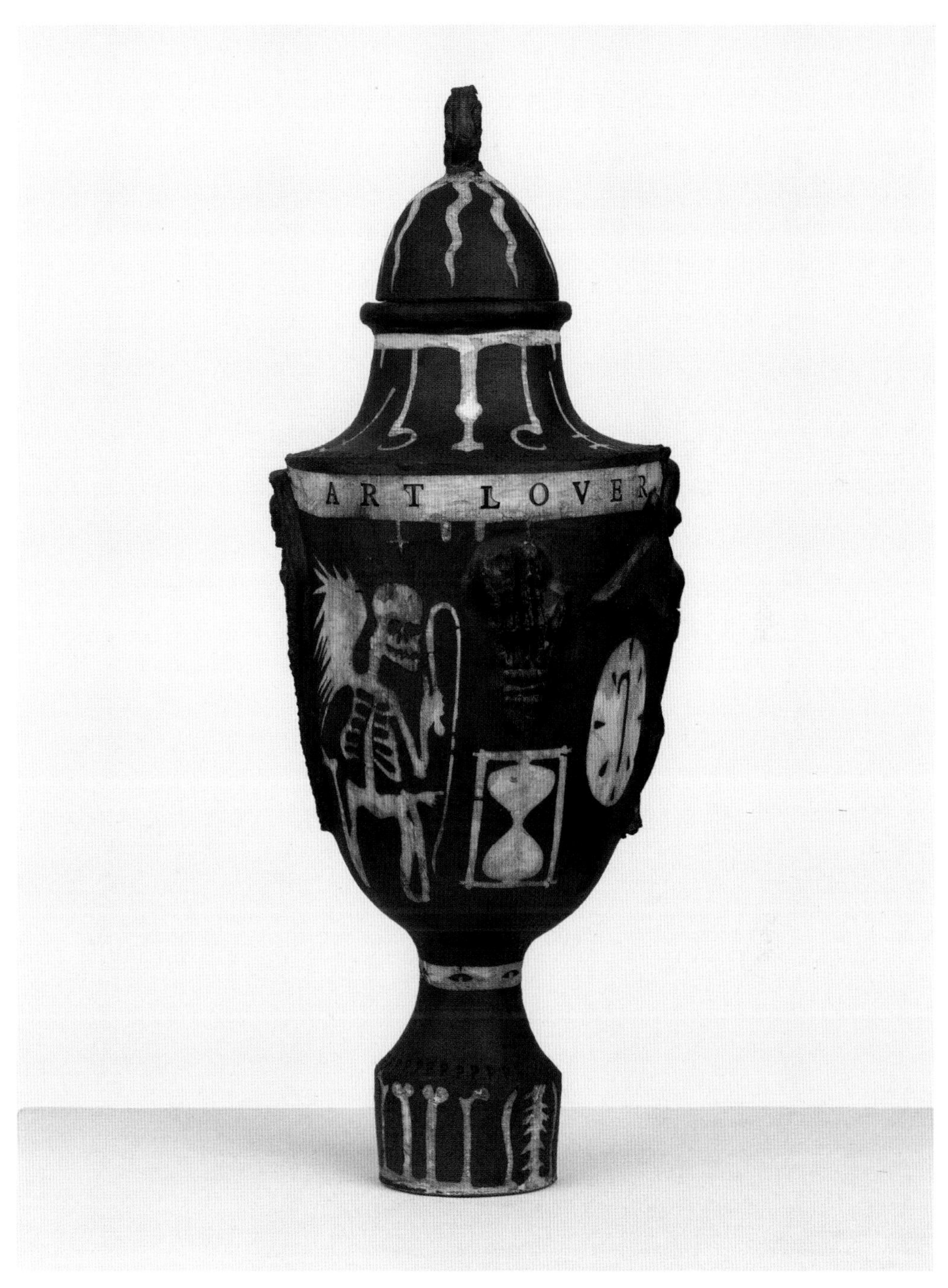

Paul Conran – Art Lover, 1985
Glazed ceramic, 45.7 × 17 cm

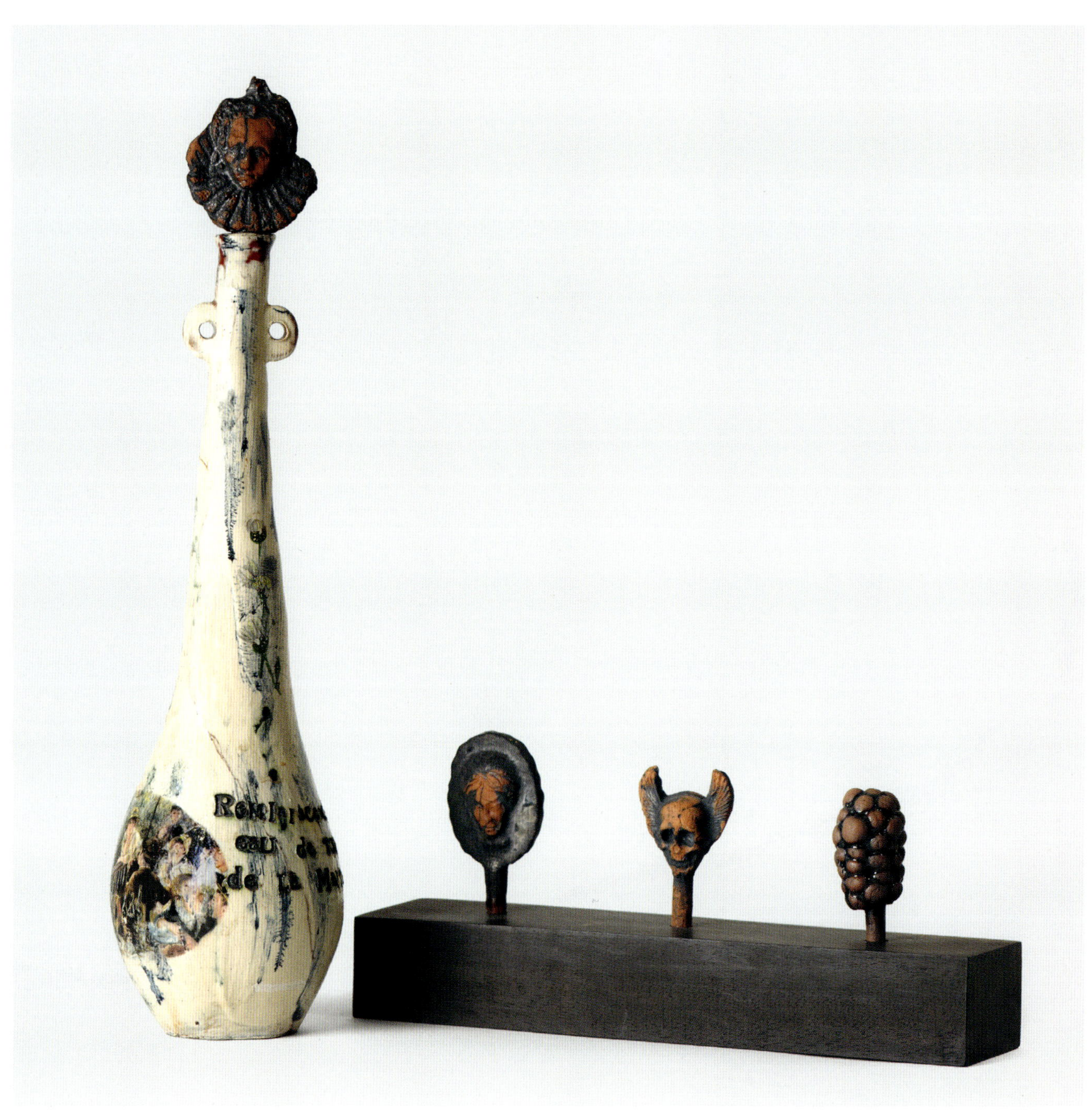

Untitled *(Perfume Bottle)*, 1985
Glazed earthenware and poppy
seed pods, 22.9 × 6.7 cm

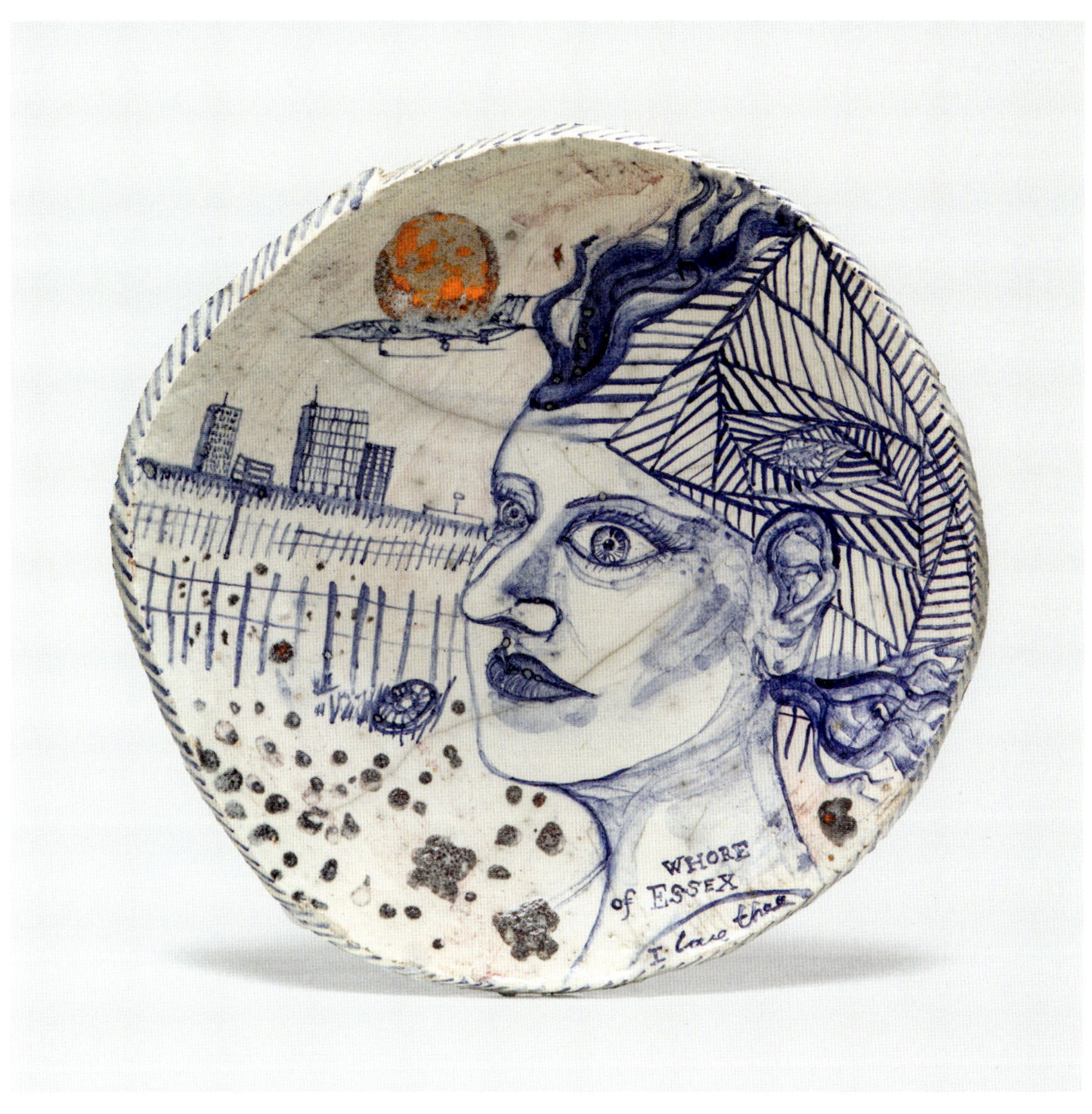

Whore of Essex, I Love Thee, 1986
Glazed ceramic, diameter 29.2 cm

This dish has features that are both common and rare in my early
work. It features typical motifs of my work at the time: the imaginary
woman, the playful abstract bits, the bleak Essex landscape and the
military jet coming in to land. What is unusual is the form, a round
dish on three legs, and the fact that it has been raku fired, where
the red-hot piece was picked out of the kiln with tongs and then
placed in sawdust, which ignited causing the cracks and unglazed
parts of the piece to absorb the metallic black carbon. Usually my
early raku pieces are much simpler than this as there is always a
high chance of the piece failing due to heat shock or the wrong
sort of chance effects.

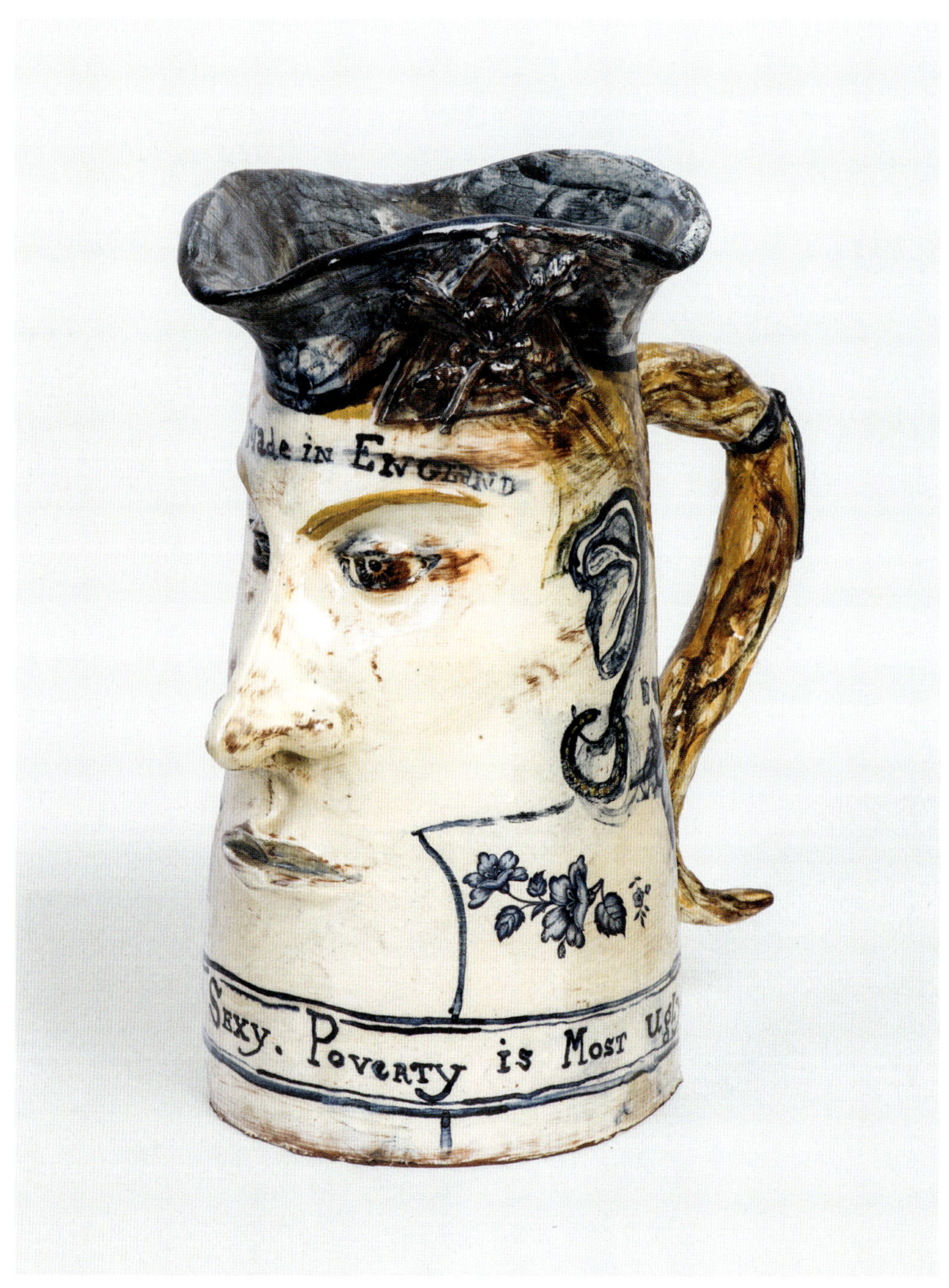

ABOVE: Untitled *(True Blue)*, 1987
Glazed ceramic, 22 × 17.8 × 15.2 cm

OPPOSITE: *The New Beauty Beyond Irony Beyond Cynicism
Beyond Perversion and All the Knowledge of Age*, 1987
Glazed ceramic, Cup: 10 × 23 × 12.5 cm
Saucer: diameter 23 cm

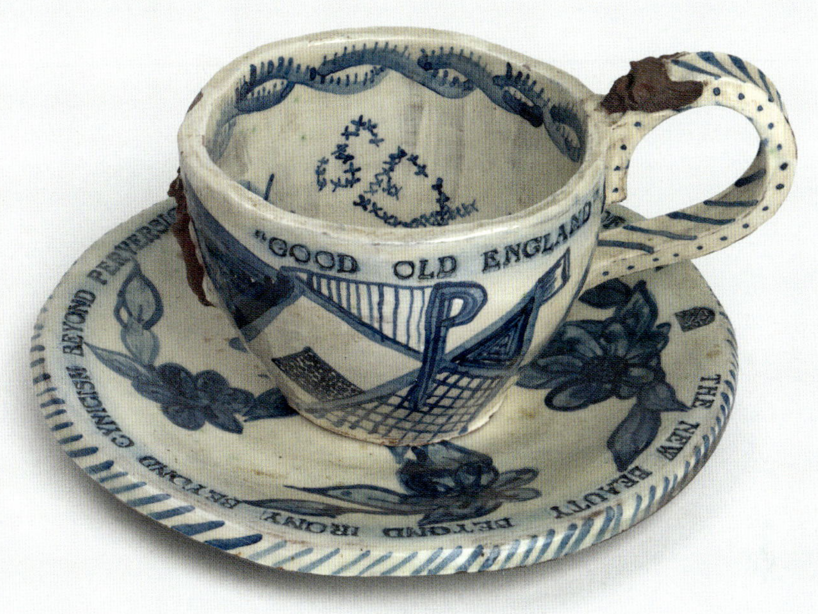
"GOOD OLD ENGLAND
THE NEW BEAUTY BEYOND IRONY BEYOND CYNICISM BEYOND PERVER

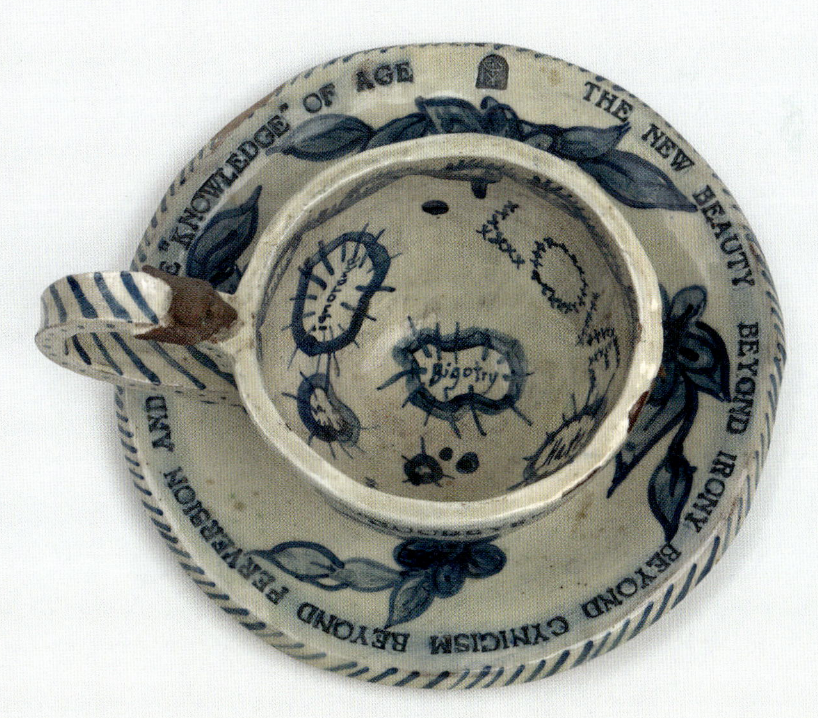
"KNOWLEDGE" OF AGE
THE NEW BEAUTY BEYOND IRONY BEYOND CYNICISM BEYOND PERVERSION AND
BIGOTRY

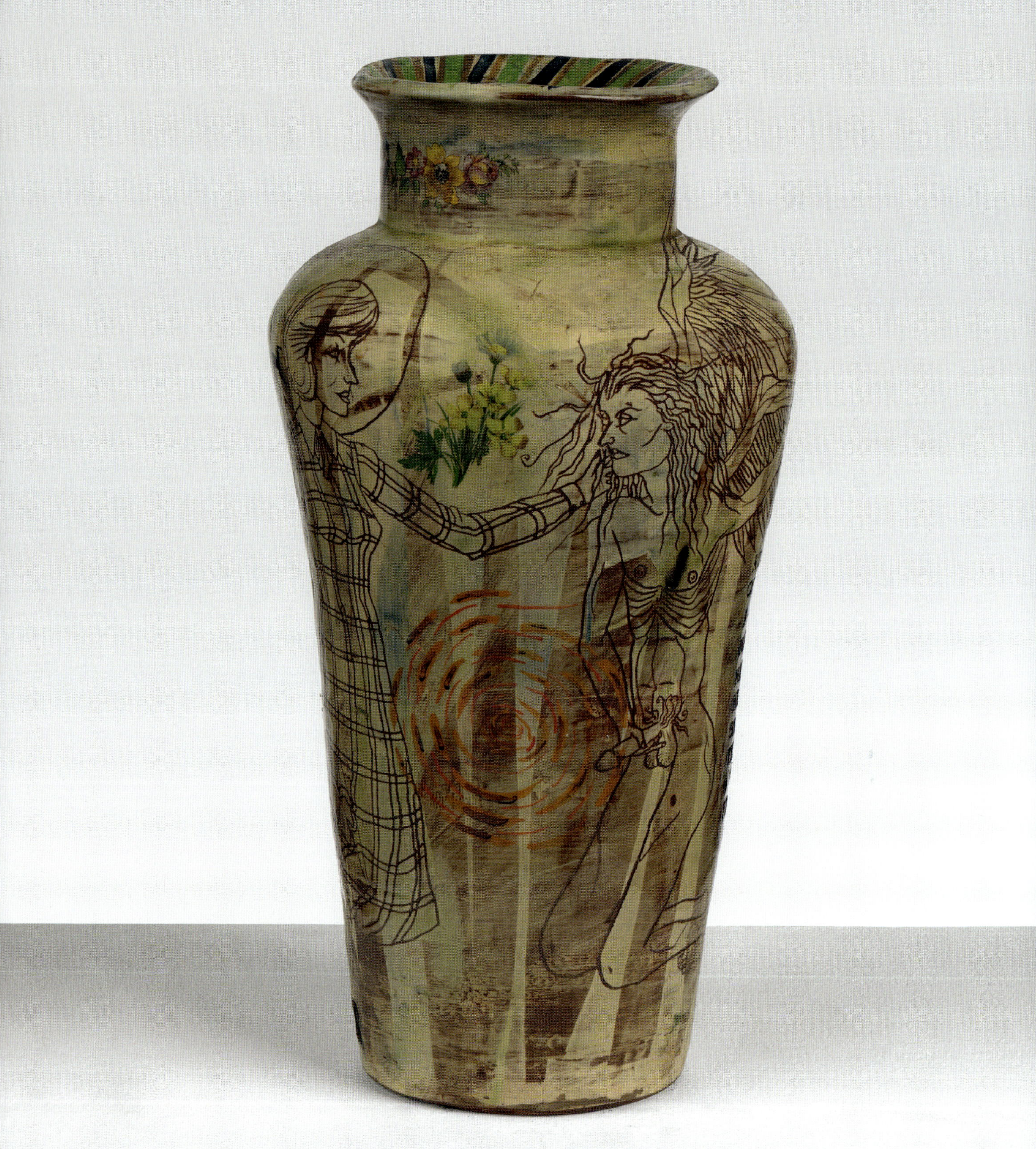

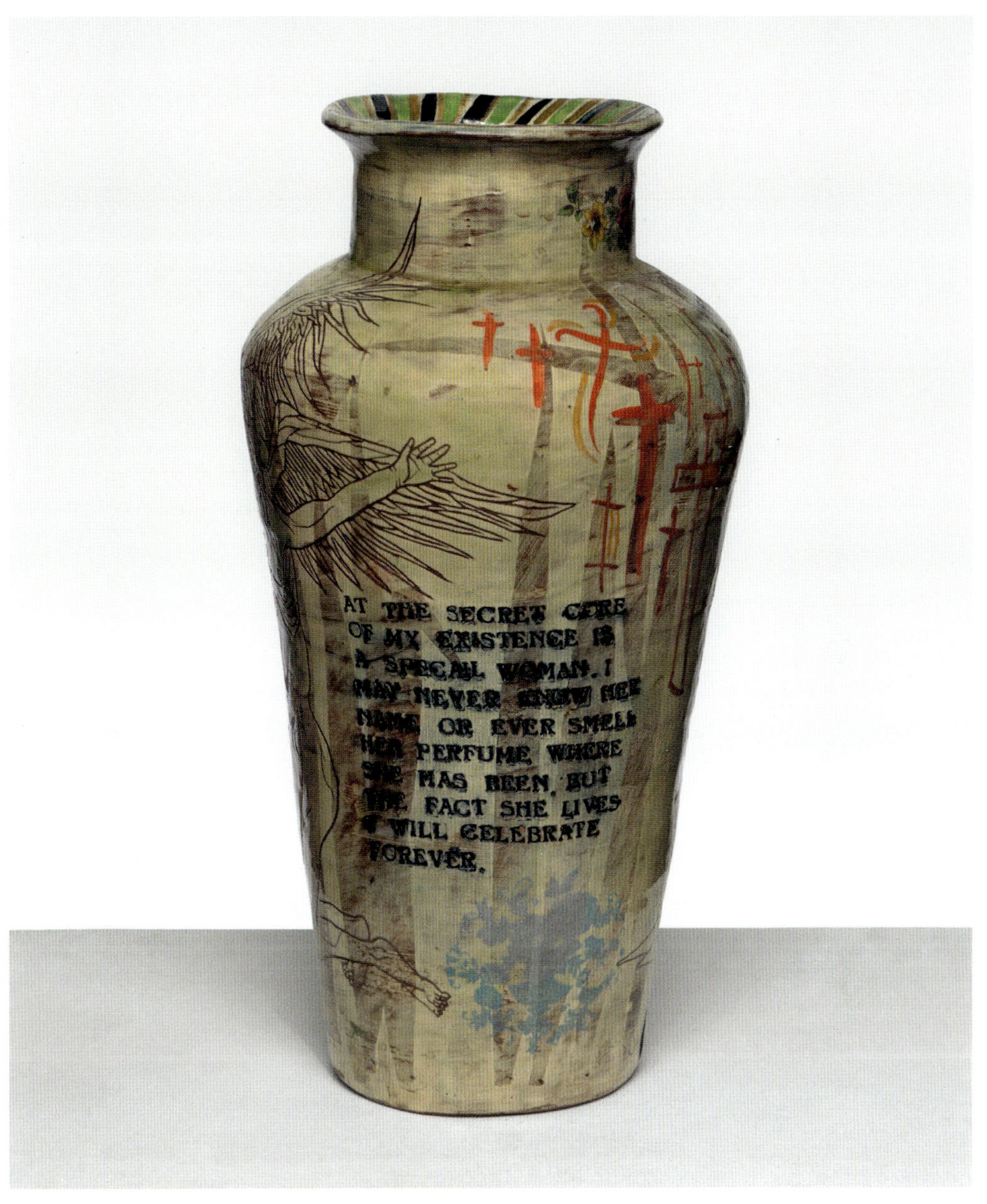

Secret Woman, 1987
Glazed ceramic, 38 × 20 cm

This pot was about my acknowledgment of Claire as a central
plank of my creative drive. I was already starting to build up
a narrative of her, a sort of internal iconography. Here, there's
an angel figure with a hard-on and Claire, wearing a dress from
the office, appears with a halo, patting the angel on the shoulder.
It's like the spirit of my femininity descending to earth and blessing
me with inspiration. There's also an elfin-looking boy in a suit,
perhaps as a more integrated idea of the male and female.

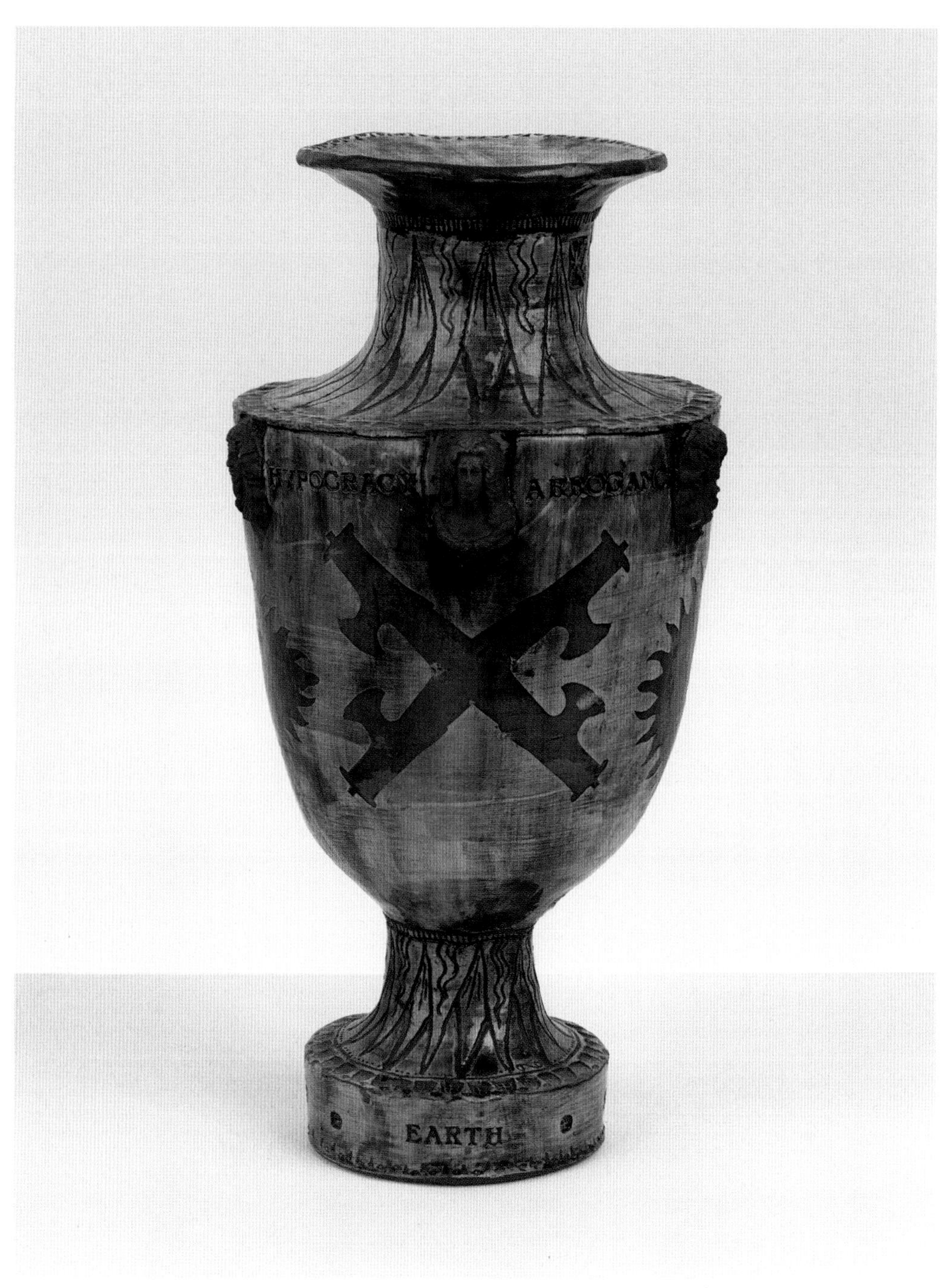

Perversion/Apathy/Arrogance/Selfishness/Ego/Hypocrisy, 1987
Glazed ceramic, 34.3 × 17.5 cm

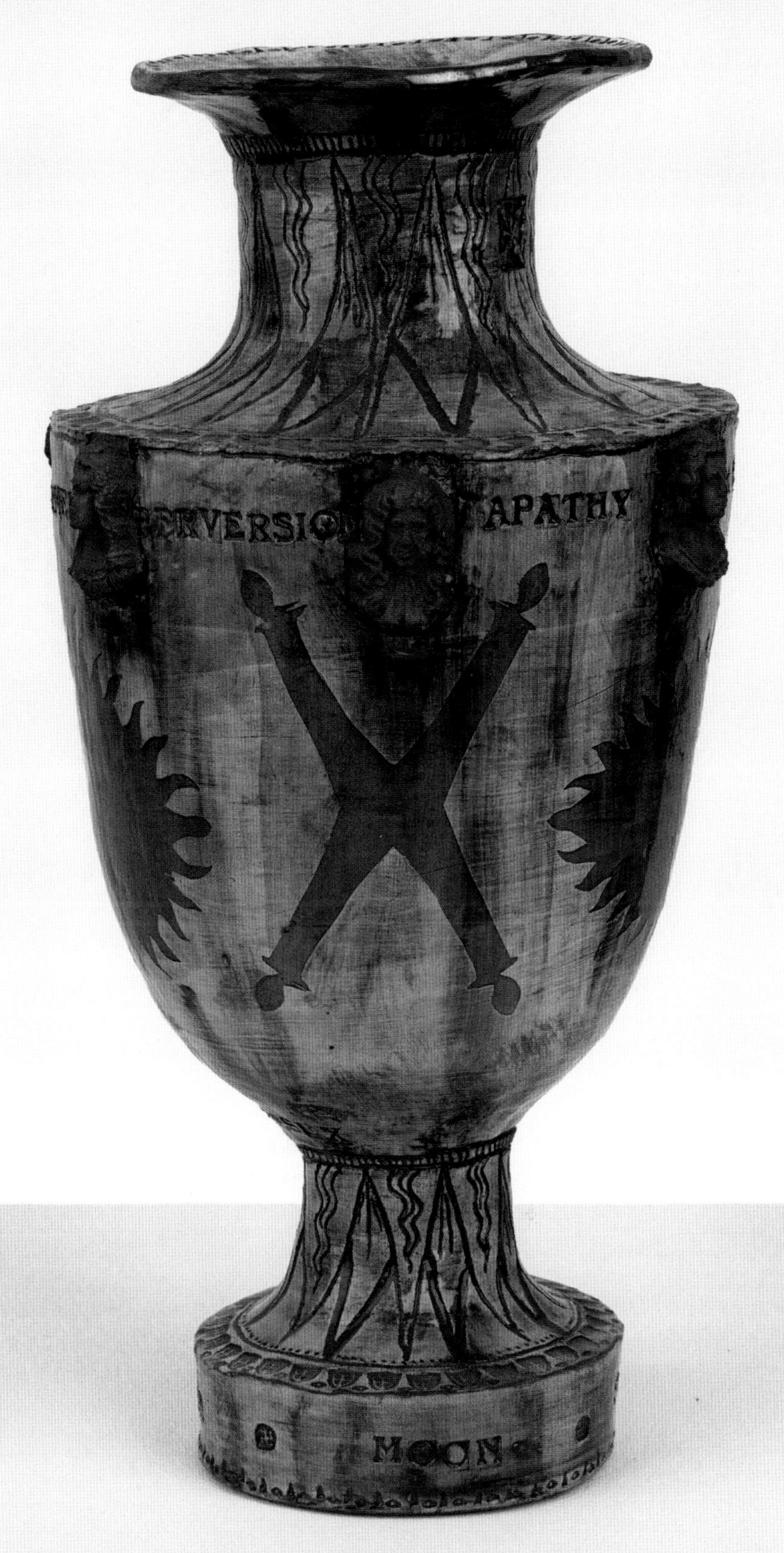
ERVERSION
APATHY
MOON

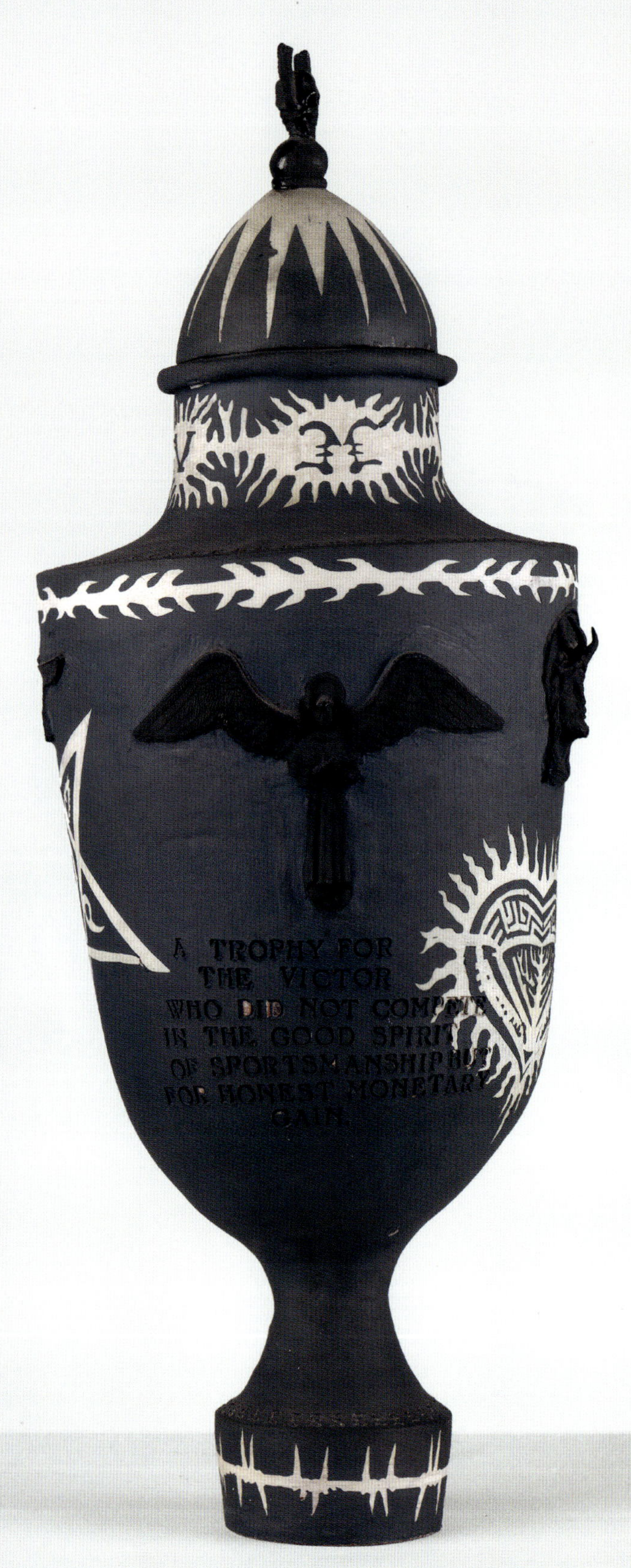
A TROPHY FOR
THE VICTOR
WHO DID NOT COMPETE
IN THE GOOD SPIRIT
OF SPORTSMANSHIP BUT
FOR HONEST MONETARY
GAIN.

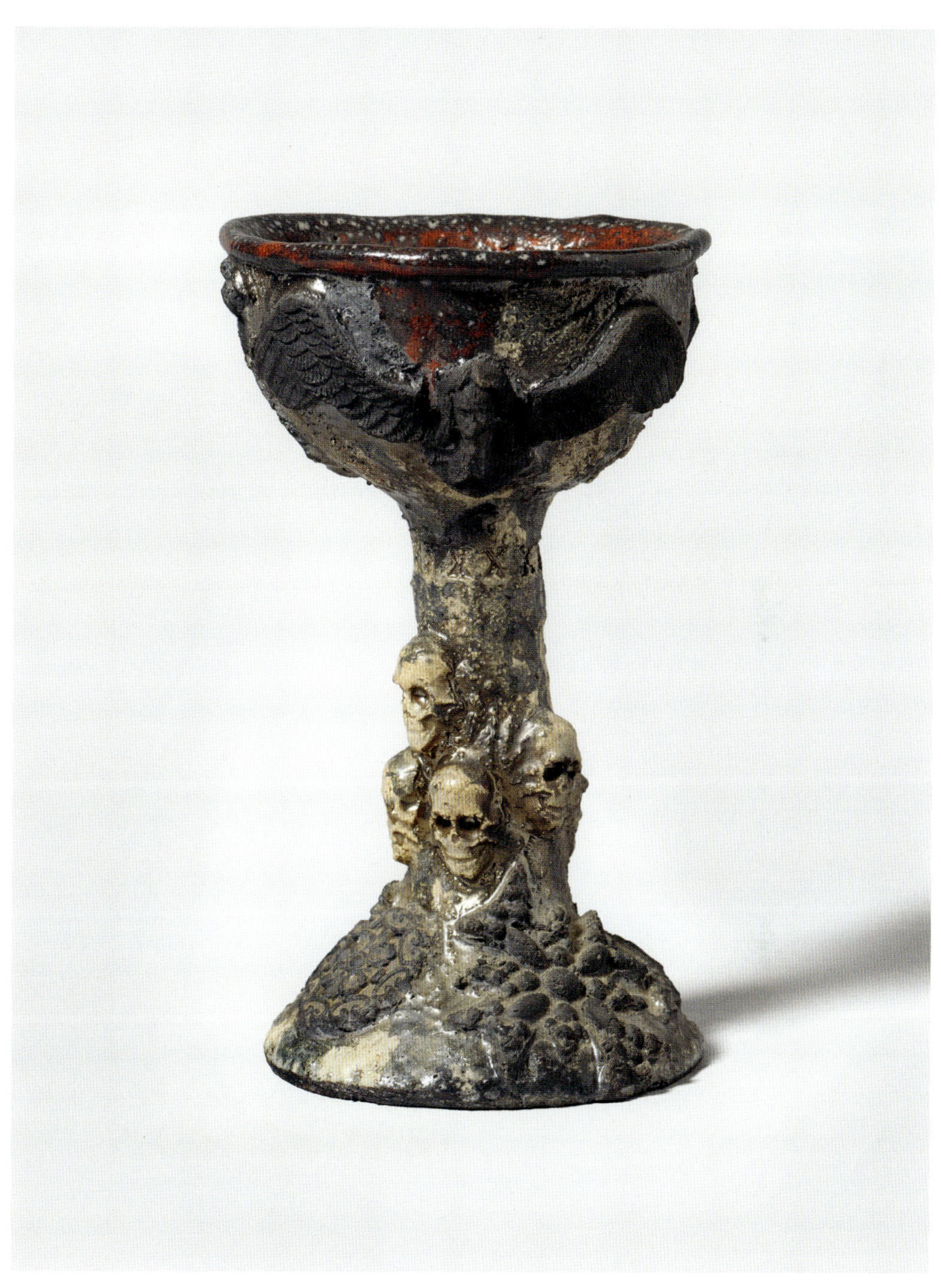

OPPOSITE: *Trophy for the Victor*, 1987
Glazed ceramic, 50.5 × 19.5 cm

ABOVE: Goblet, 1987
Raku ceramic with seven lead pieces
19 × 11 cm

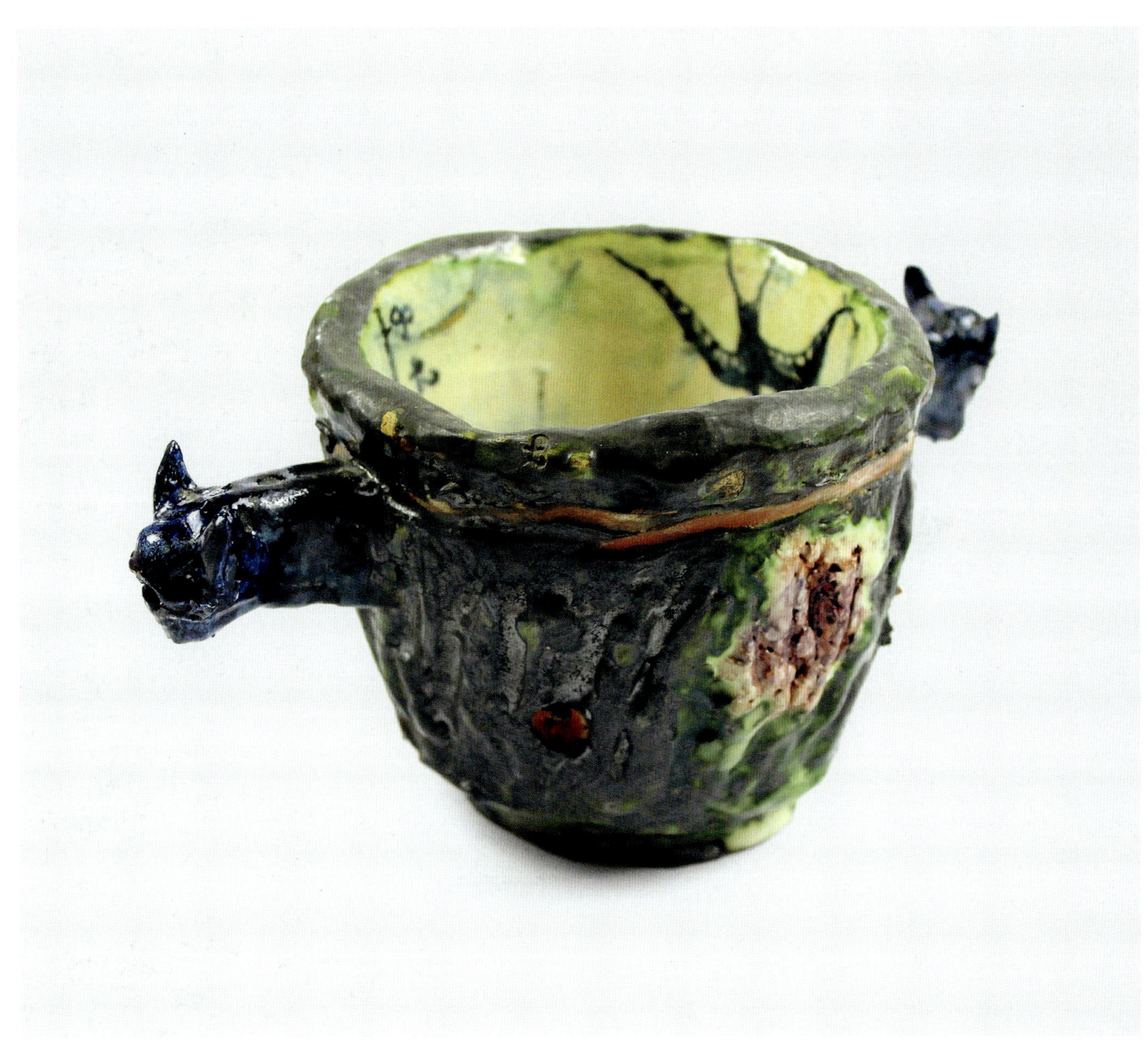

ABOVE: Two-Handled Porringer with Demonic Skulls, 1987
Glazed ceramic, 11 × 21 cm

OPPOSITE: *I Hate Poetry*, 1987
Glazed ceramic, 15 × 9 × 19 cm

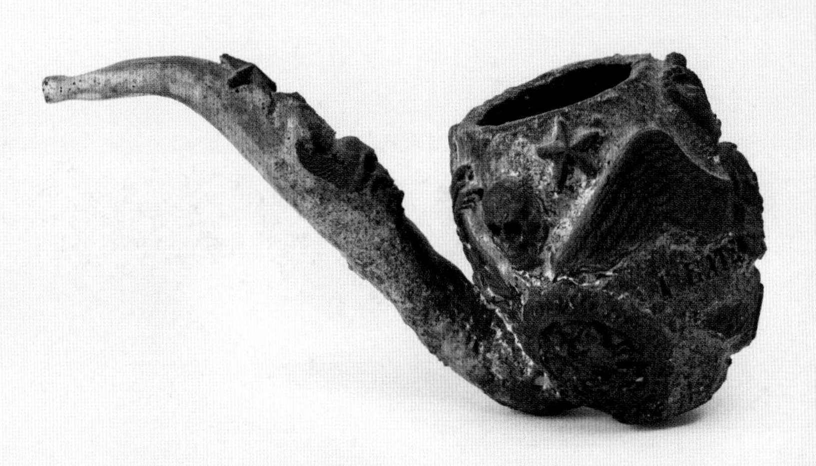

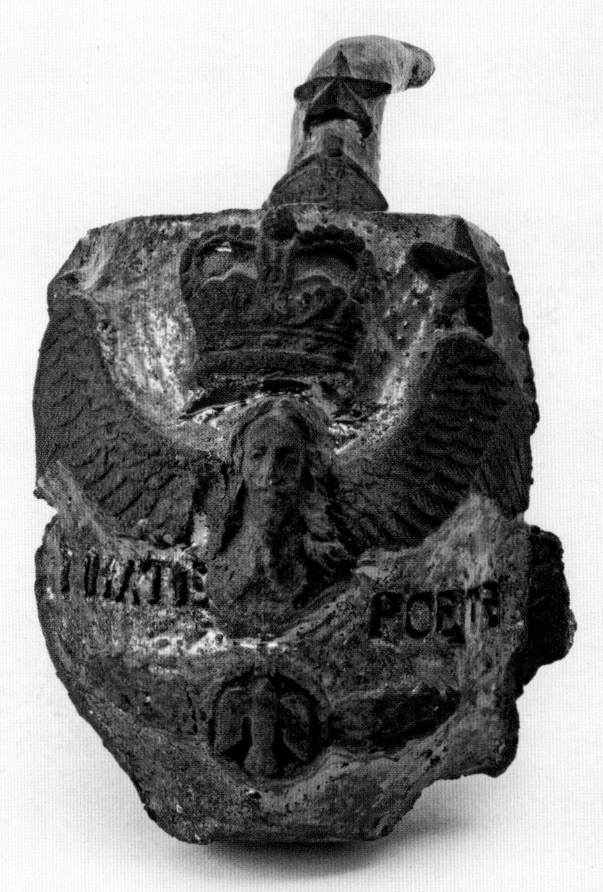

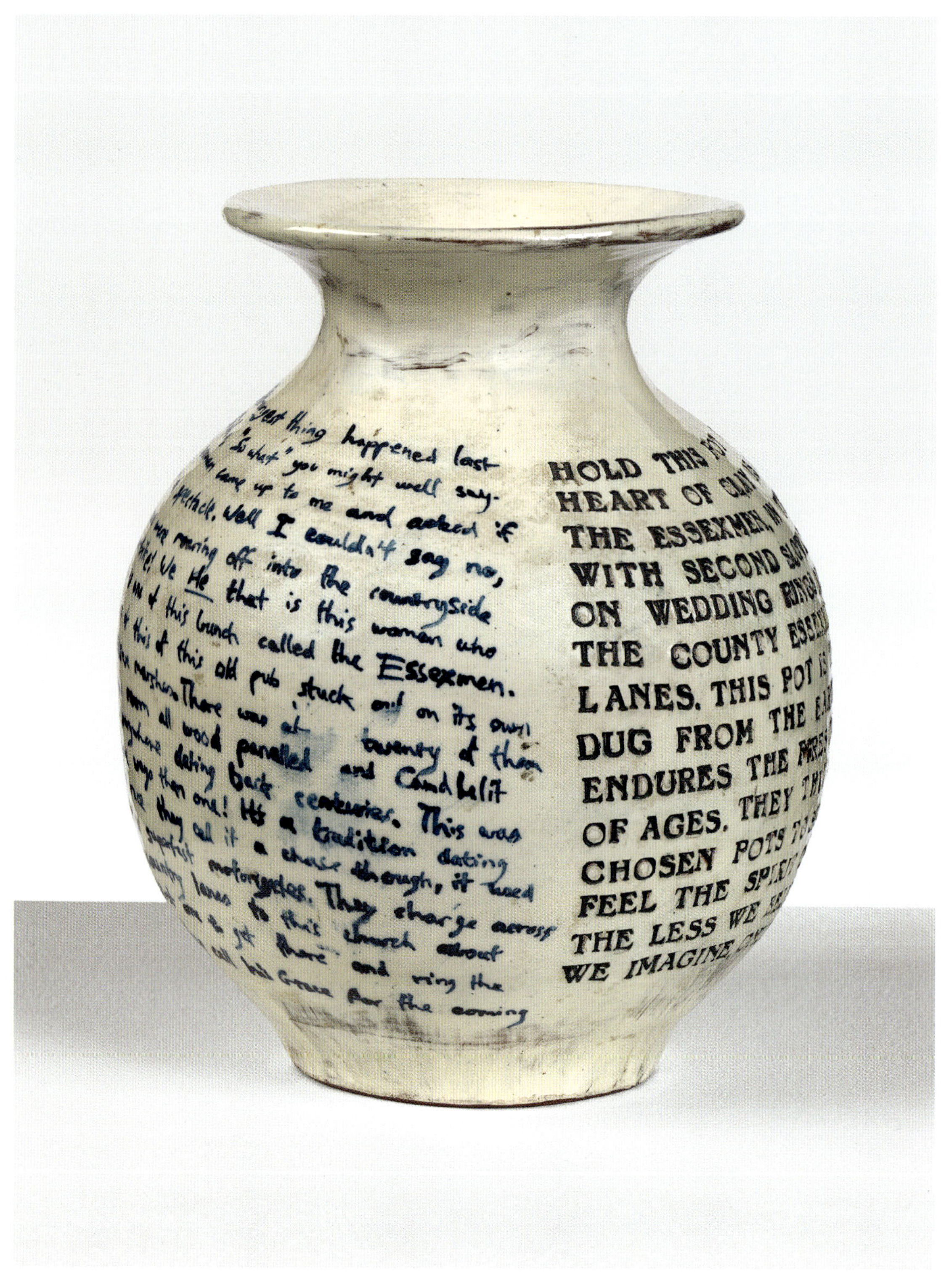

Untitled, 1987
Glazed ceramic, 24 × 22 cm

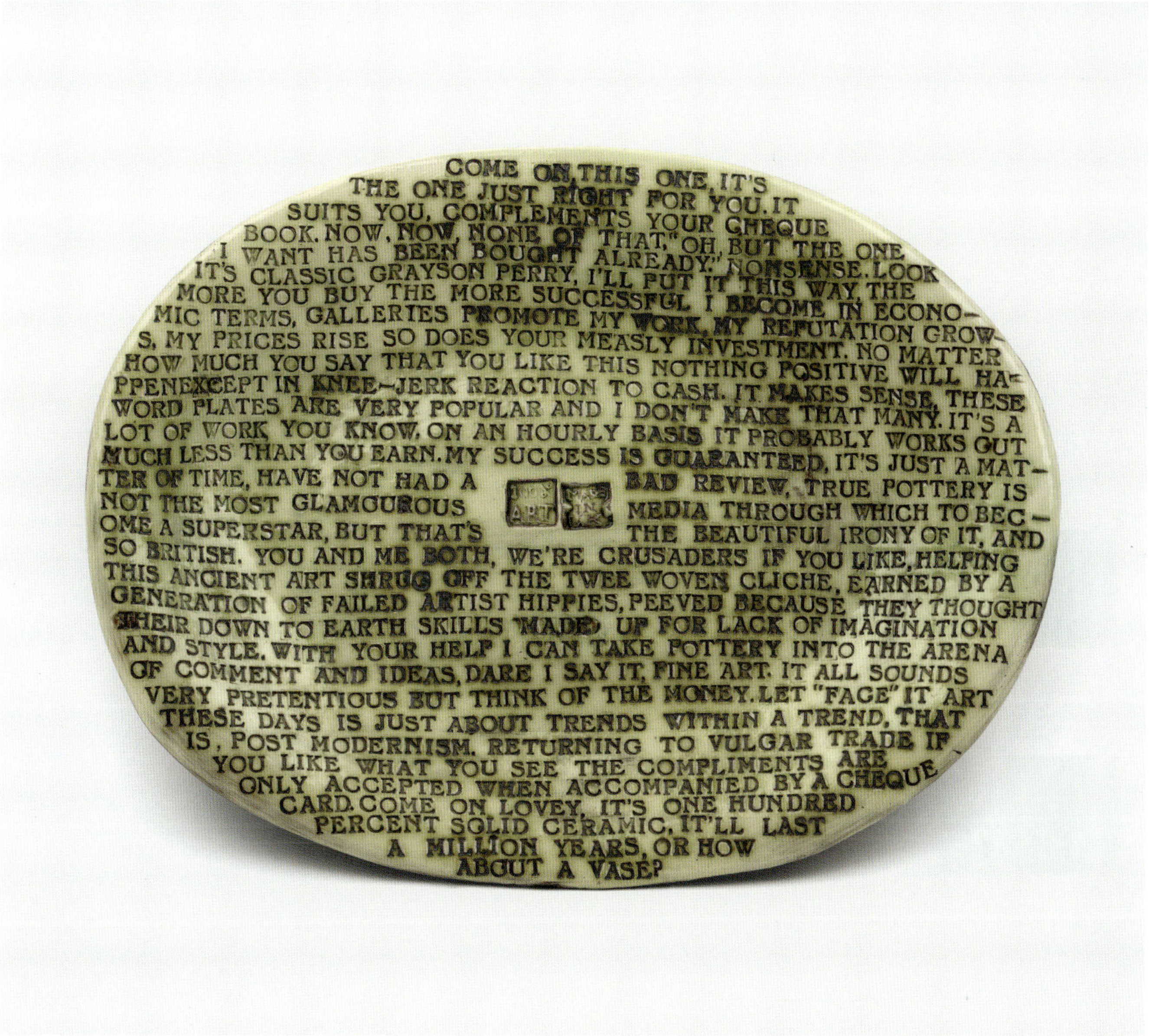

Sales Pitch, 1987
Glazed ceramic, 27.5 × 35.7 cm

Right from my very earliest ceramics I used words a lot. I found
it easier to be funny with words but I enjoyed the look of
text as well. This plate is a kind of minimalist joke, an artwork
trying to sell itself. Looking back thirty years it all still rings
true. I was a cocky bastard. I love the tone of desperation that
creeps in towards the end; I really needed the cash to buy my
next motorbike. In the centre are two of my pre-1992 potter's
marks, '100% ART' and 'MADE IN U.K.'.

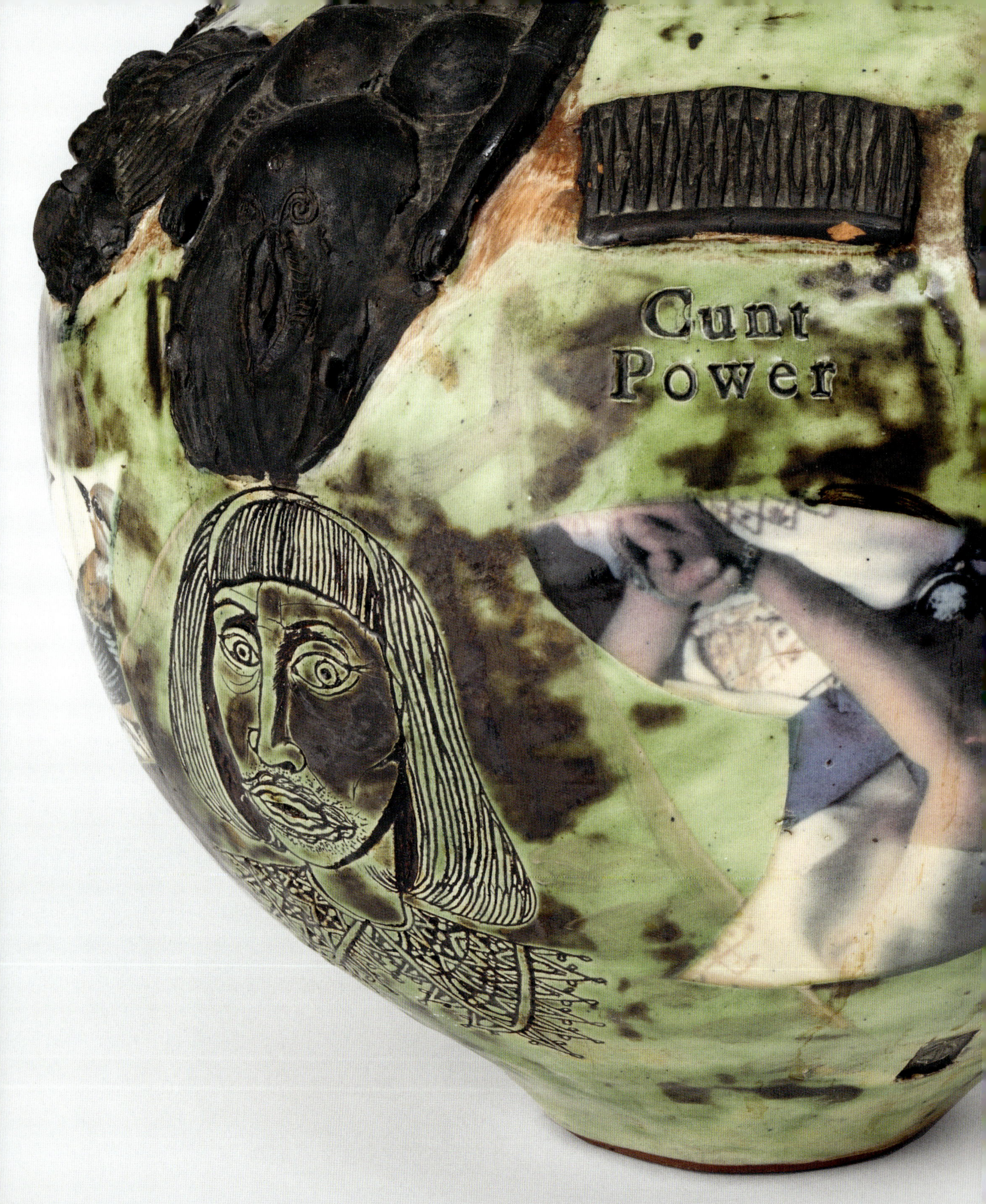

Cunt
Power

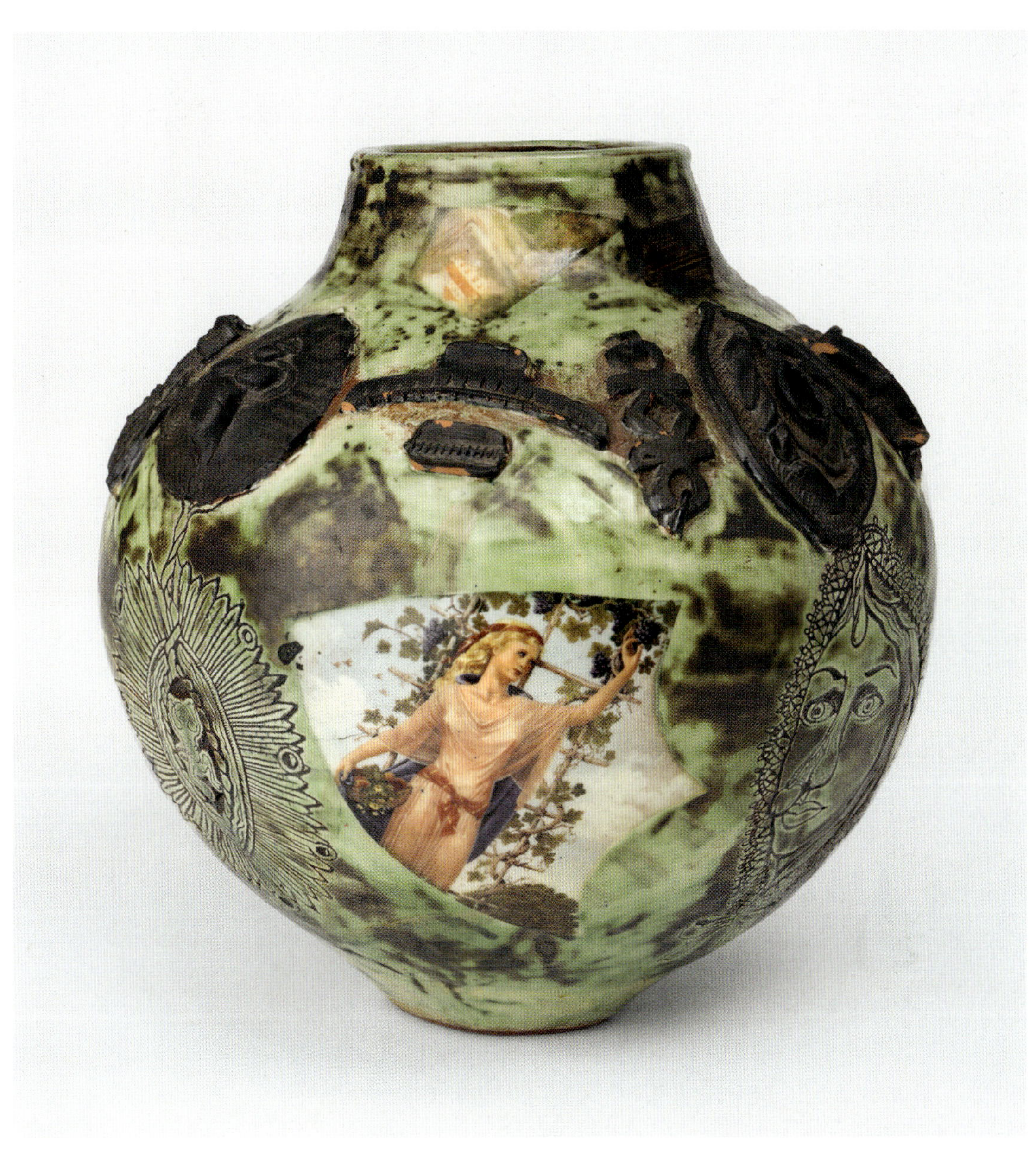

Cunt Power, 1987
Glazed ceramic, 31 × 30 cm

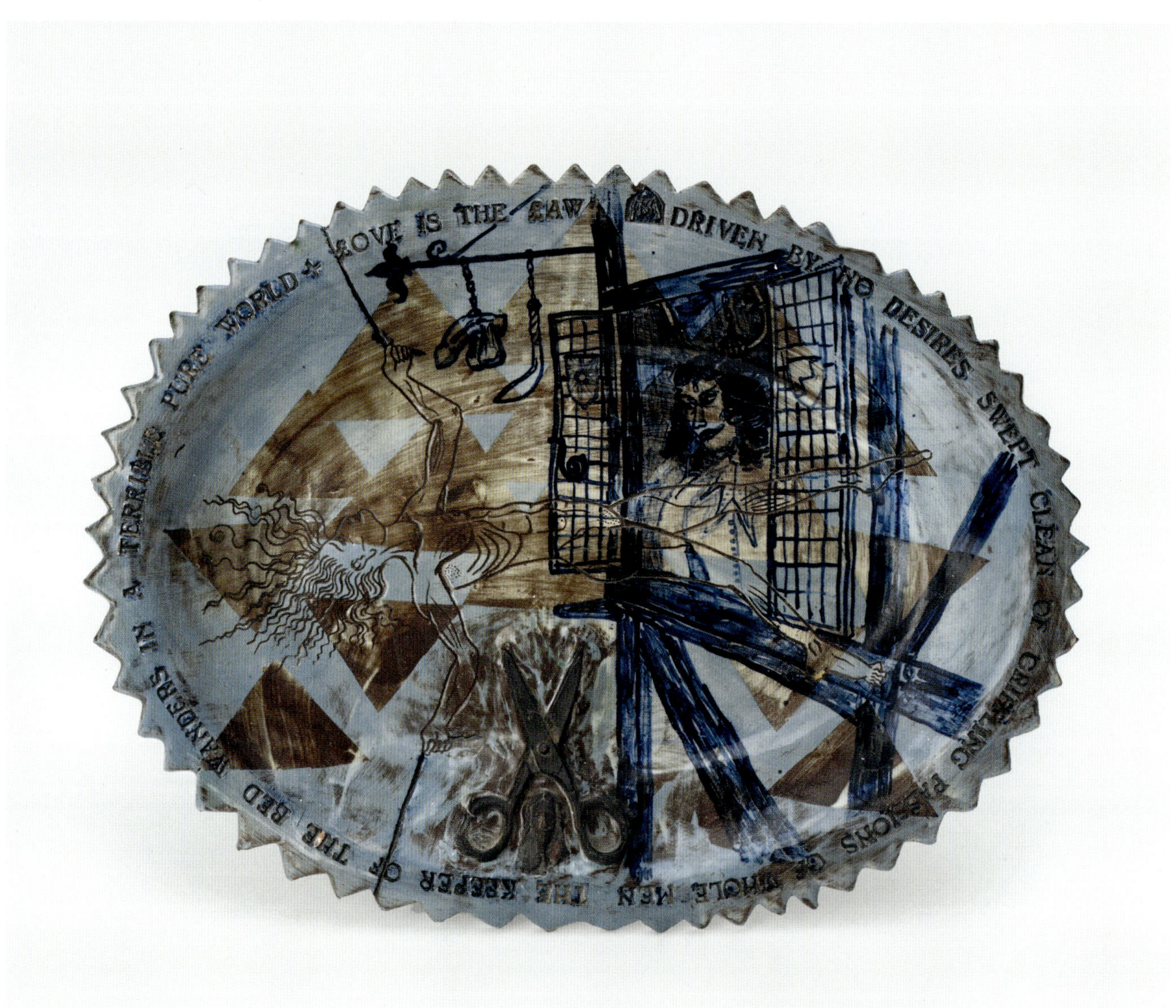

The Keeper of the Bed, 1987
Glazed ceramic, 28 × 35.5 cm

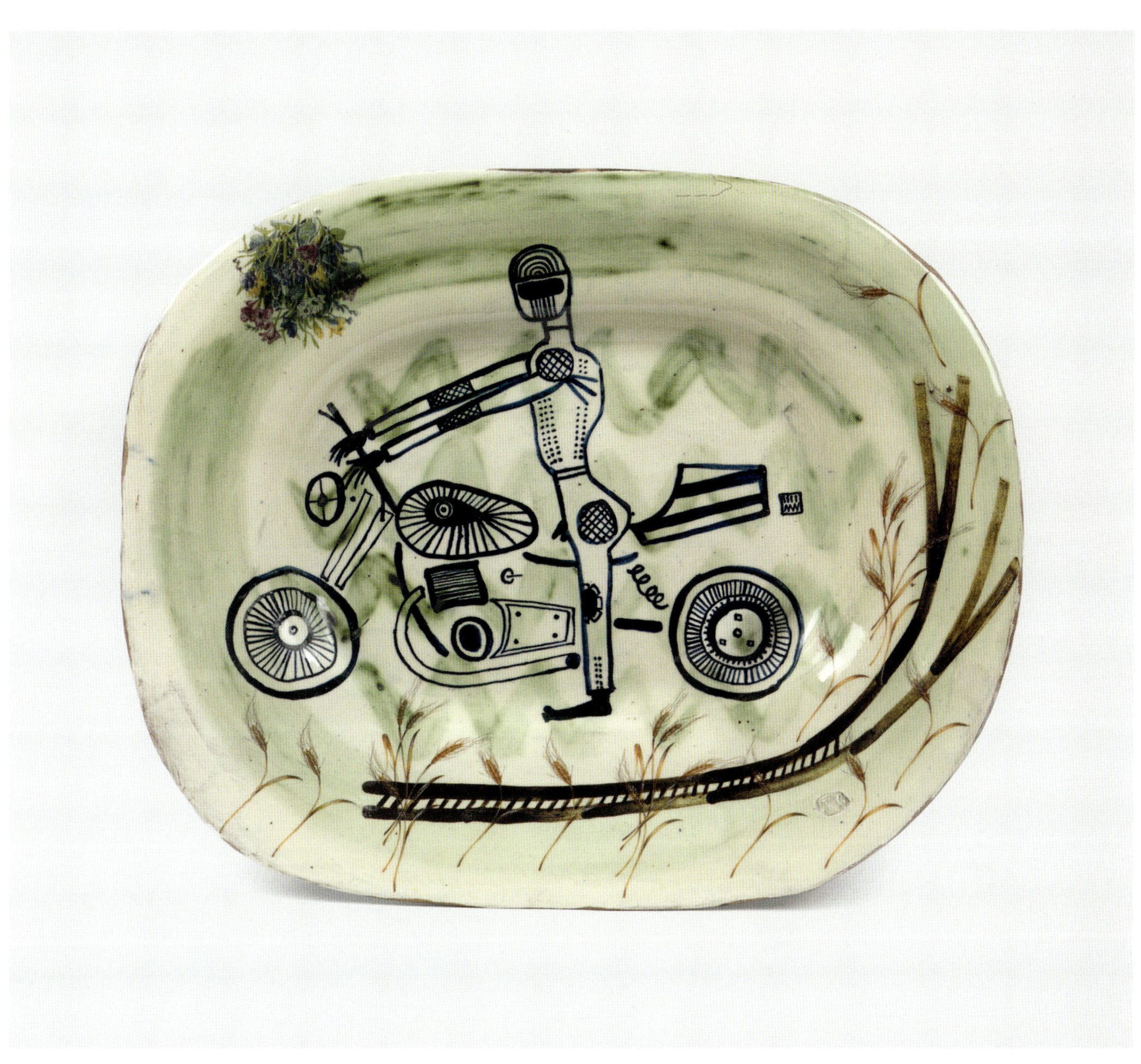

Untitled, 1987
Glazed ceramic, 28 × 46 cm

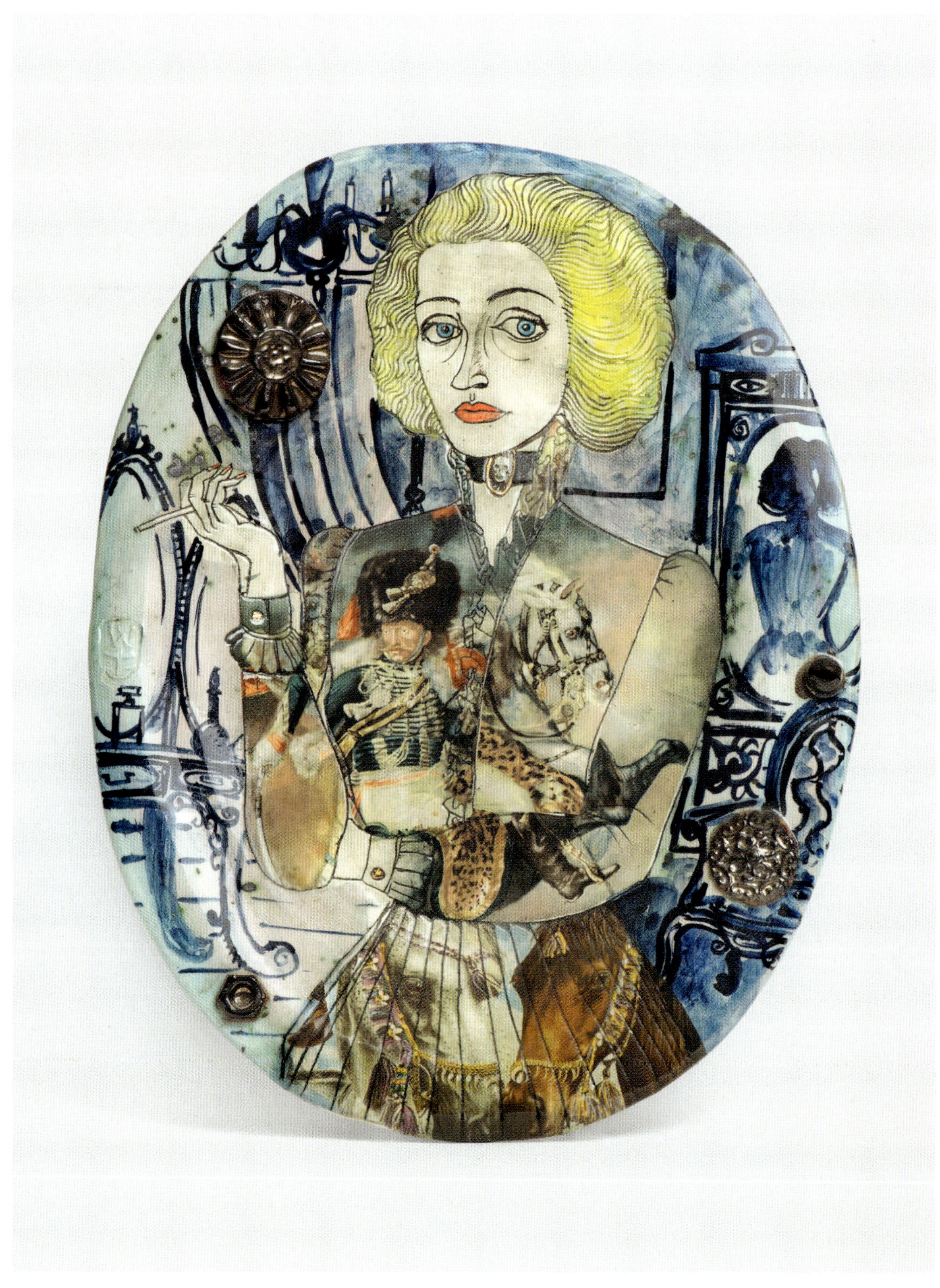

Claire as a Soldier, 1987
Glazed ceramic, 36 × 27 cm

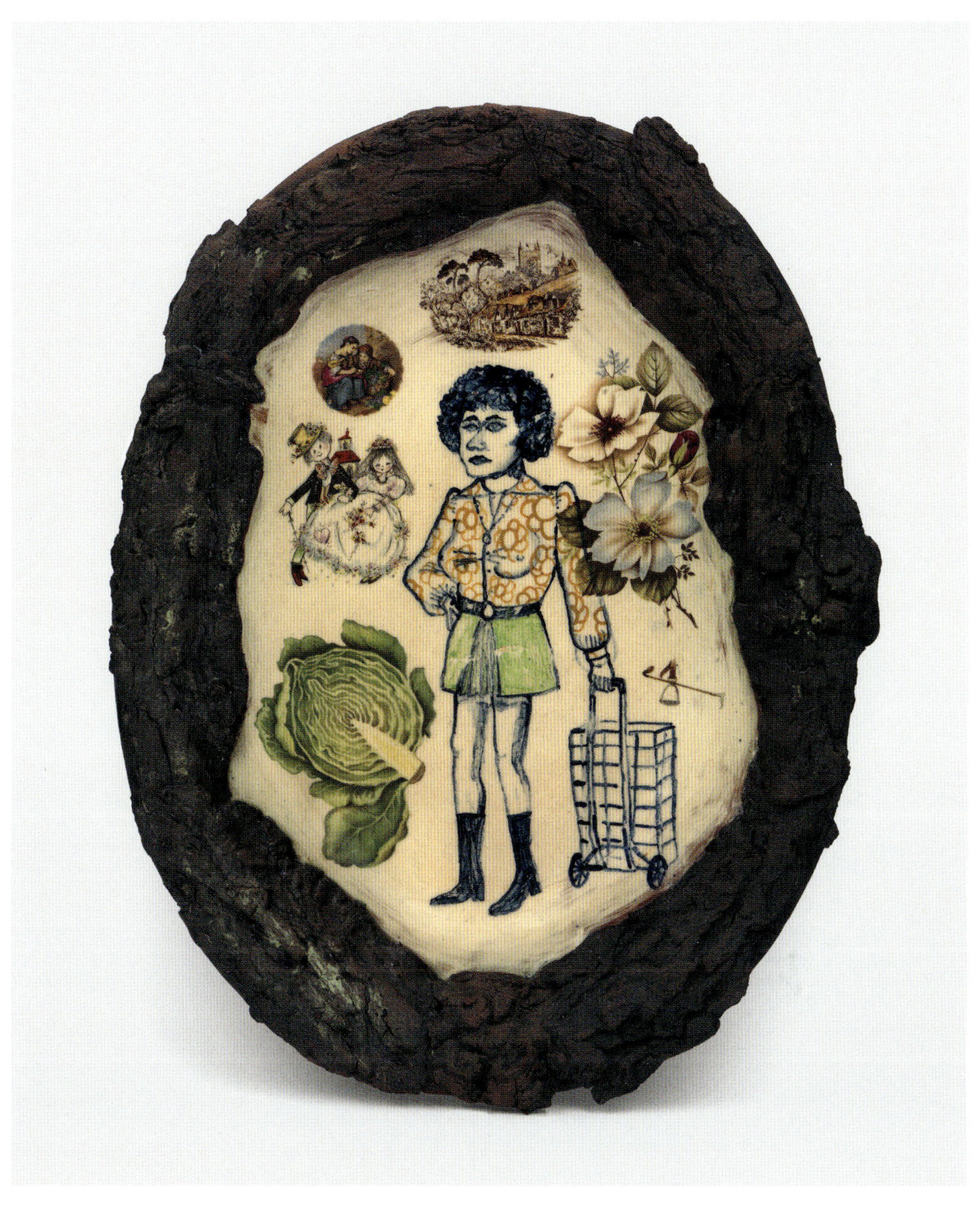

Untitled, 1988
Glazed terracotta, 36.8 × 28.3 cm

Class and taste are such deep unconscious processes that they often play a part in our sexual fantasies, adding emotional resonance to imagined scenarios. On this plate a transvestite dressed in dated but sexually provocative clothes is out pulling an old ladies shopping trolley to add further delicious humiliation. The kitsch stock imagery that surrounds her hints at working-class interiors of my parents' generation. The border, made from sprig moulds of bark, is very redolent of faeces, which was probably intentional.

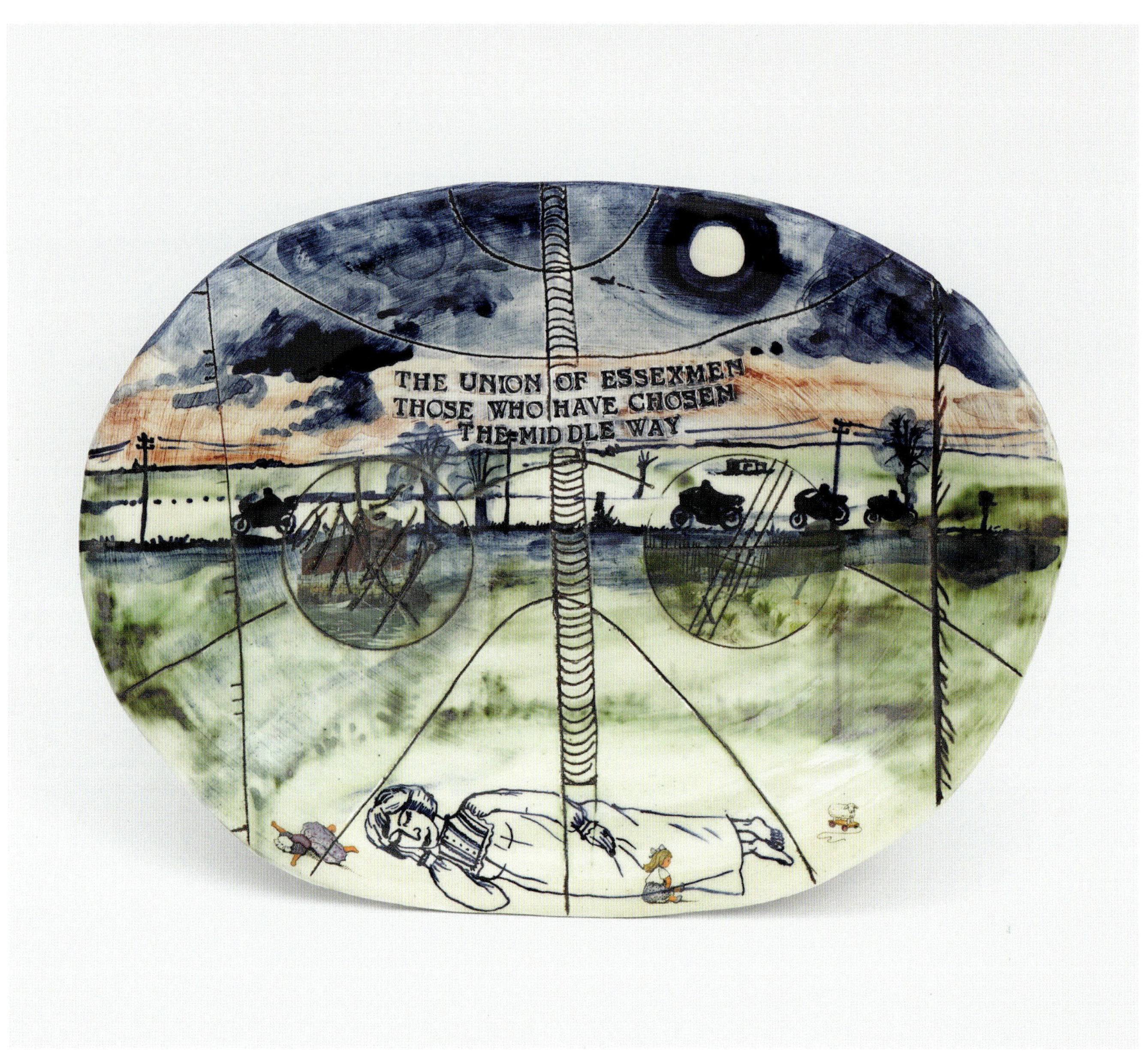

ABOVE: *The Union of Essexmen*, 1988
Glazed ceramic, 27.6 × 36.8 cm

OPPOSITE: *Armageddon Feels
so Very Re-assuring*, 1988
Glazed ceramic, 16.5 × 13 cm

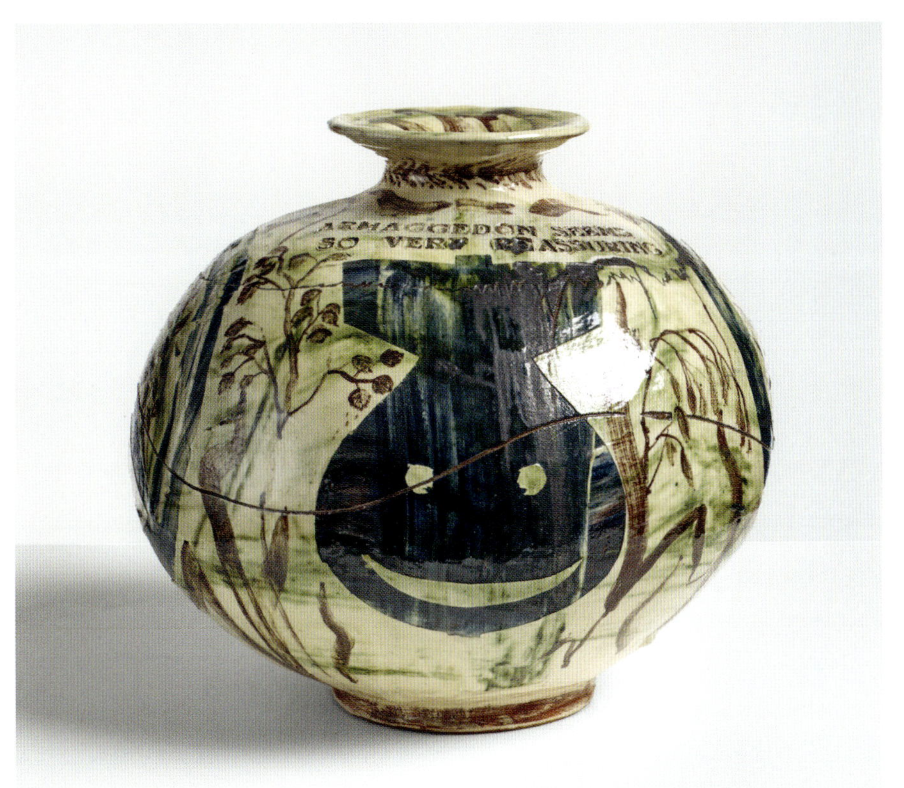
ARMAGGEDON SEEMS
SO VERY REASSURING

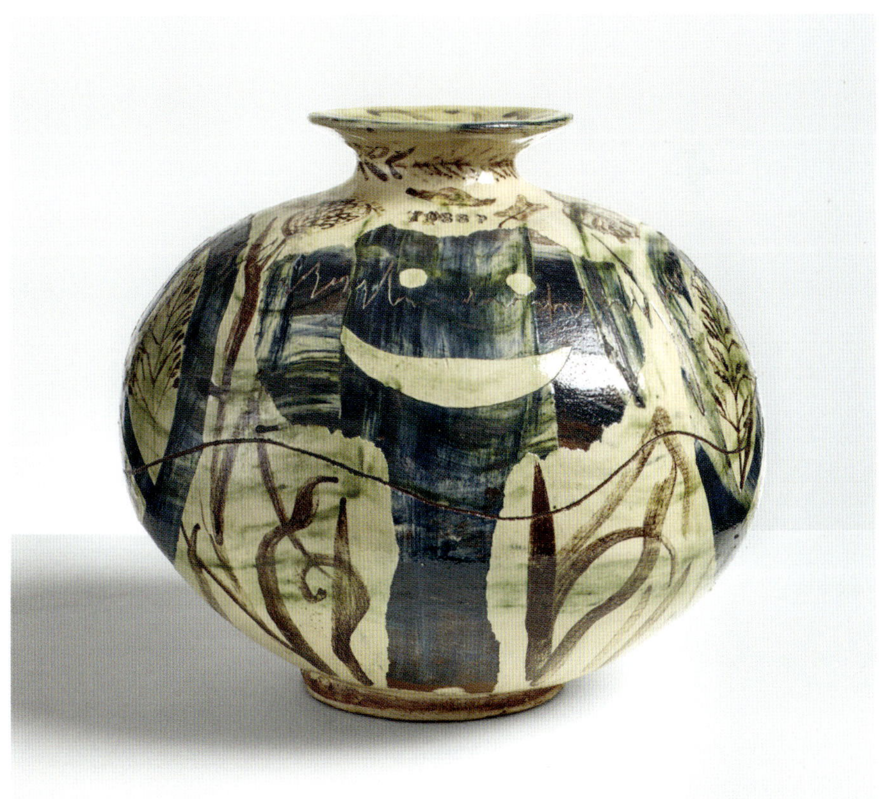
1988

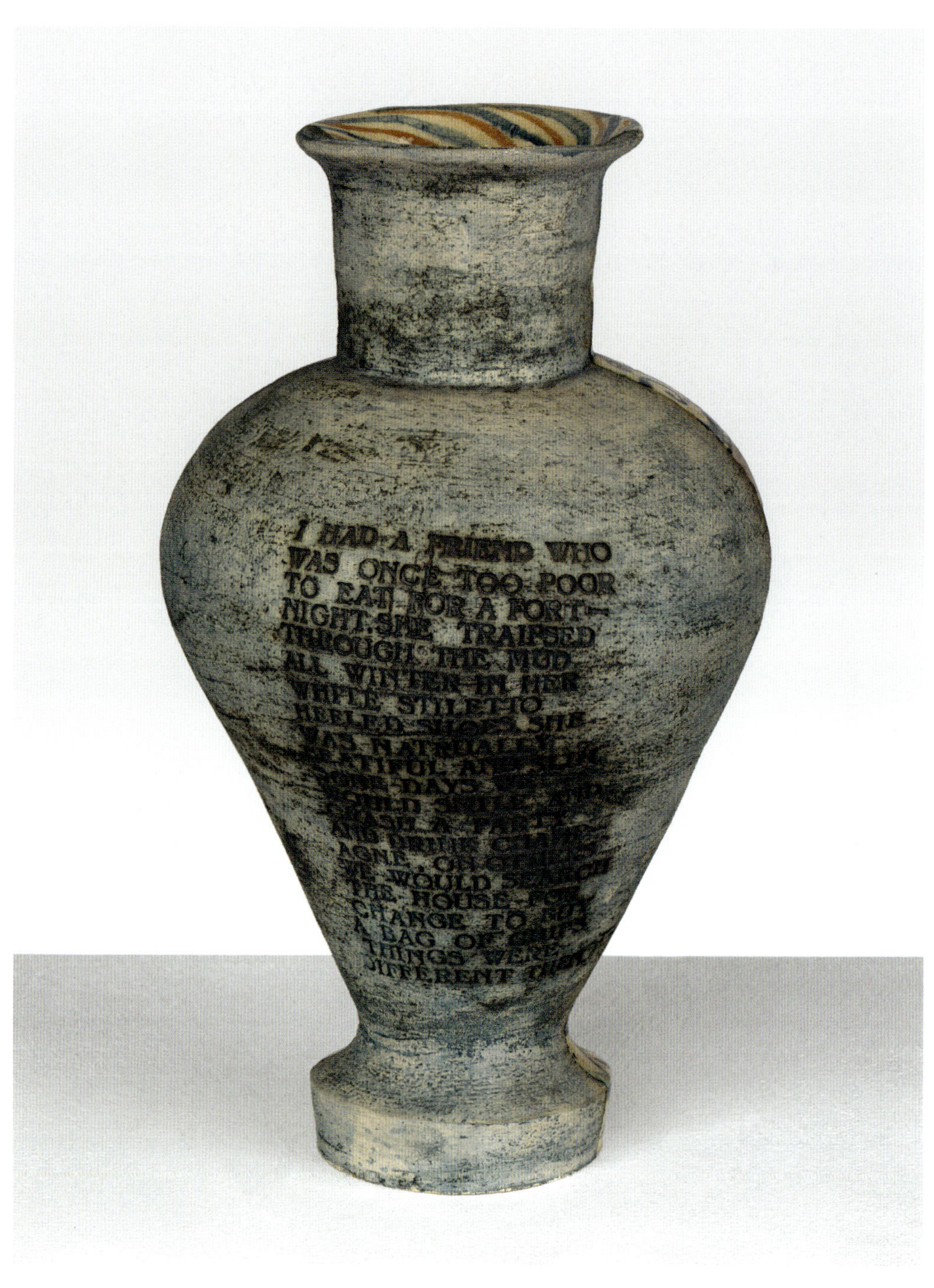

Untitled, 1988
Glazed ceramic, 37 × 21 cm

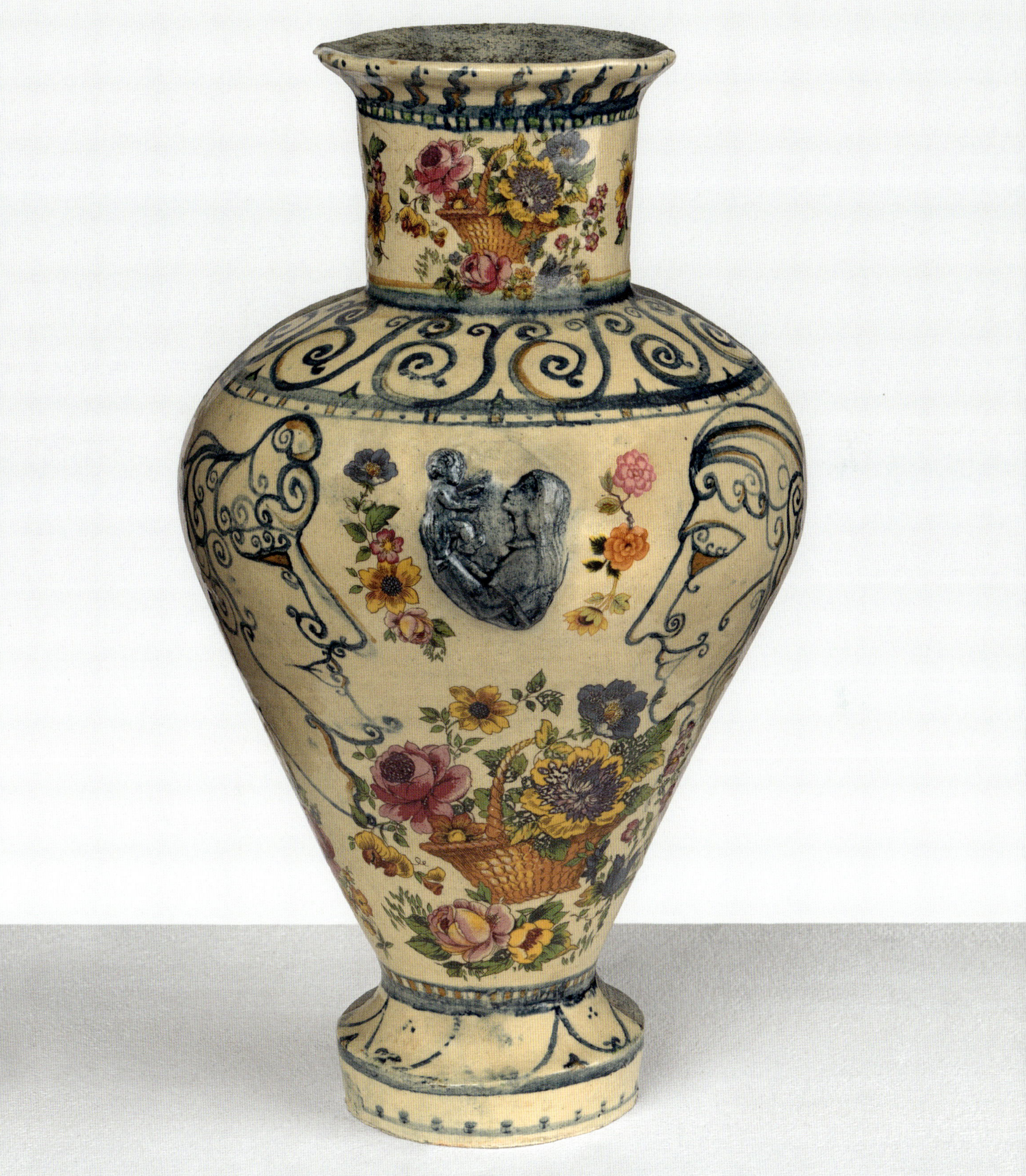

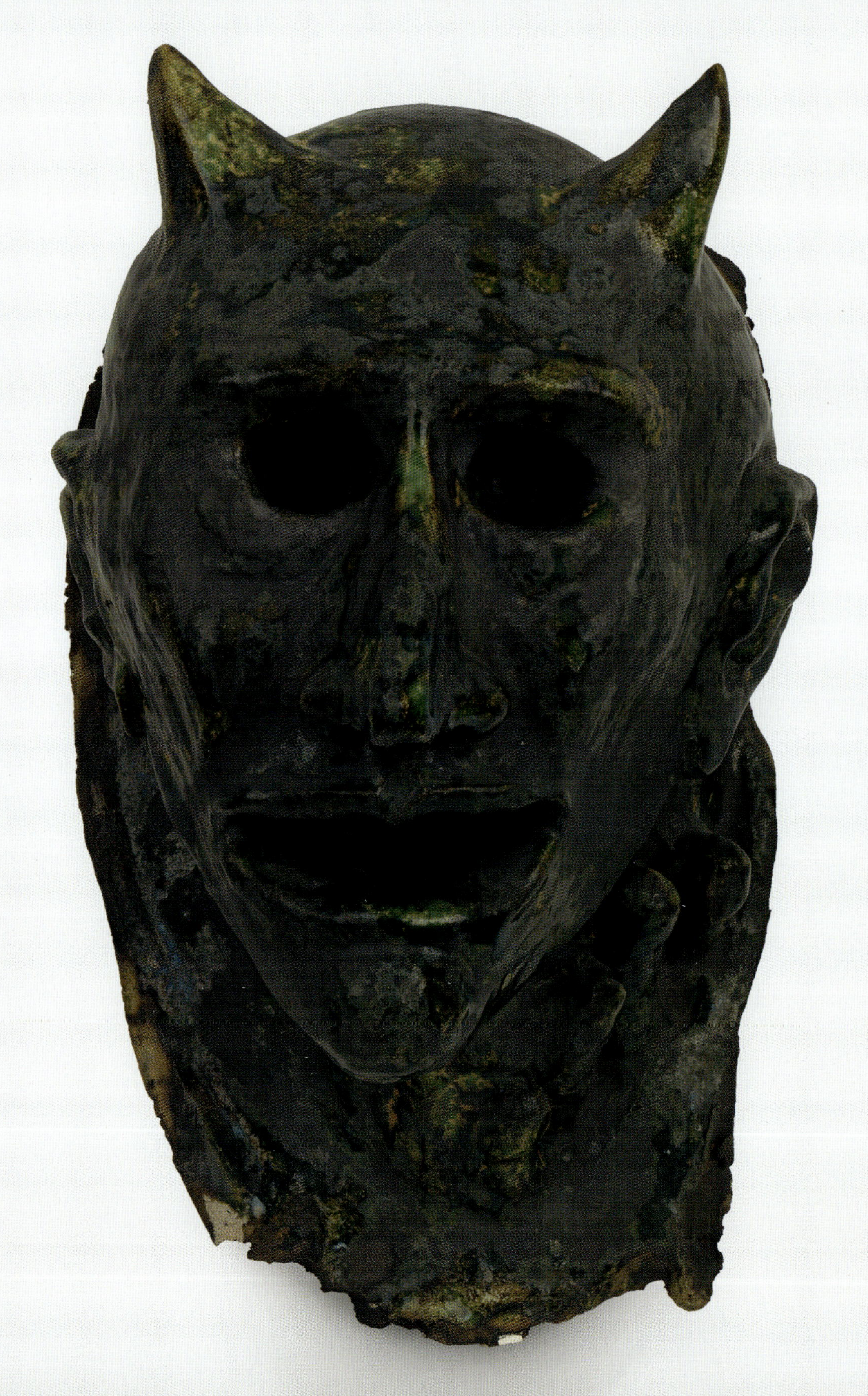

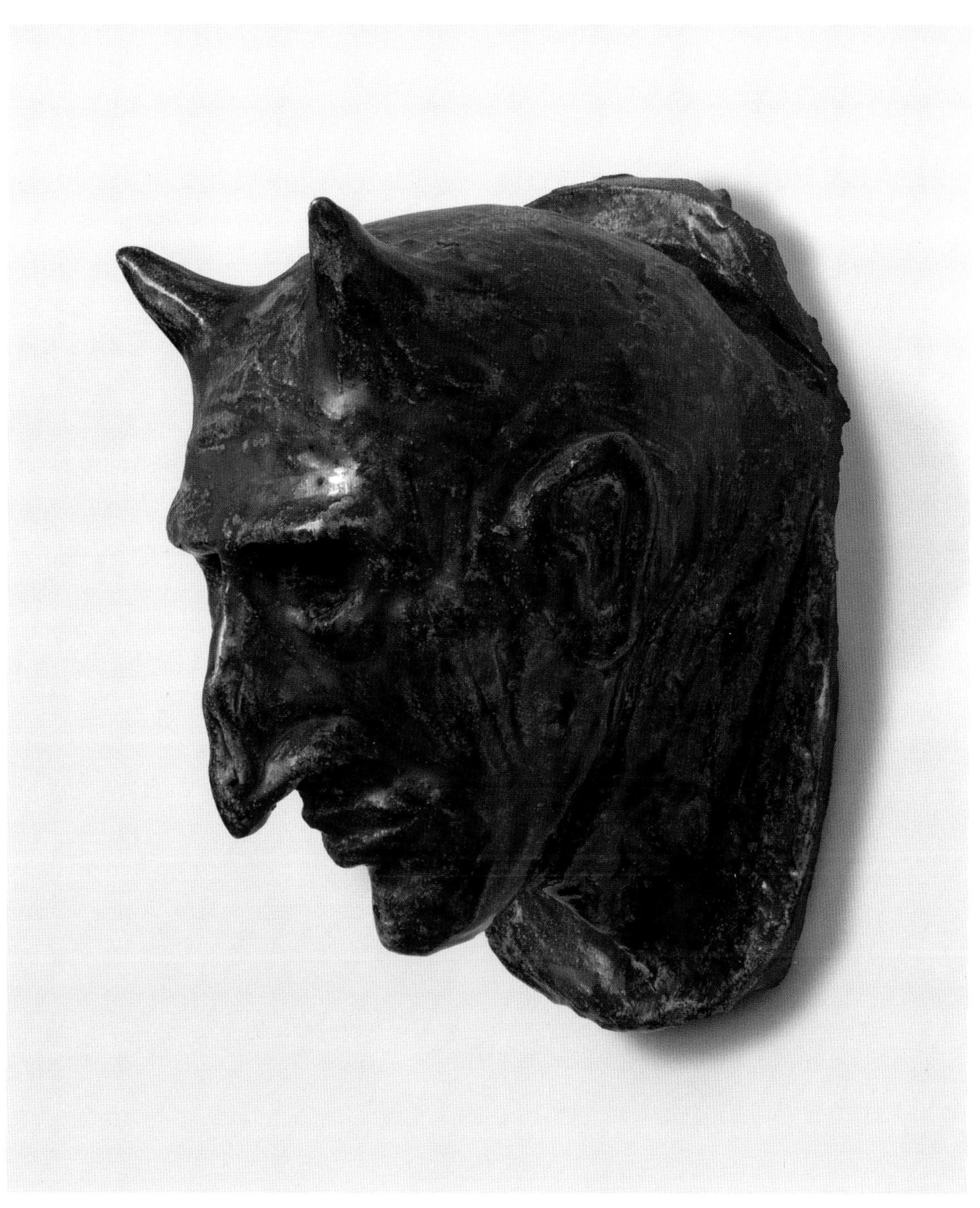

ABOVE: *Grotesque Devil Head*, 1988
Glazed ceramic, 29 × 17.5 × 20.5 cm

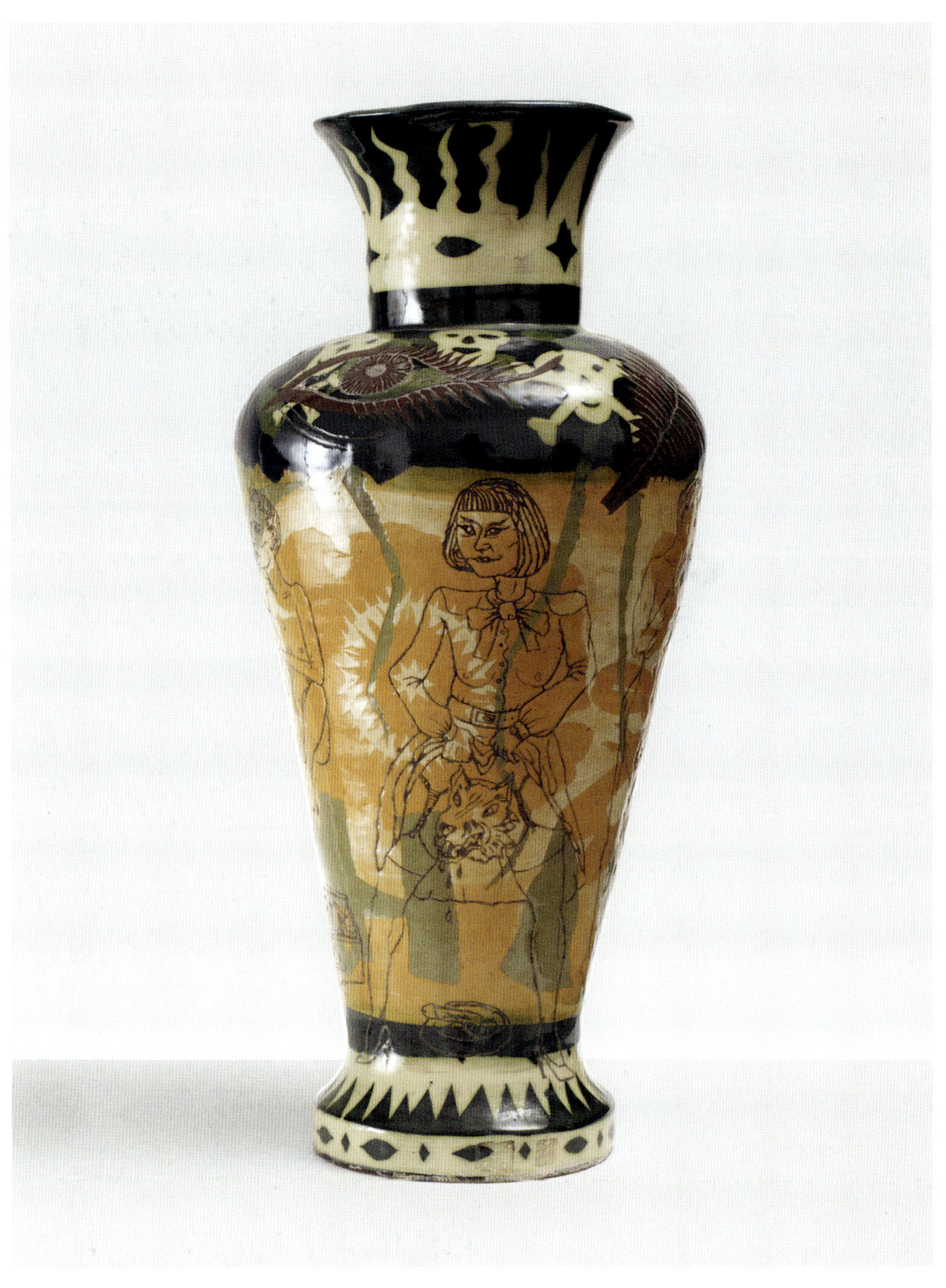

Beneath Every Stone is Life, 1988
Glazed ceramic, 46.5 × 21 cm

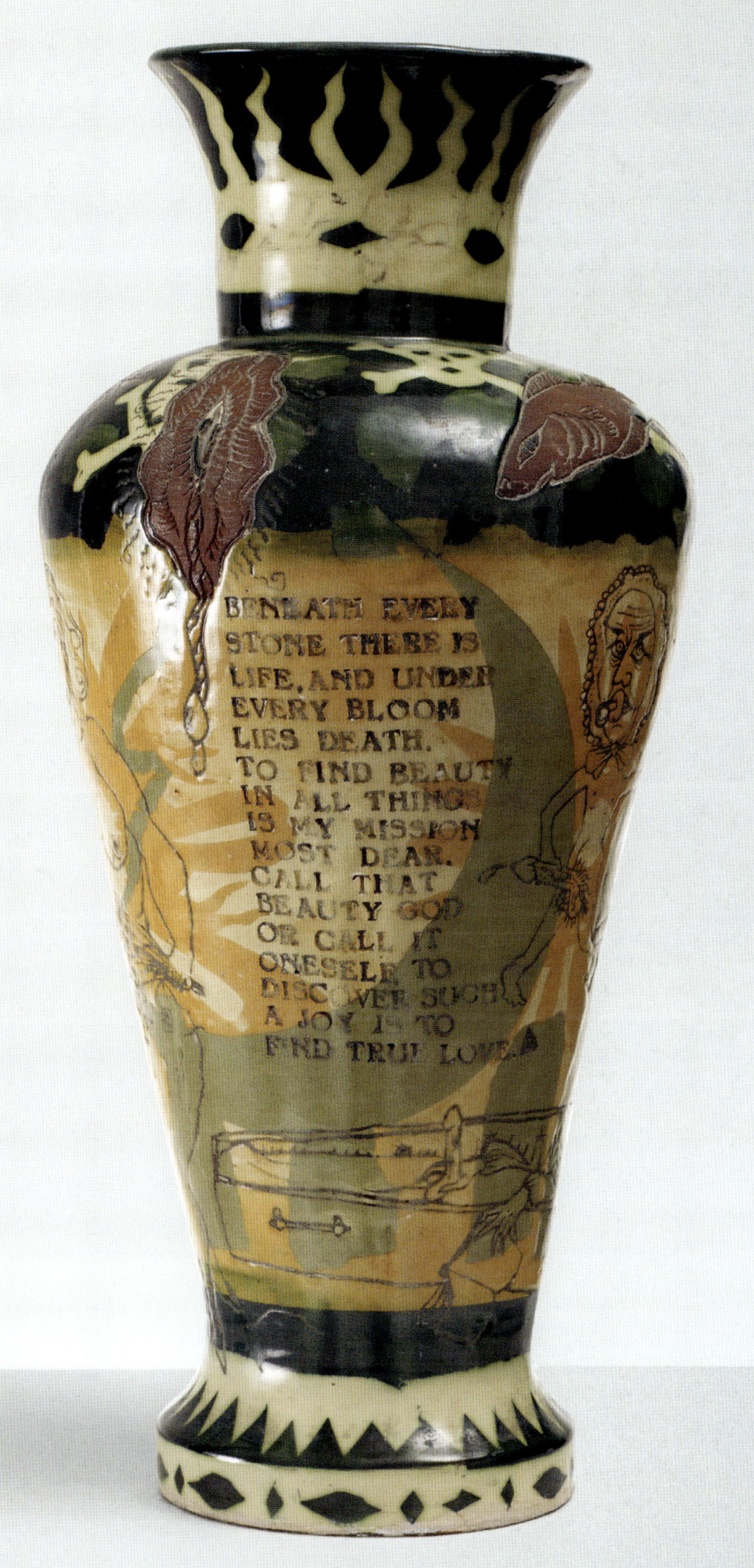
BENEATH EVERY
STONE THERE IS
LIFE, AND UNDER
EVERY BLOOM
LIES DEATH.
TO FIND BEAUTY
IN ALL THINGS
IS MY MISSION
MOST DEAR.
CALL THAT
BEAUTY GOD
OR CALL IT
ONESELF TO
DISCOVER SUCH
A JOY IS TO
FIND TRUE LOVE.

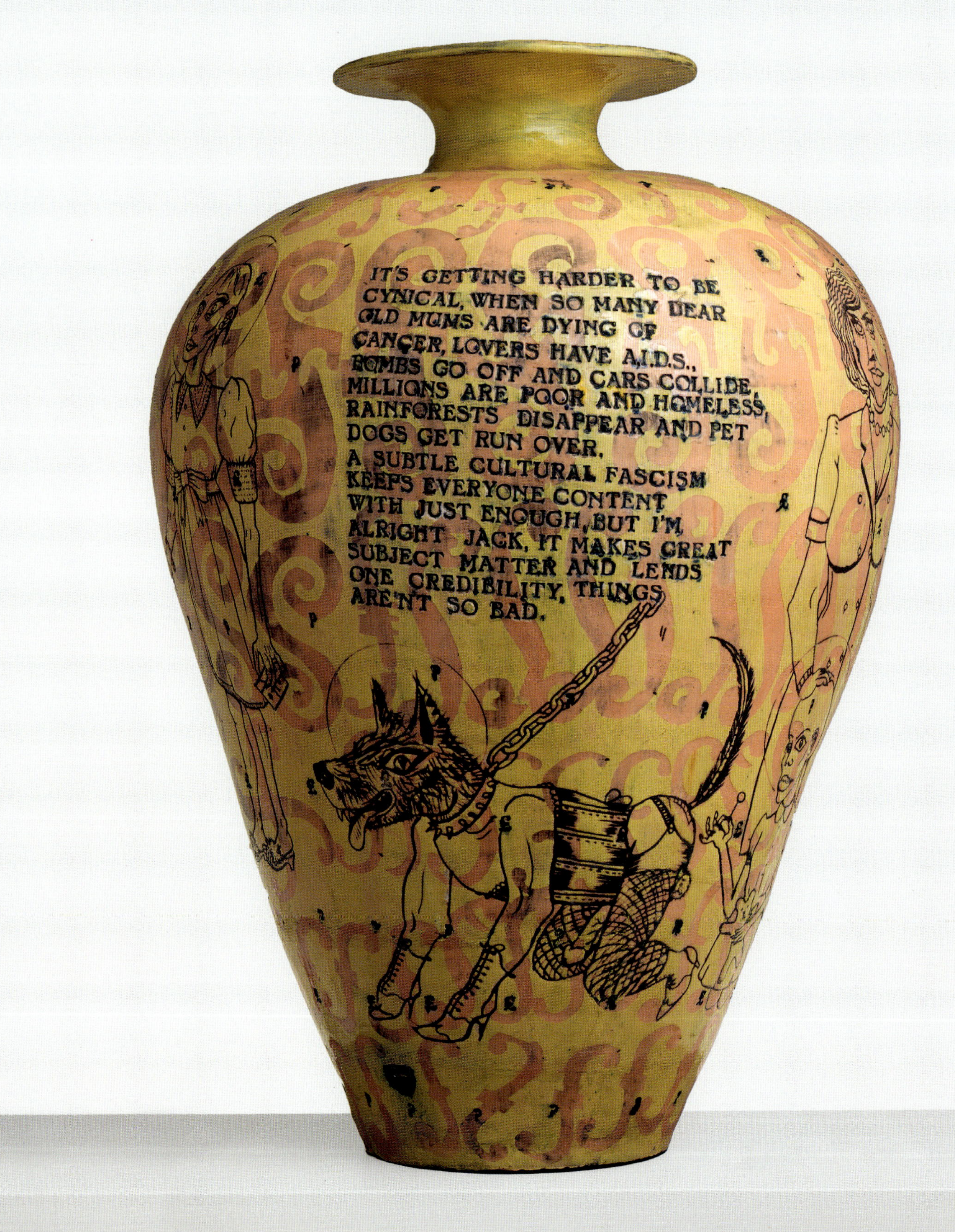

IT'S GETTING HARDER TO BE
CYNICAL, WHEN SO MANY DEAR
OLD MUMS ARE DYING OF
CANCER, LOVERS HAVE A.I.D.S.,
BOMBS GO OFF AND CARS COLLIDE,
MILLIONS ARE POOR AND HOMELESS,
RAINFORESTS DISAPPEAR AND PET
DOGS GET RUN OVER.
A SUBTLE CULTURAL FASCISM
KEEPS EVERYONE CONTENT
WITH JUST ENOUGH, BUT I'M
ALRIGHT JACK, IT MAKES GREAT
SUBJECT MATTER AND LENDS
ONE CREDIBILITY, THINGS
AREN'T SO BAD.

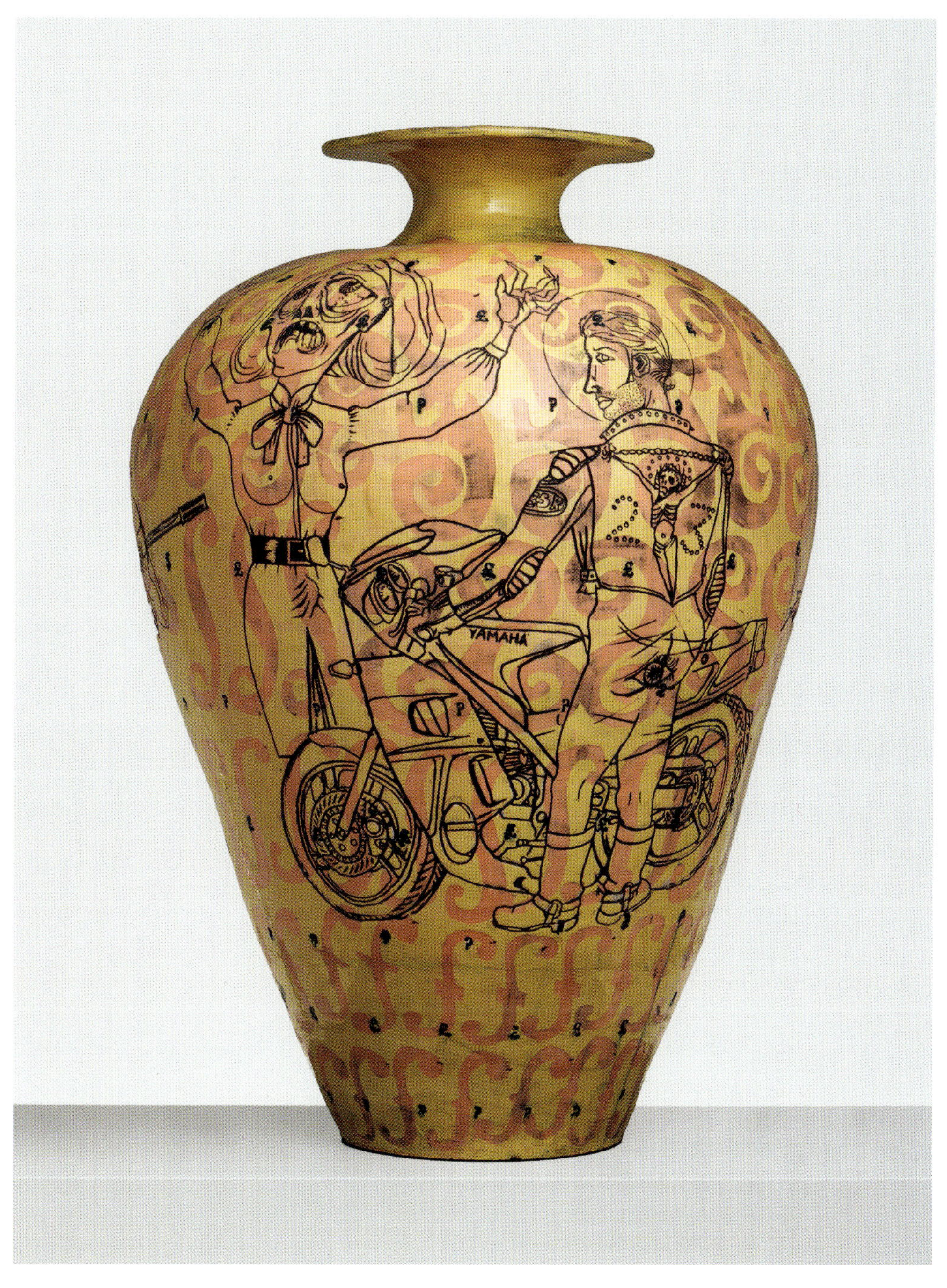

It's Getting Harder to be Cynical, 1988
Glazed ceramic, 46.3 × 30.2 cm

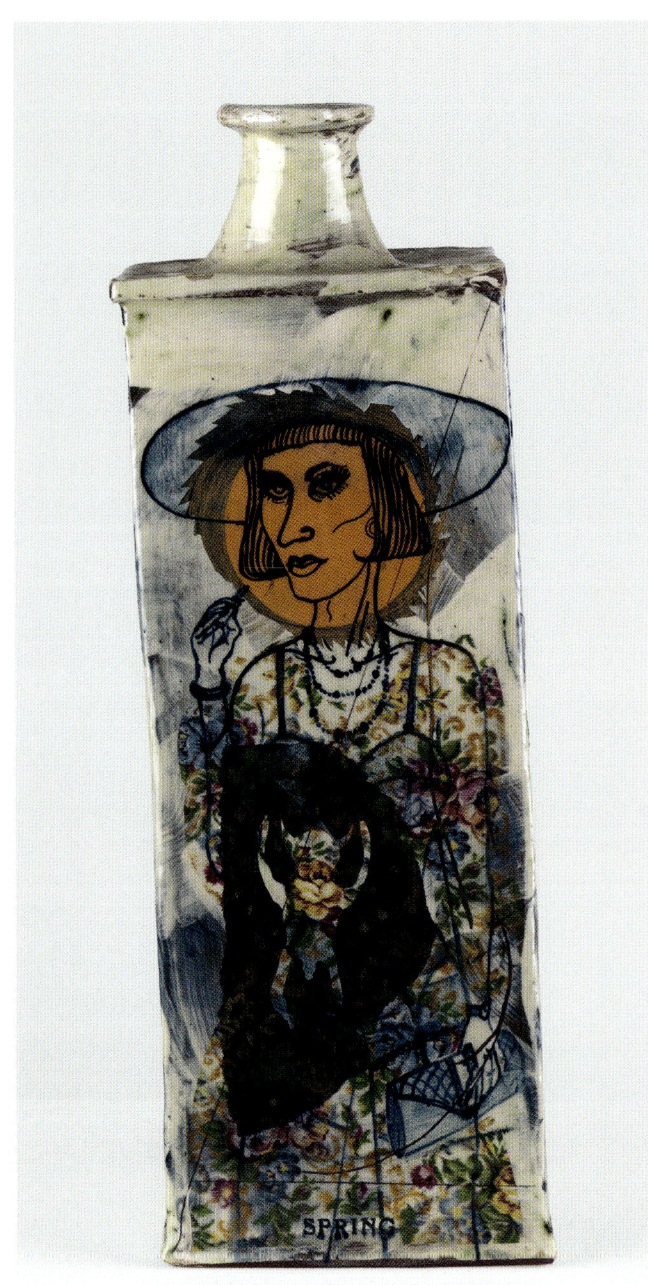

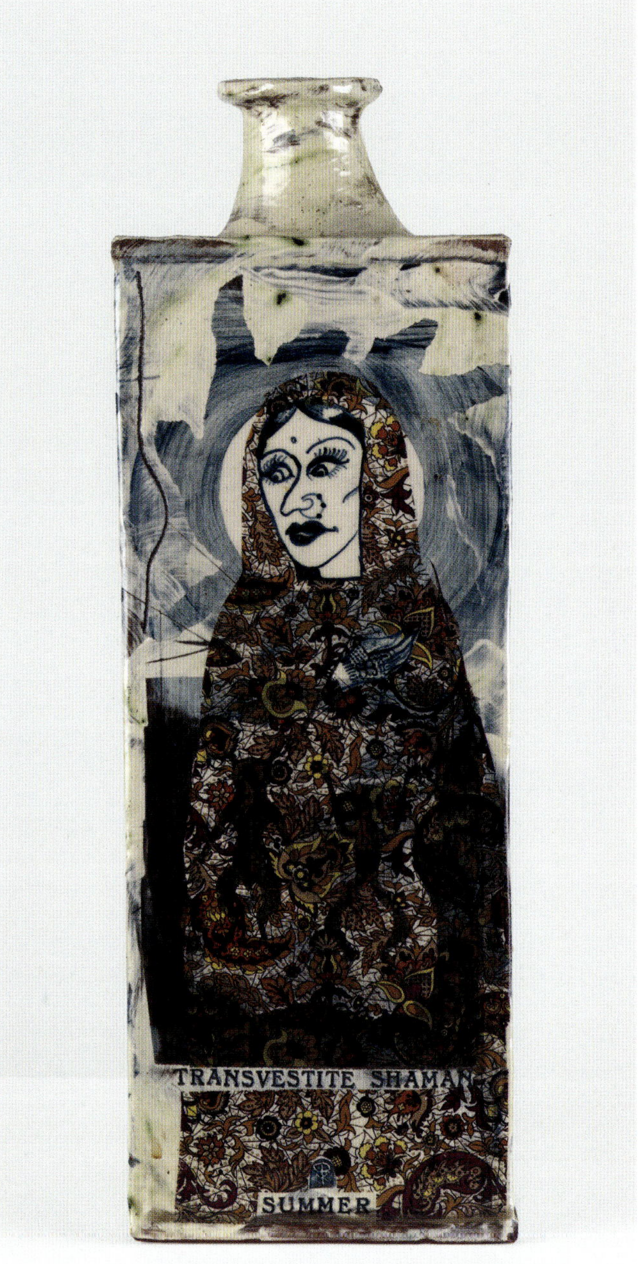

Four Seasons, 1988
Glazed ceramic, 46.9 × 15.5 cm

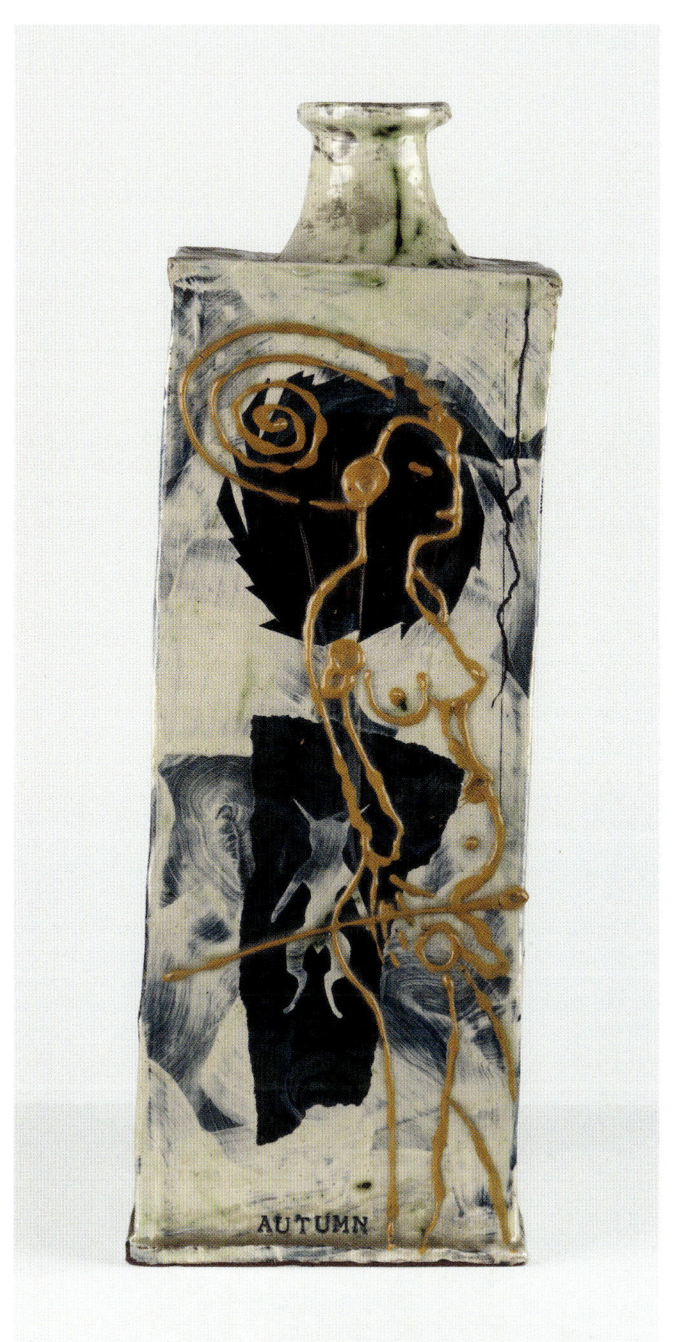
AUTUMN

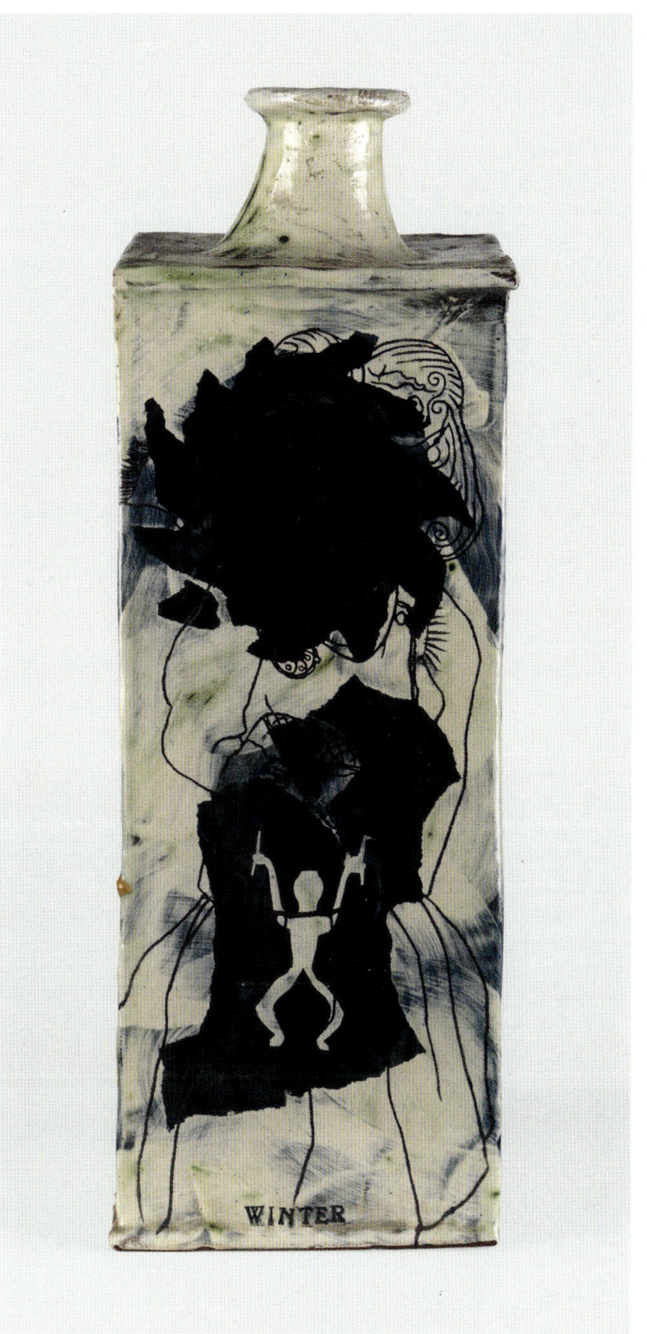
WINTER

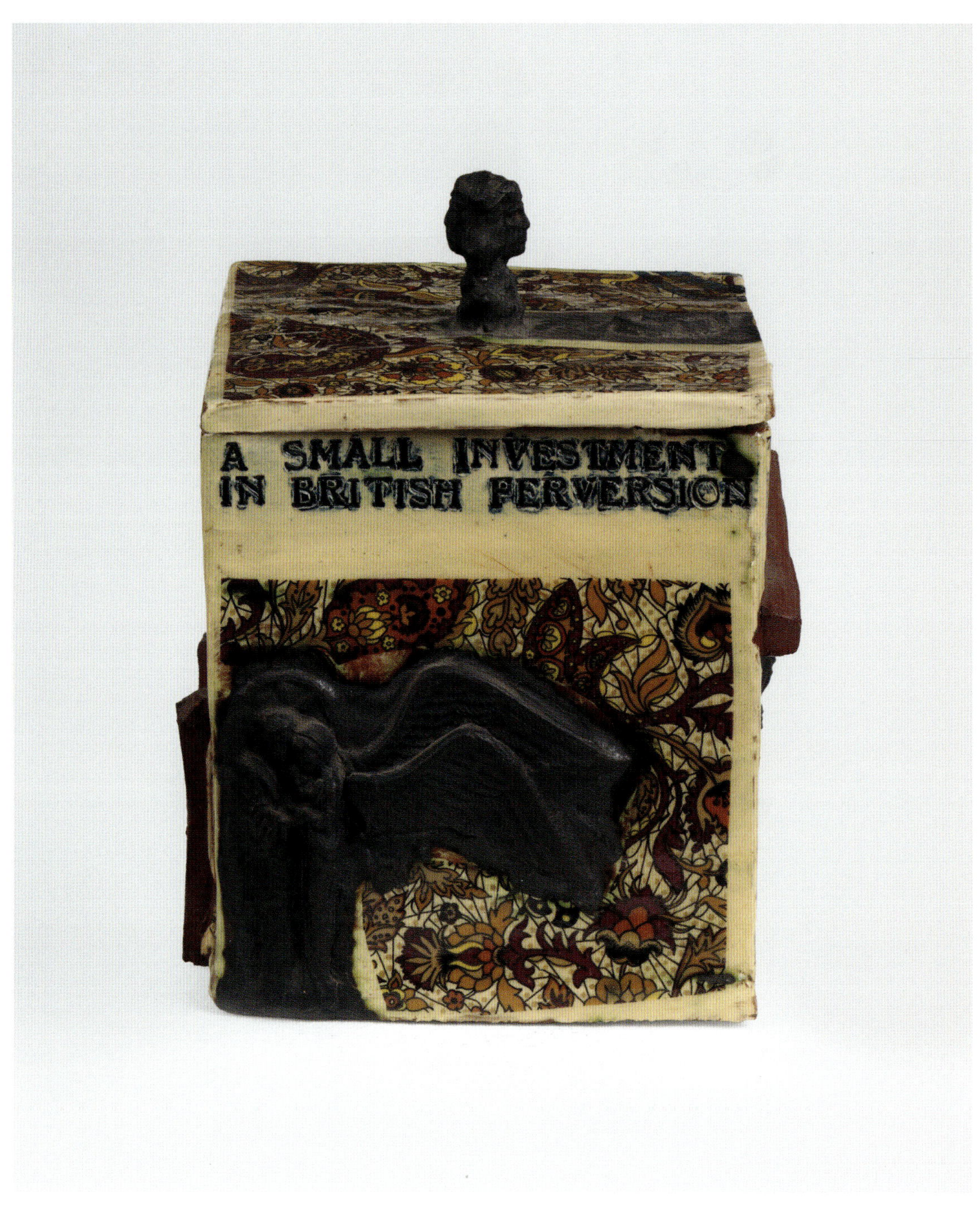

ABOVE: *A Small Investment in British Perversion*, 1988
Glazed ceramic, 17.5 × 13.5 cm

OPPOSITE: *Skull*, 1989
Glazed ceramic, 15 × 13 × 18 cm

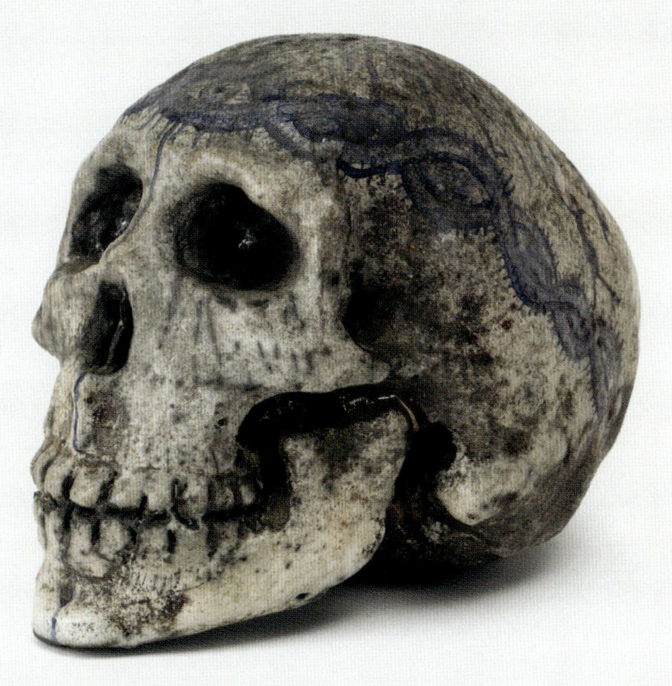

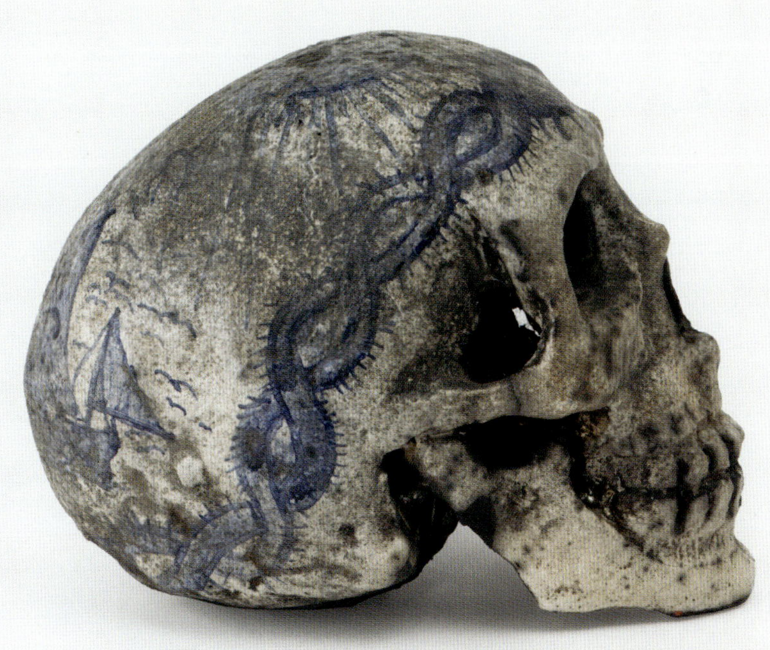

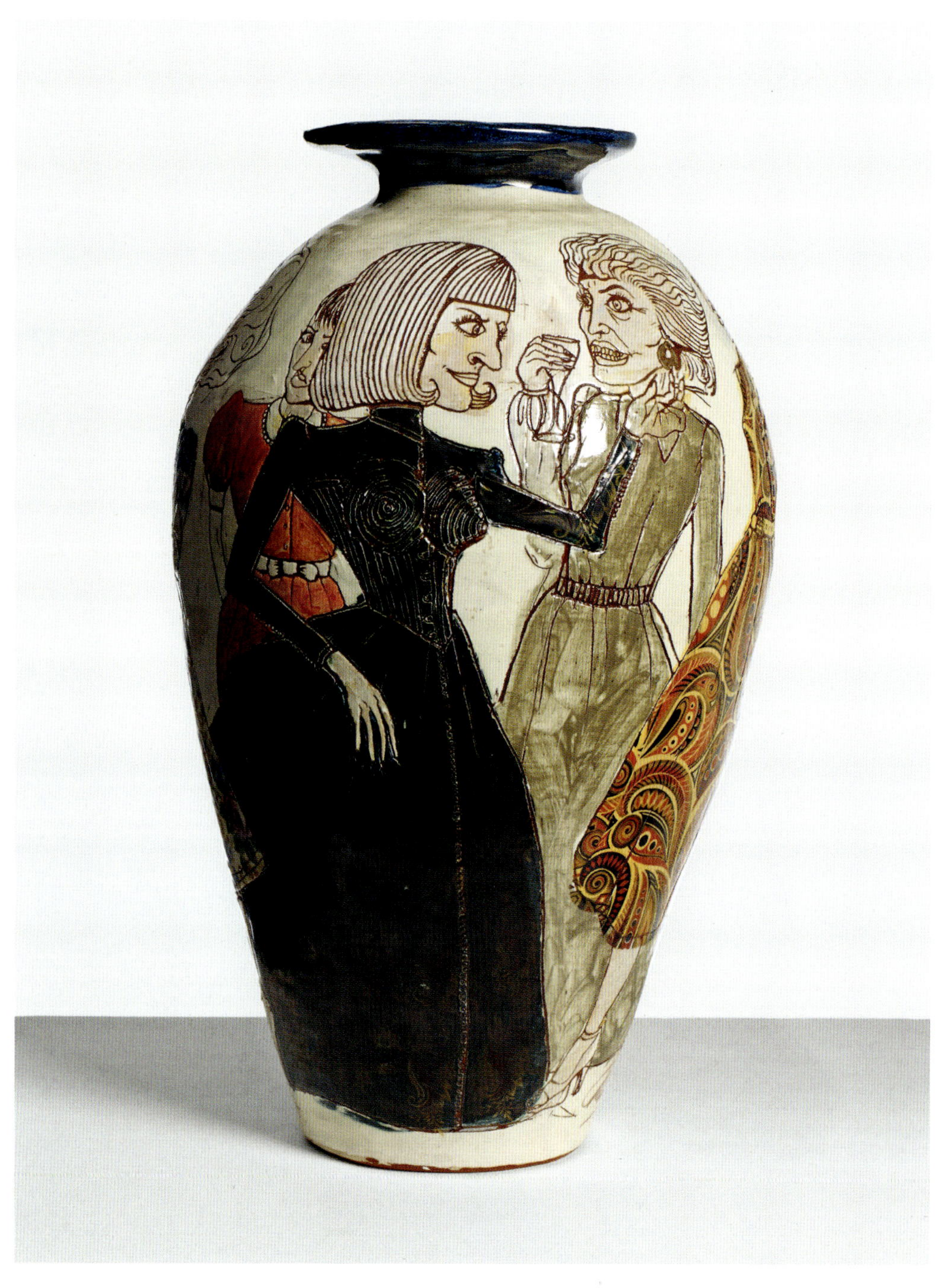

Cocktail Party, 1989
Glazed ceramic, 41 × 22 cm

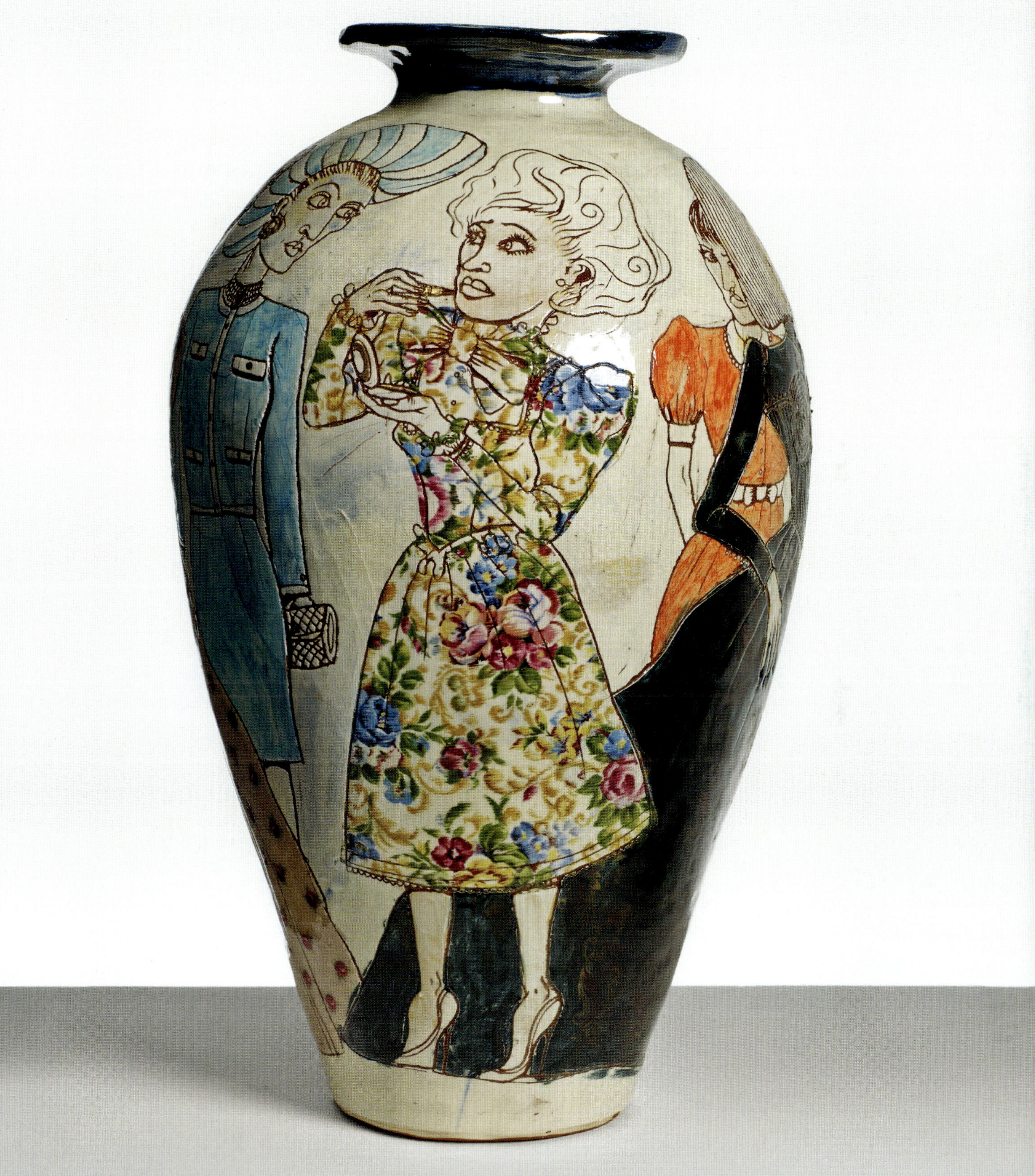

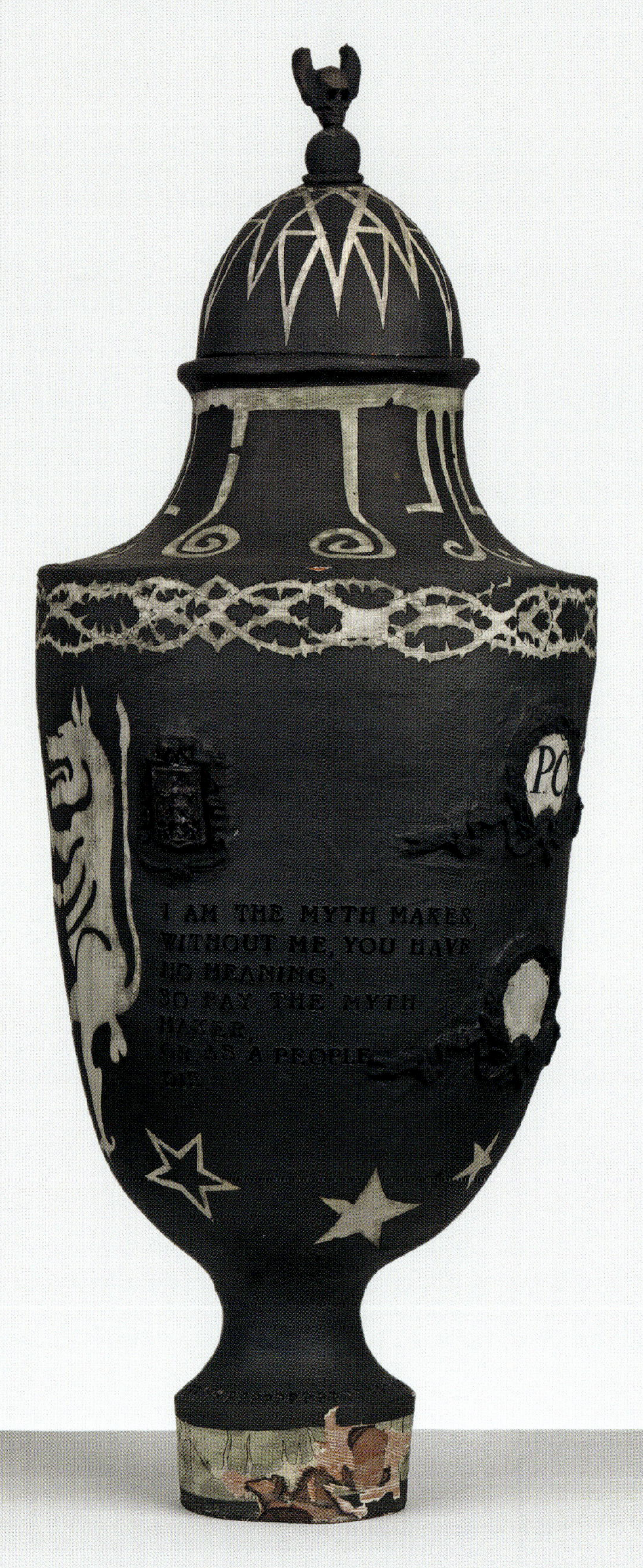

I AM THE MYTH MAKER,
WITHOUT ME, YOU HAVE
NO MEANING,
SO PAY THE MYTH
MAKER,
OR AS A PEOPLE
DIE.
PO

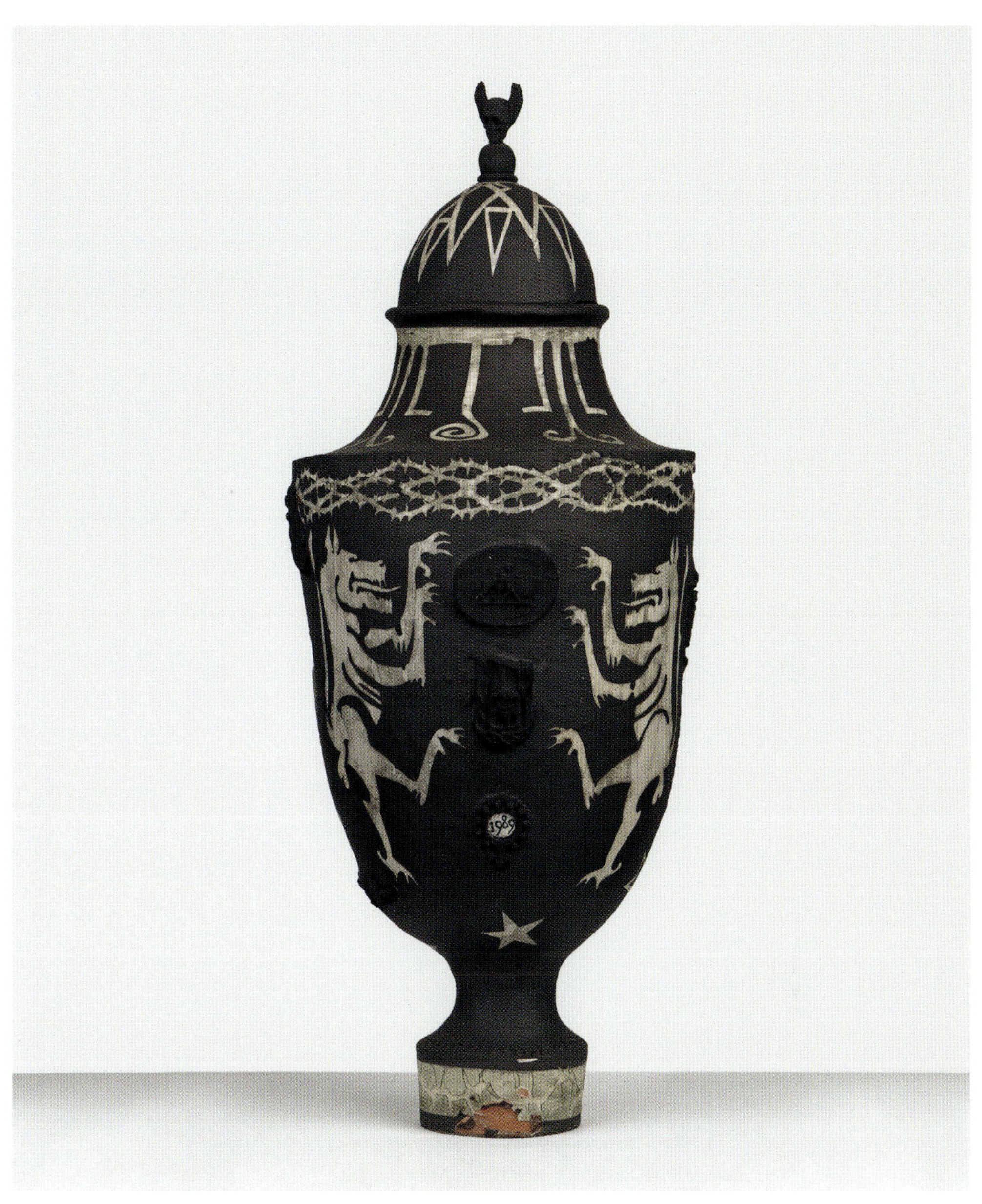

I am the Myth Maker, 1989
Glazed ceramic, 58.4 × 22.5 cm

I made a lot of these unglazed blue grey funereal urns decorated
with papercut stencils and sprig mouldings. The exhortation to
'pay the myth maker' speaks of how obsessed I was with earning
money. Yet ironically I stopped making pots in this style, despite
them being a guaranteed seller, because I got bored of making
them. I like the motto on this one. It has the arrogance of youth
but it is also true. Artists are the myth makers. The arts create
templates that help people find meaning in their lives.

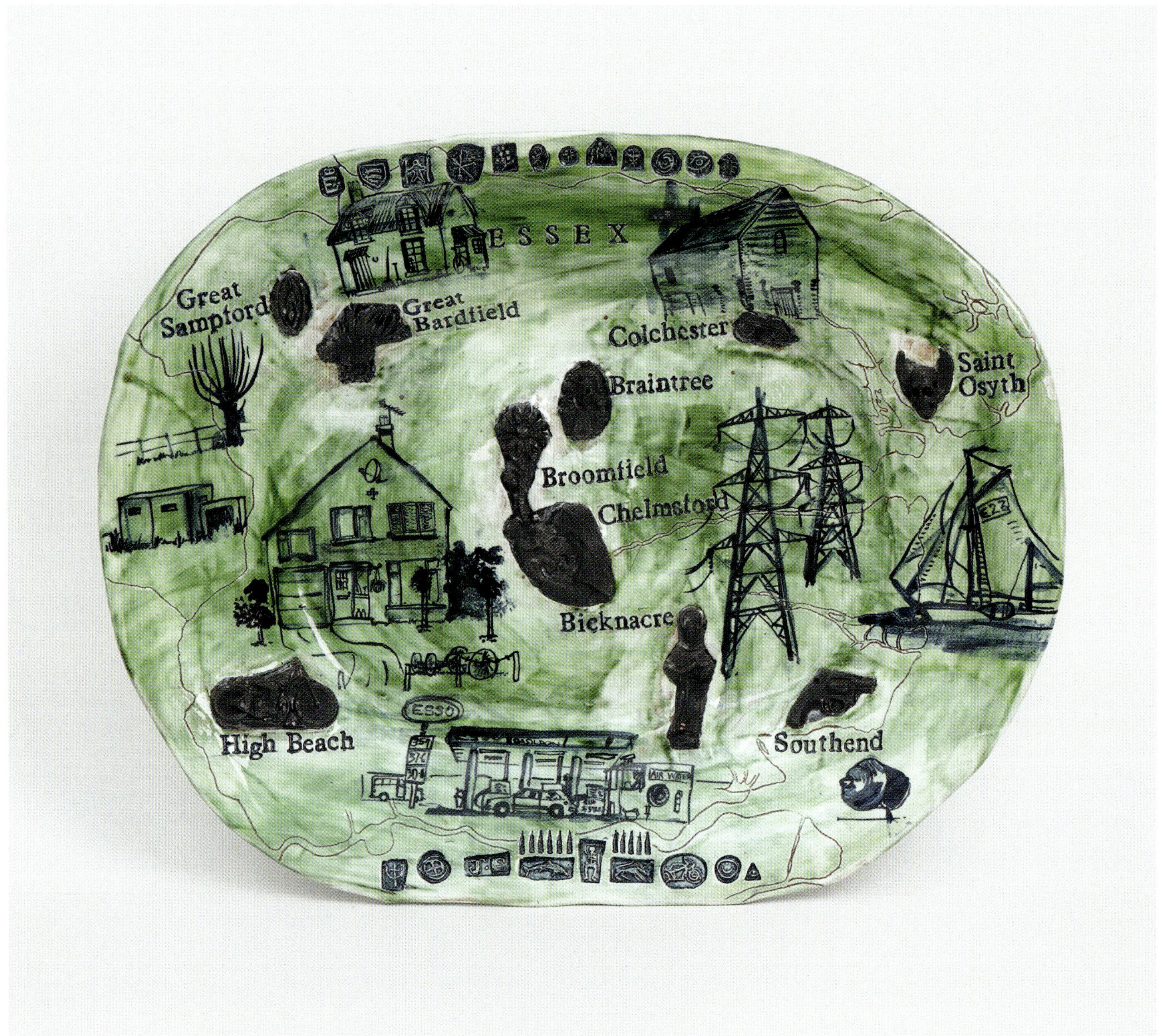

Map of Essex, 1990
Glazed ceramic, 38 × 47.5 cm

Looking at my early work, I am amazed how many of the themes that were to become important in my career were present in these youthful ceramics. This plate must be one of the first map pieces I made, a form that I have used often in the last fifteen years or so. The stamped place names mainly refer to locations significant in my life. 'High Beach' (*sic*) is the site of the bikers' tea hut in Epping Forest where I spent an awful lot of time in the 1990s. The painting of the suburban house is where I grew up in Bicknacre and the building above 'Colchester' is St Peter-on-the-Wall, one of Britain's oldest churches and an inspiration for the House for Essex (2015) I designed with Charles Holland.

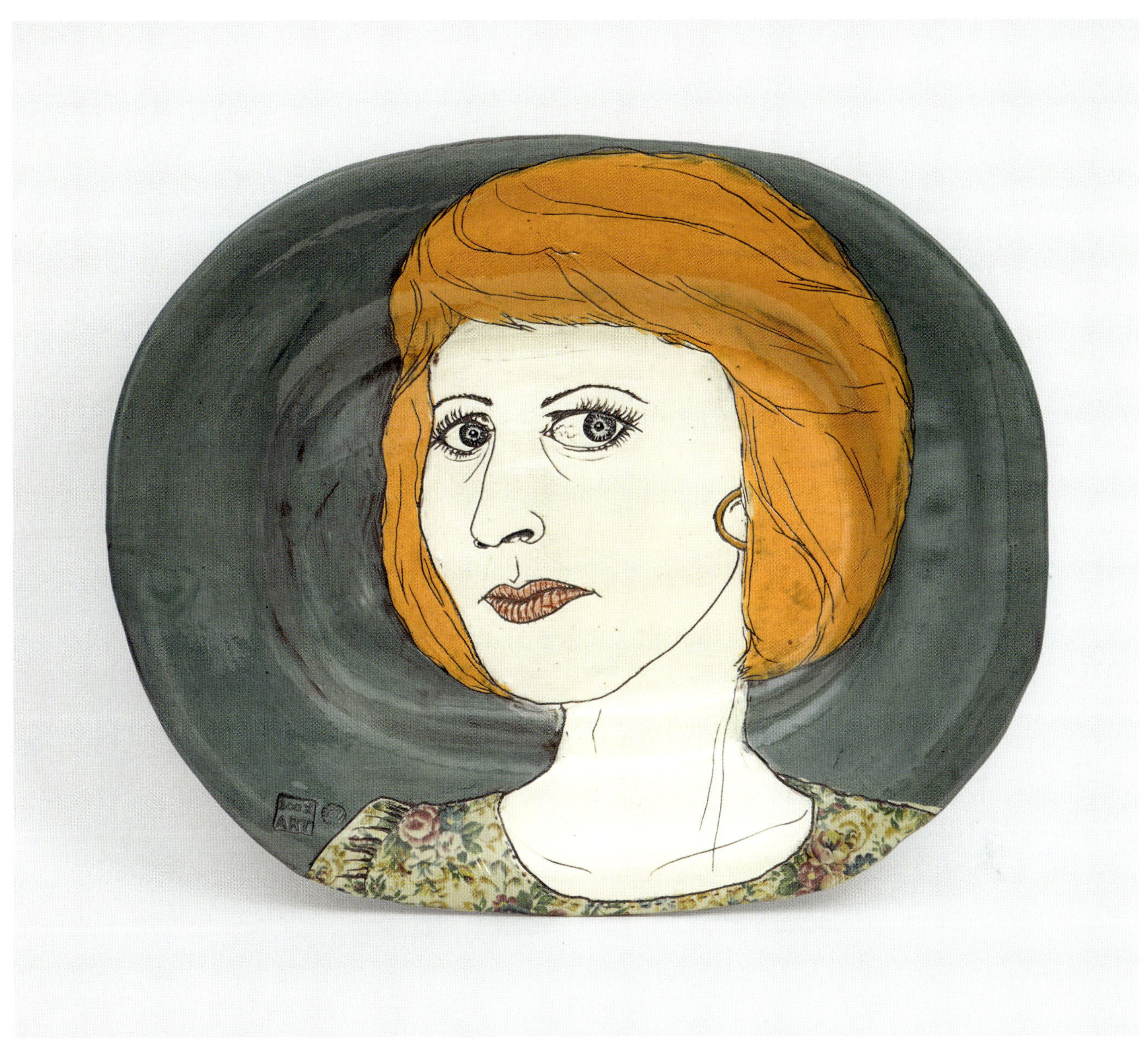

Newsreader, 1990
Glazed ceramic, 38.5 × 47 cm

This is one of a pair of large dishes featuring portraits of female
television newsreaders who at the time represented an aspirational
form of femininity for me: superbly groomed, mature, in command.
As a transvestite I was constantly seeking out female role models to
emulate. I was still very much in my wanting-to-pass-as-a-real-woman
phase of cross-dressing. I drew the portraits from memory but I was
thinking of Jan Leeming and, in this case, Sue Lawley.

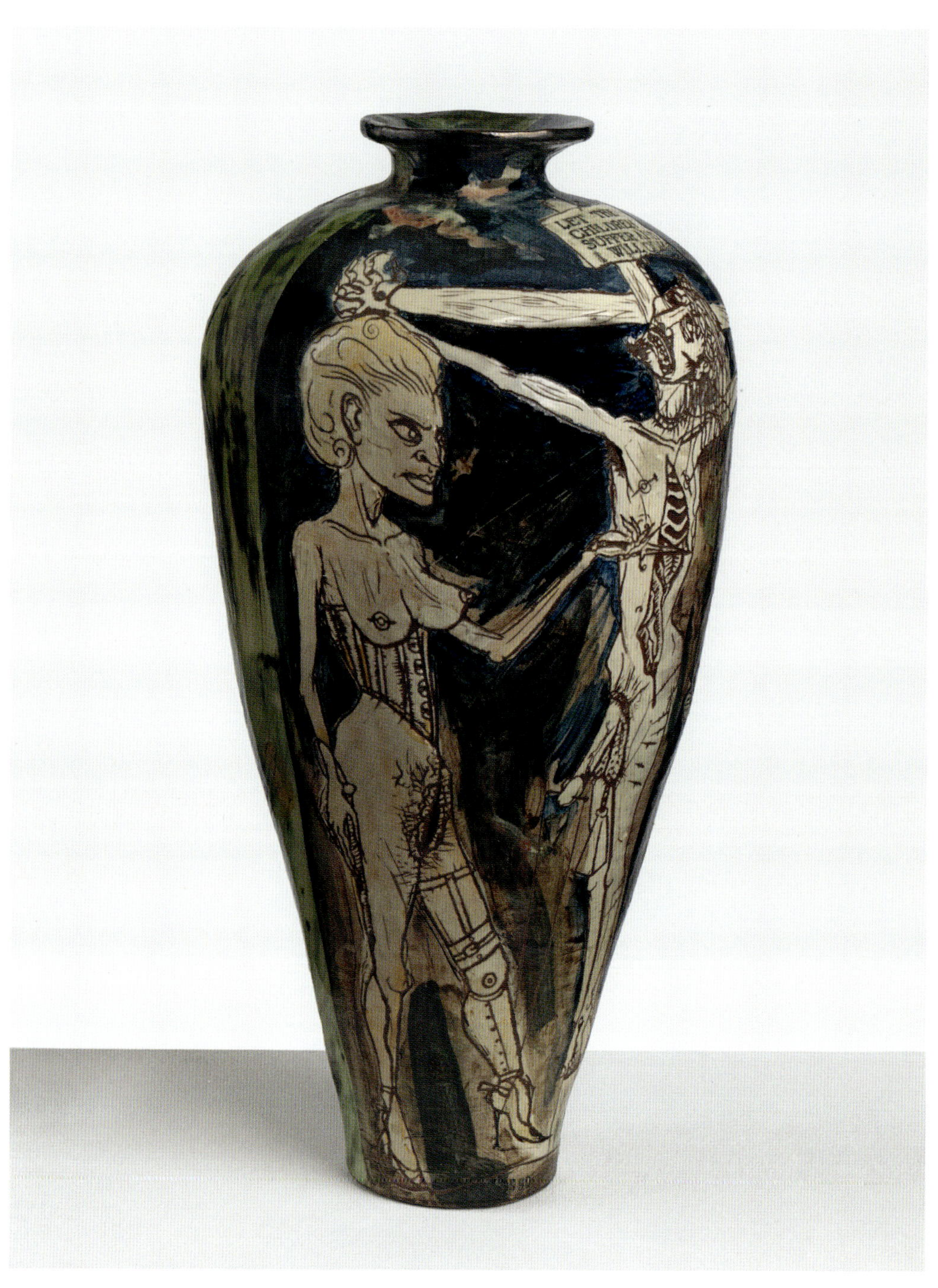

ABOVE: Untitled, 1990
Glazed ceramic, 51 × 23.5 cm

OPPOSITE: *I am Angry like the Wind*, 1990
Glazed ceramic, 43 × 27 cm

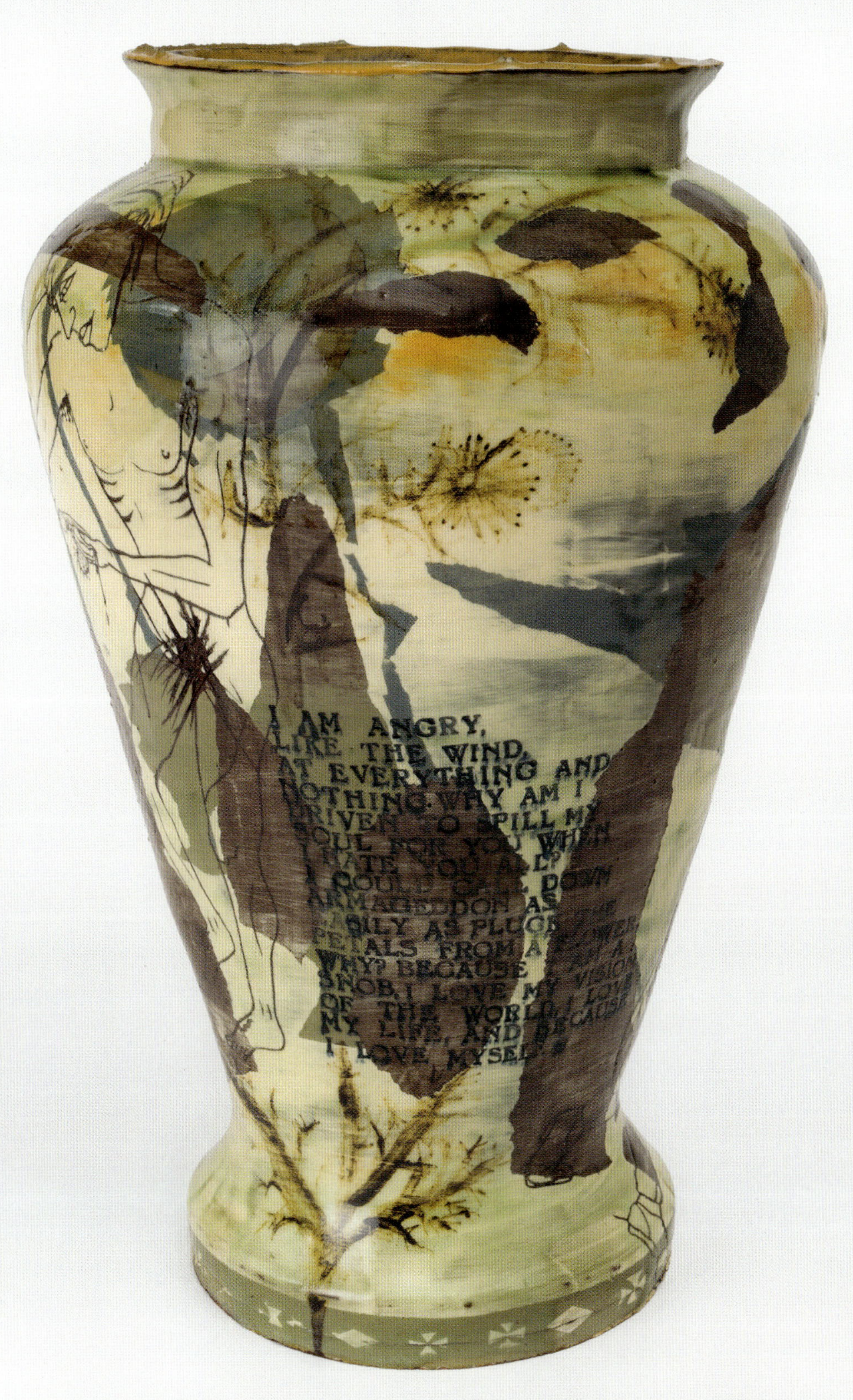
I AM ANGRY,
LIKE THE WIND,
AT EVERYTHING AND
NOTHING. WHY AM I
DRIVEN TO SPILL MY
SOUL FOR YOU WHEN
I HATE YOU ALL?
I COULD CALL DOWN
ARMAGEDDON AS
EASILY AS PLUCK
PETALS FROM A FLOWER.
WHY? BECAUSE I AM A
SNOB. I LOVE MY VISION
OF THE WORLD. I LOVE
MY LIFE, AND BECAUSE
I LOVE MYSELF.

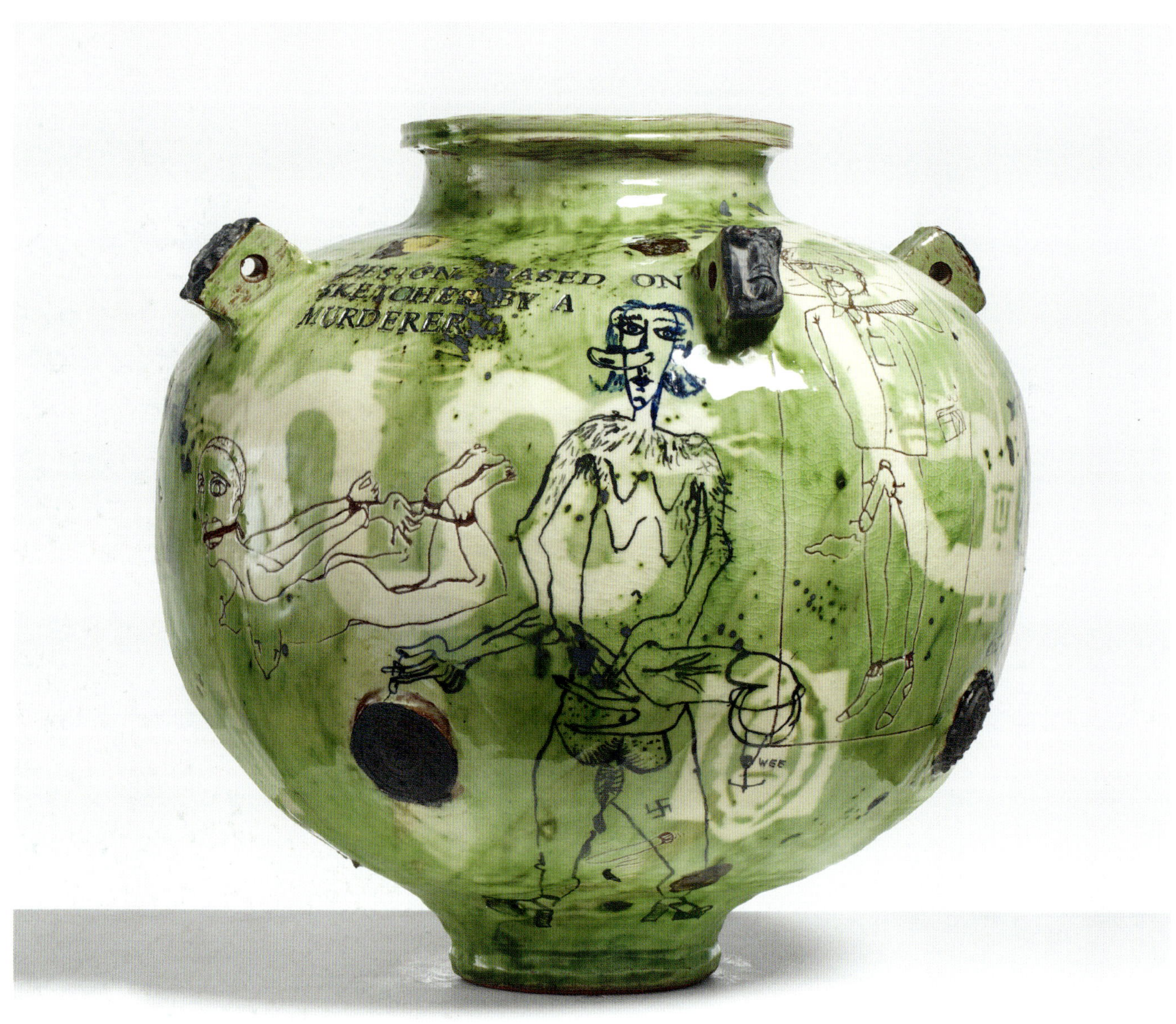

Design Based on Sketches by a Murderer, 1990
Glazed ceramic, 35 × 34 cm

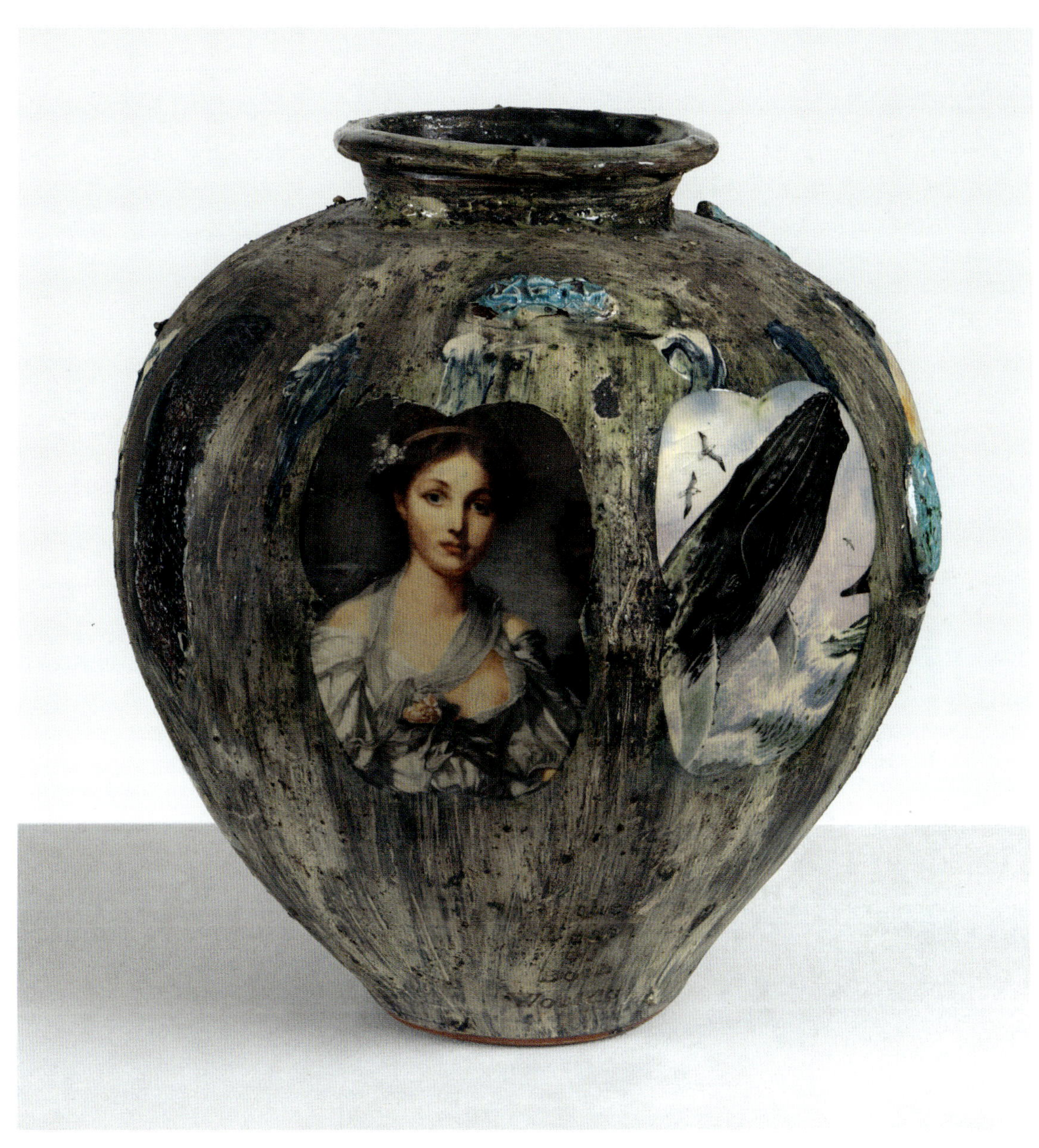

Untitled, 1990
Glazed ceramic, 32.5 × 31 cm

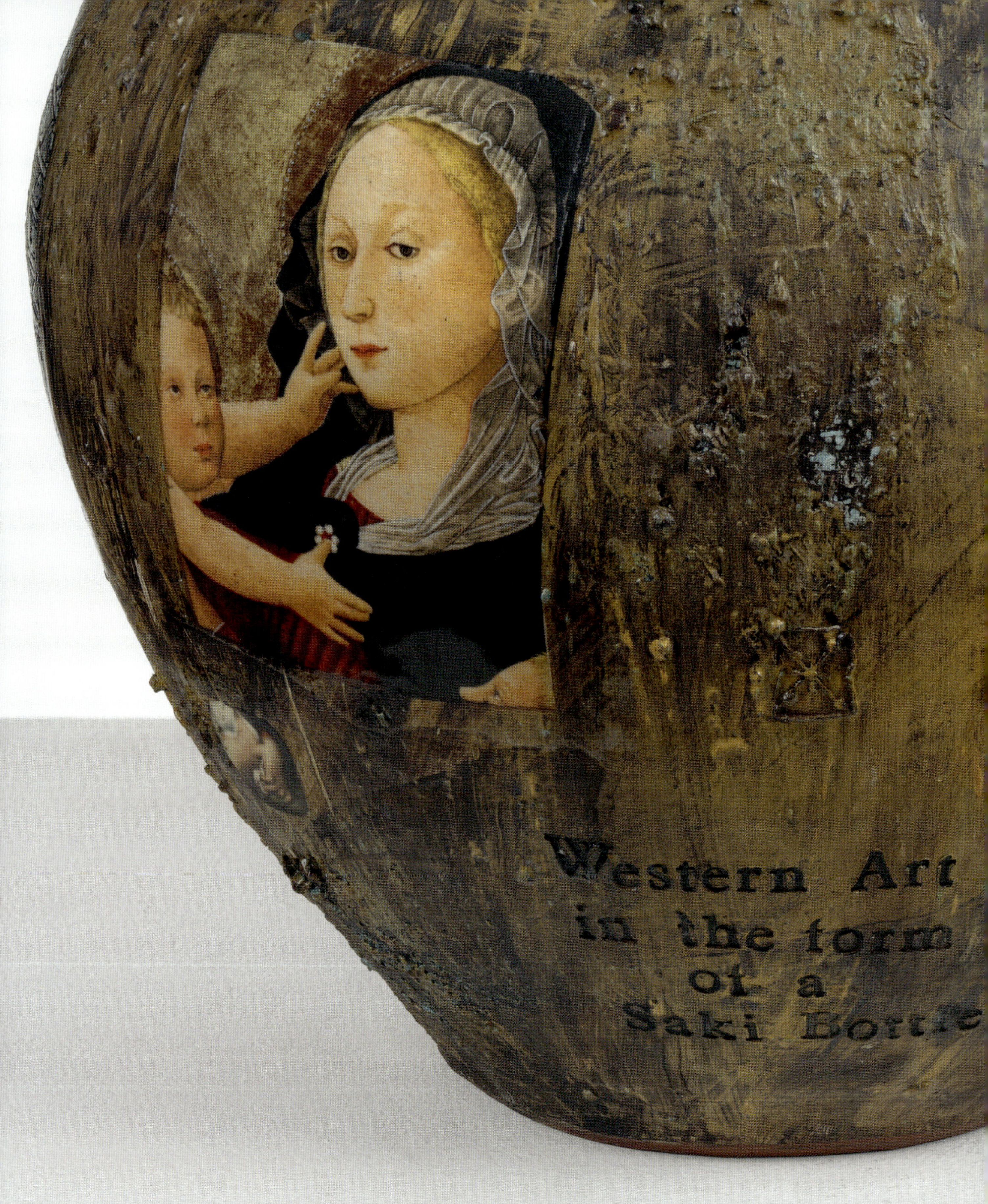
Western Art
in the form
of a
Saki Bottle

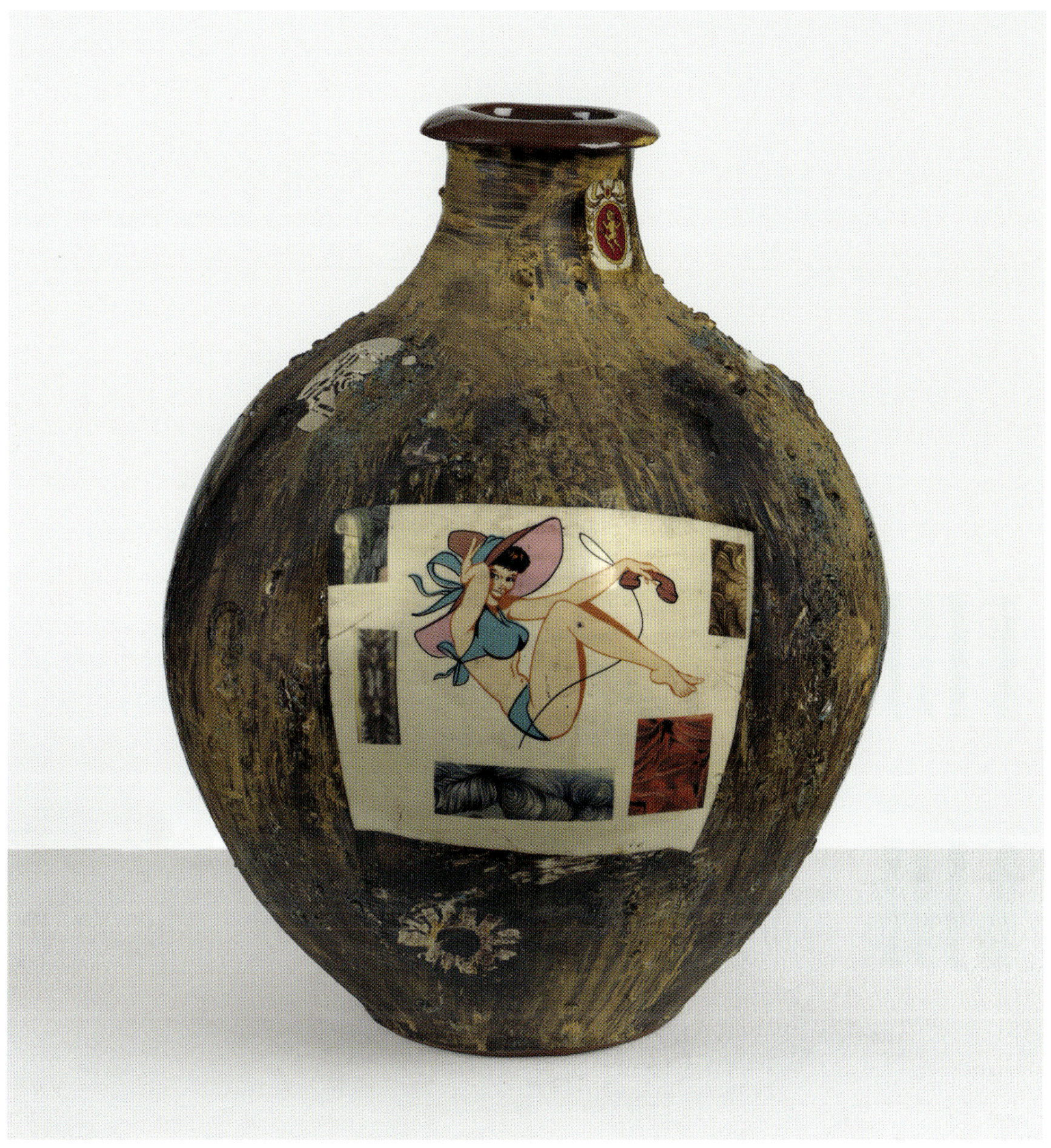

Western Art in the Form of a Saki Bottle, 1992
Glazed ceramic, 34 × 29 cm

This vase pushed forward my relationship with pottery a bit. I was starting to get a handle on where I felt I stood within the long history of ceramics, and what place I felt there was for irony within this tradition.

I was looking at a lot of Japanese teaware and Edo period ceramics. In Japan, there is a great reverence for the peasant aesthetic. The organic aspects of craft pottery, the dribbles, cracks and crumbles, have become central to the Japanese rustic tradition. They loved it when the ash that flew around the wood-fired kiln would chance to land in the glaze, forming little lumps and discolourations. I copied a little saki bottle out of a book and tried to imitate its ash texture.

To make it more obvious that my surface was fake, I cut holes in it, like a curtain through which you could see various images, including a scene of a child in a kitchen pleading with its mother. I was playing with the idea of the authenticity of the rusticated surface in the ceramics. Both my drawings and the supposedly 'natural' surface of my vase are contrived: the only 'authentic' thing here is the feelings behind my drawings. The kitsch images I included were another way of abusing this revered tradition.

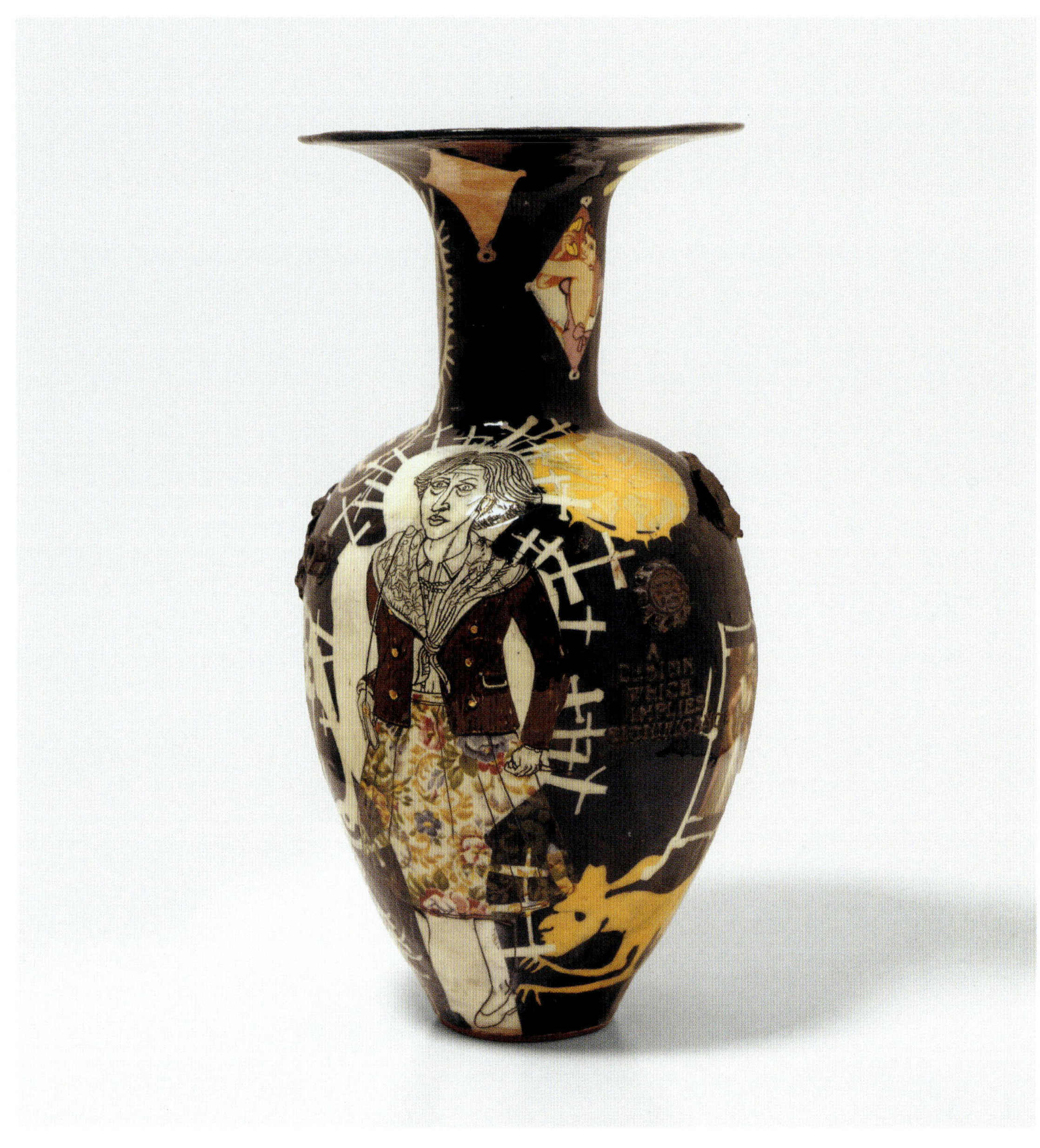

A Design which Implies Significance, 1992
Glazed ceramic, 39 × 16 cm

This vase has a surreal, rather incoherent jumble of images on it: a Hogarthian print of street-sellers; Claire in her Sloane Ranger clothes wielding a dagger; the christening photo of Prince Harry with the Queen and Princess Diana; and an upside-down floating transvestite who's been castrated. The form is vaguely oriental. The papercut shapes of strange figures are almost Picassoesque, including one with a penis for a brain. There's a strange animal creature with a human face, a sort of pig devil. The title was me suggesting that it all had some greater meaning. I used to have a conflicted attitude to craftsmanship and decoration. Nowadays, I'm much more unapologetic about it but then I still felt I had to cover my back, to be sure I was seen as a conceptual artist and not as a craftsman.

Even early on, though, I did have self-imposed standards. I couldn't ever have pots that were cracked to the extent that it threatened their integrity. A little crack in the edge of a pot doesn't bother me too much but a great big one running through the middle does. The first thing you do when you open the kiln is to hit a pot. If it makes a bright, ringing sound, that's great – but if it responds with a dull thud, you worry, because it means it's got a severe crack in it. That's a heart-rending moment, but thankfully it doesn't happen too often these days.

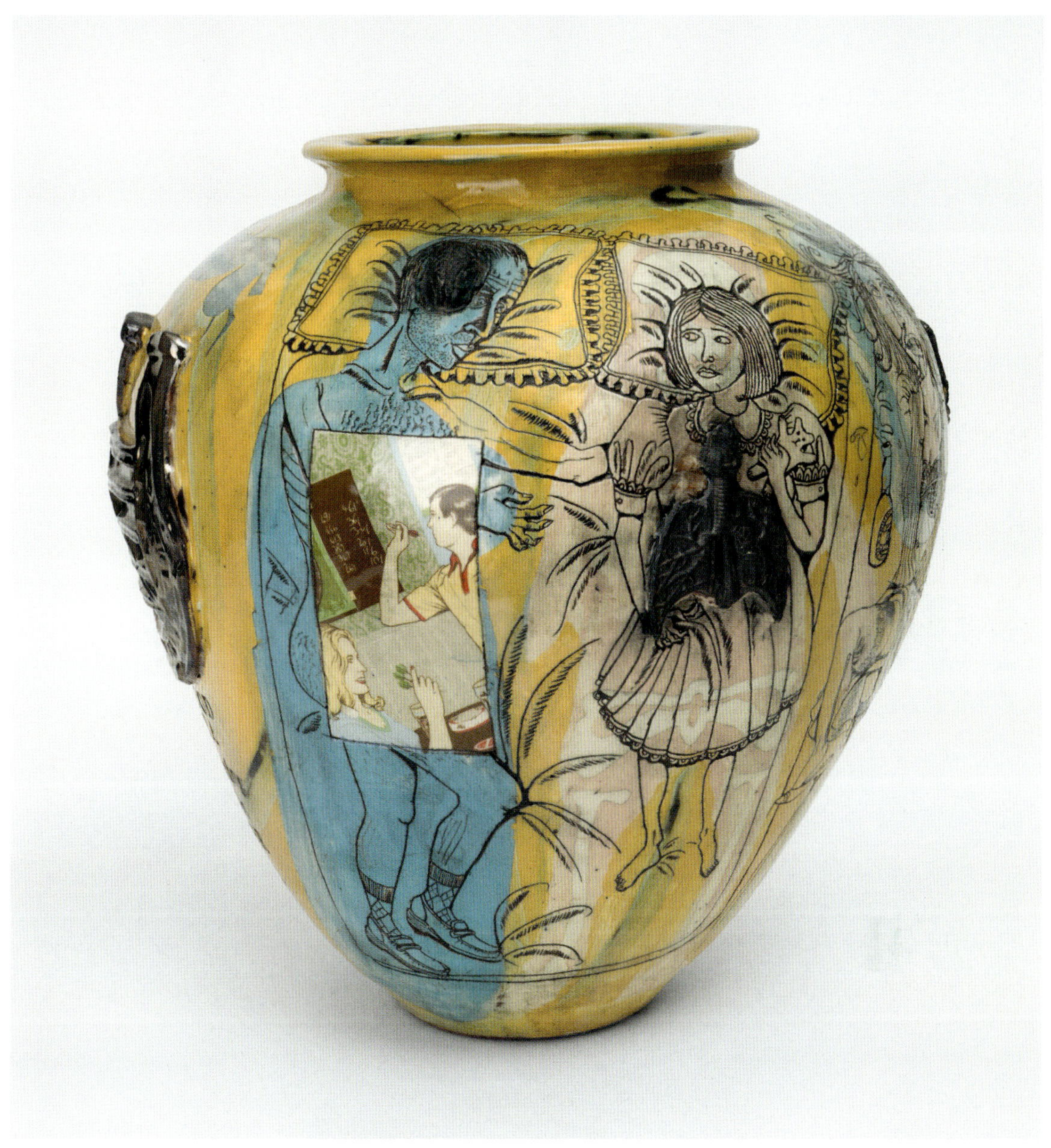

Childhood Trauma Manifesting Itself in Later Life, 1992
Glazed ceramic, 34 × 33 cm

My daughter, Flo, was born about the time I made this vase so
I was thinking a lot about being a parent. I had a lot of fear about
passing the psychological legacy of my own upbringing on to
her. This is still six years before I started having psychotherapy
but there were many discussions with my wife about not acting
out any childhood demons around our newborn. As parents we
often find our children trigger emotional memories of our own
experience of being the same age.

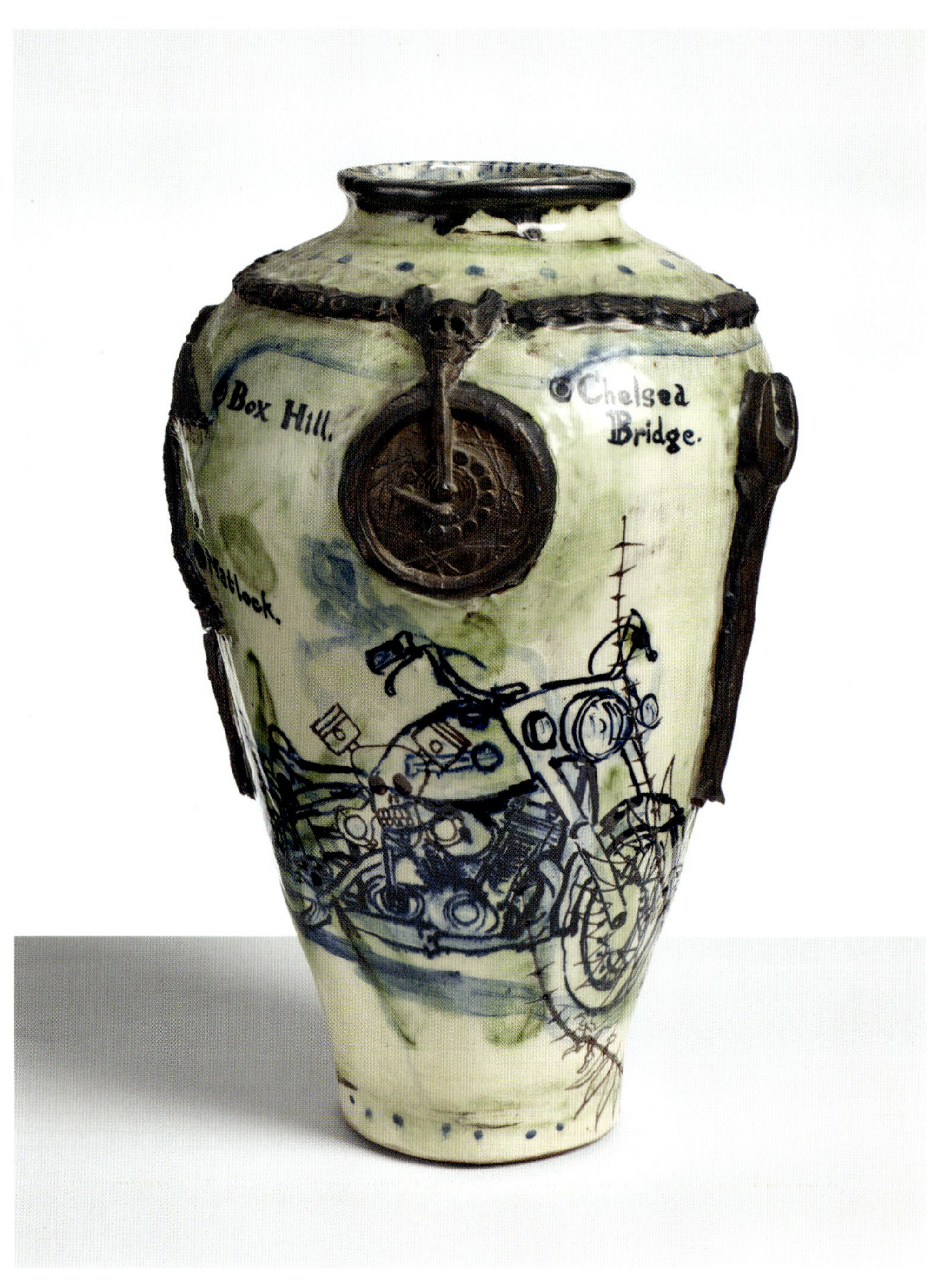

Biker Pot, 1992
Glazed ceramic, 33 × 21 cm

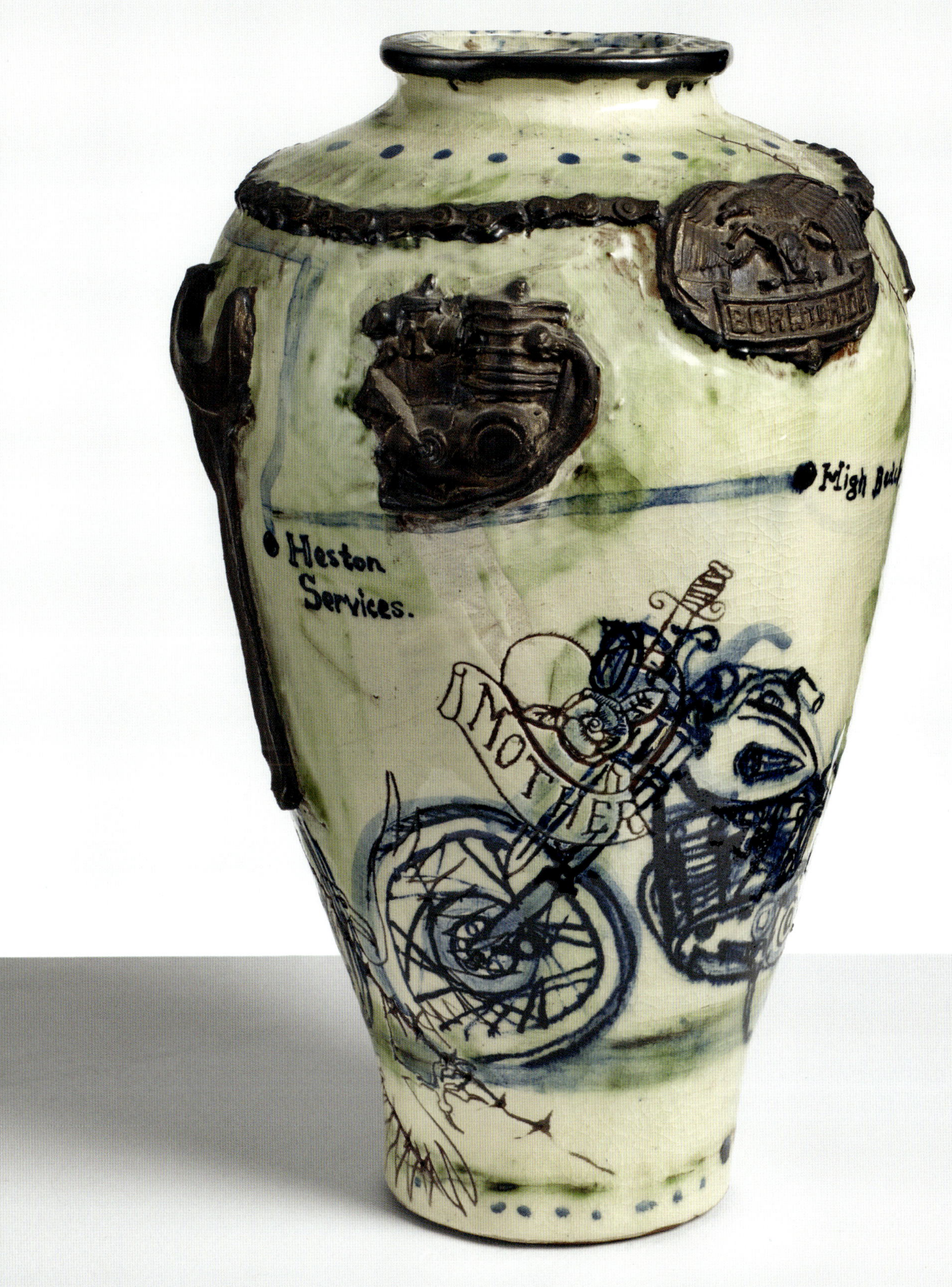

BORN TO RIDE
High Bedu
Heston Services.
MOTHER

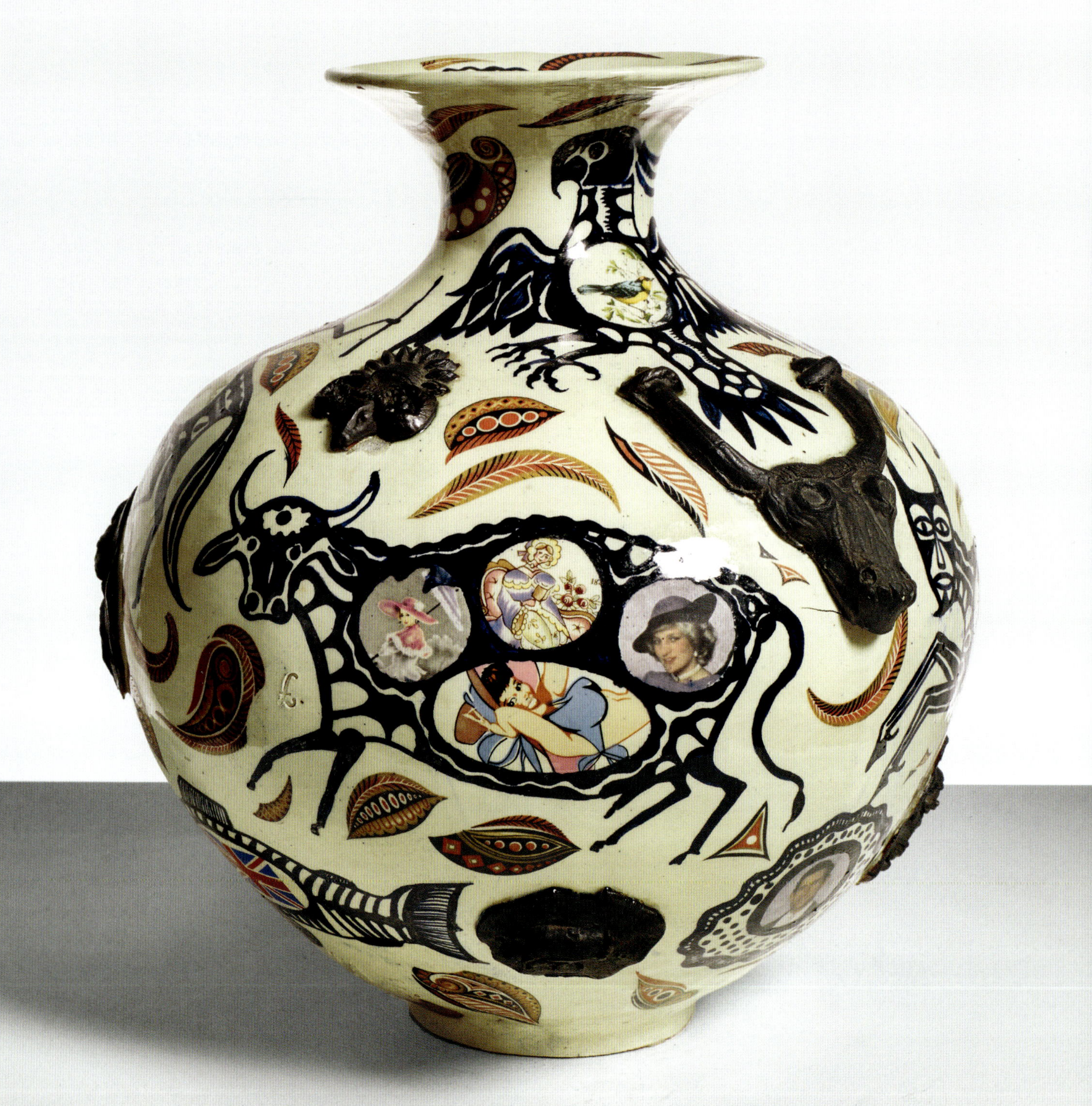

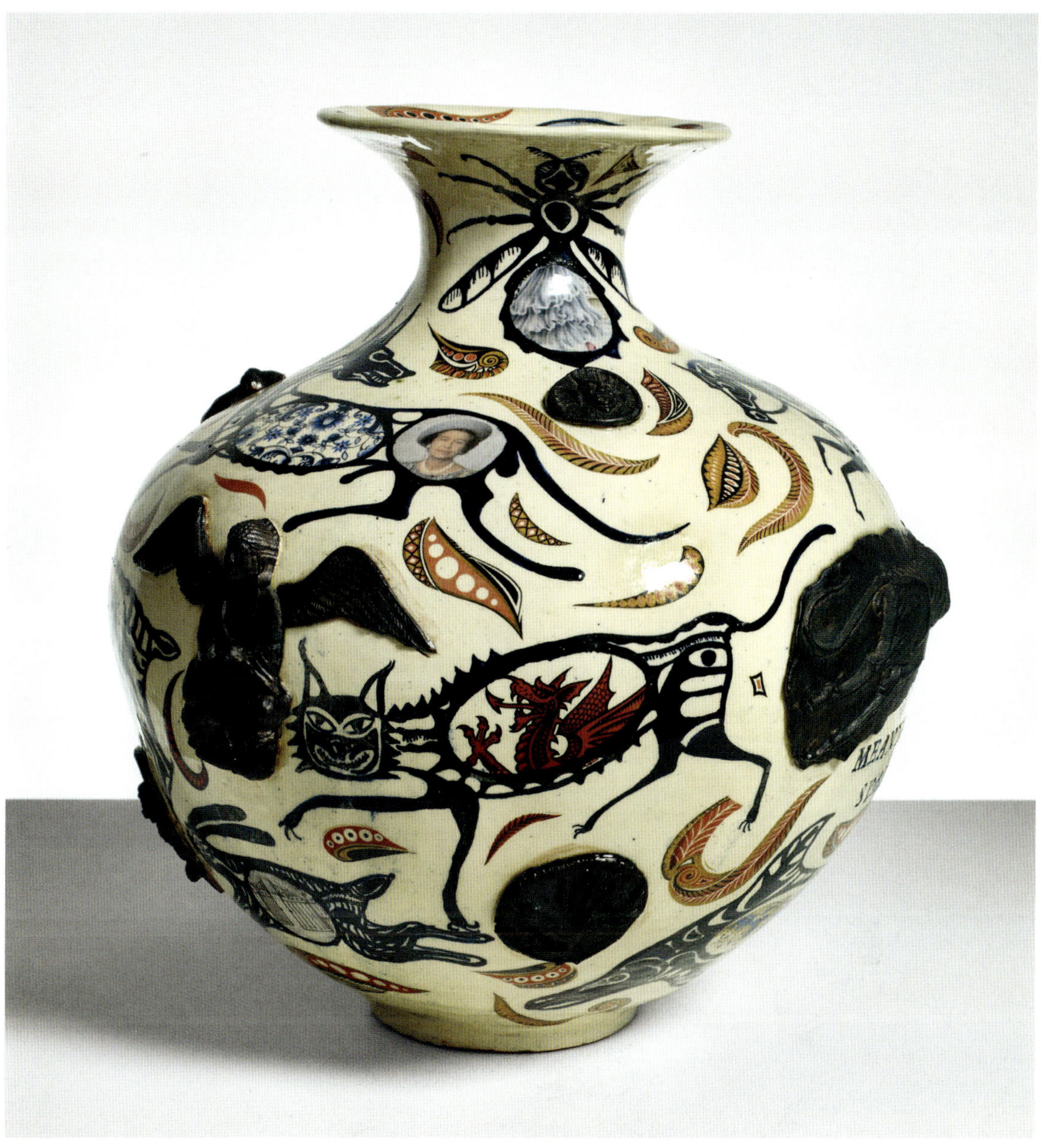

Meaningless Symbols, 1993
Glazed ceramic, 36 × 35 cm

There is a tension in making a piece of contemporary ceramics in a medium that has such a strong history of decorativeness. I can joke with Chris Ofili about how much we love making decorative art, and we can agree that it's a noble and profound thing to do. But if you had asked me about the term 'decorative' when I made this pot, I would have found it a loaded word and seen it as derogatory. My title was defensive: I was getting in there first with the idea that everything is meaningless, and that it's all just a melange of style and no substance. What I'm coming to realize as I age is that profundity comes about by letting go, by not worrying about being meaningful.

This pot would have been white, with just the sprig moulds attached, before it was fired. I then painted the animals in cobalt oxide with the spaces for the transfers left blank. It was not a typical combination of techniques for me at the time.

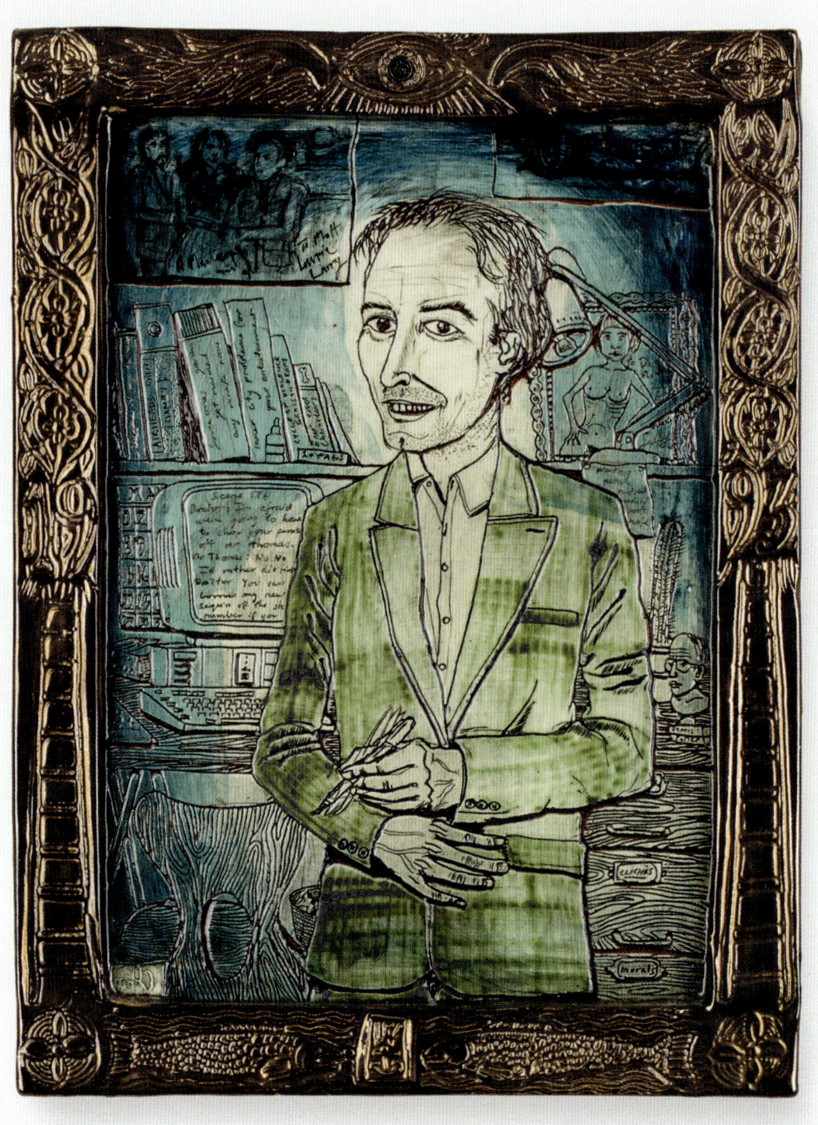

ABOVE: *Portrait of Matthew Bardsley*, 1993
Glazed ceramic, 36 × 26 cm

OPPOSITE: *Phallic Woman*, 1993
Glazed ceramic, 52 × 21 cm

154

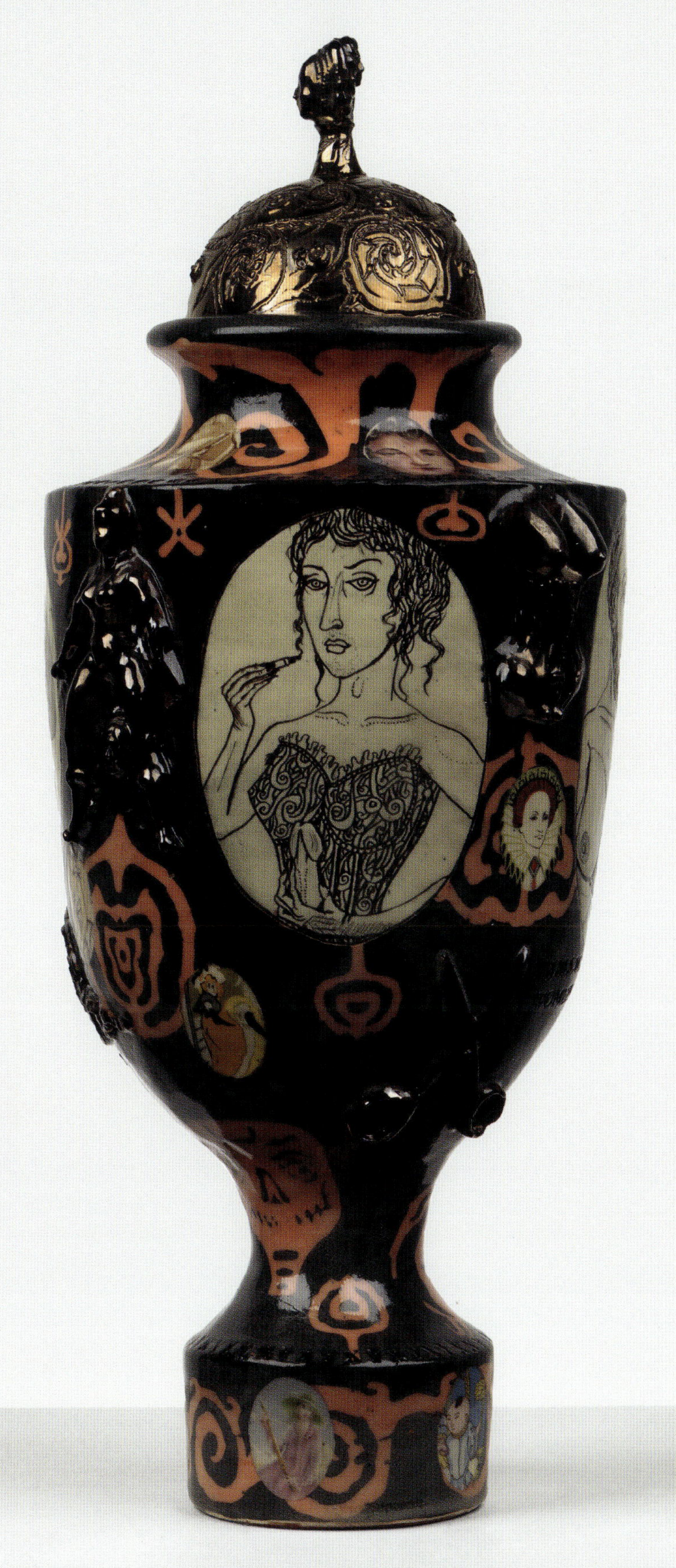

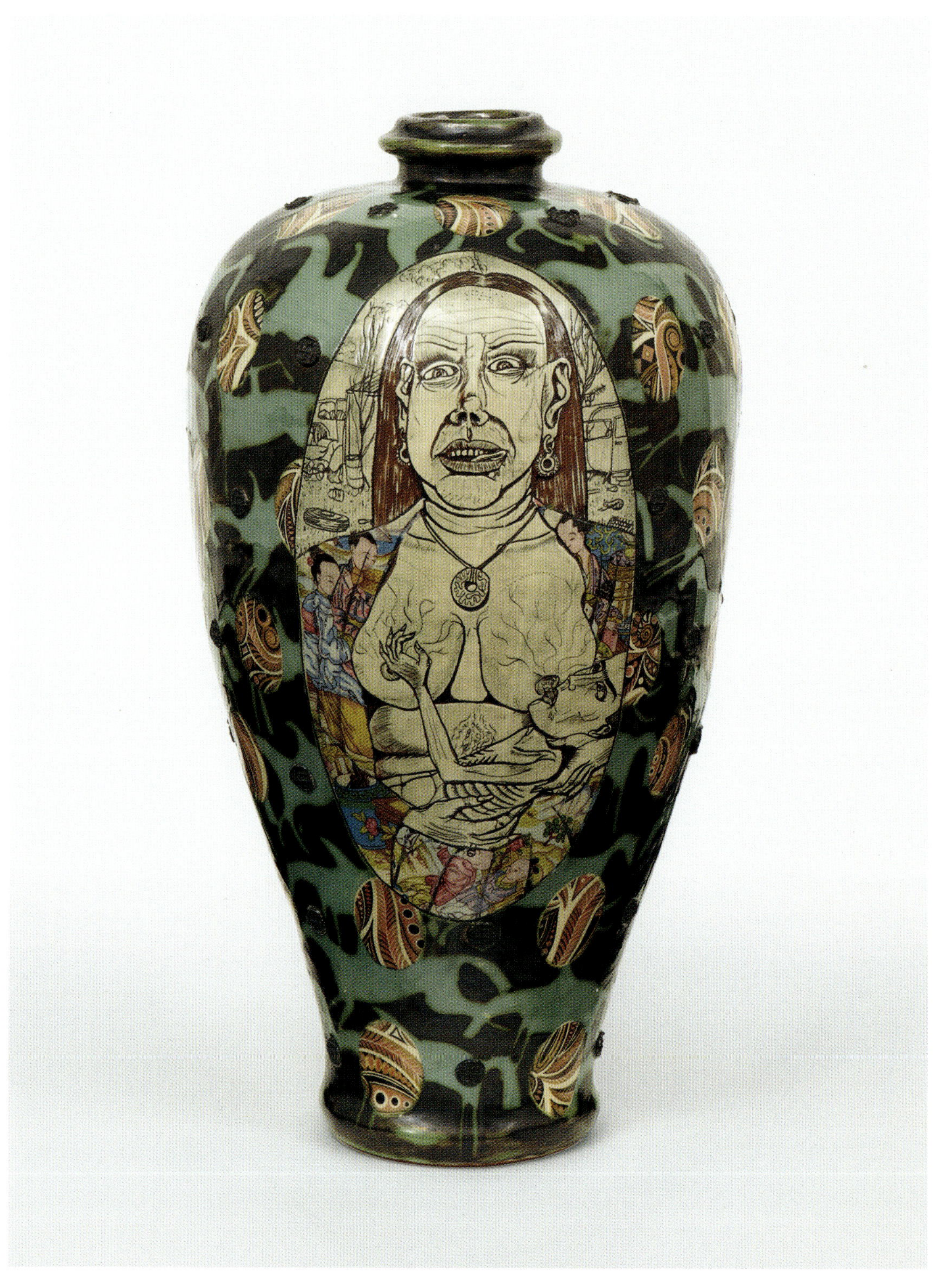

Spirit Jar, 1994
Glazed ceramic, 45.7 × 20.3 cm

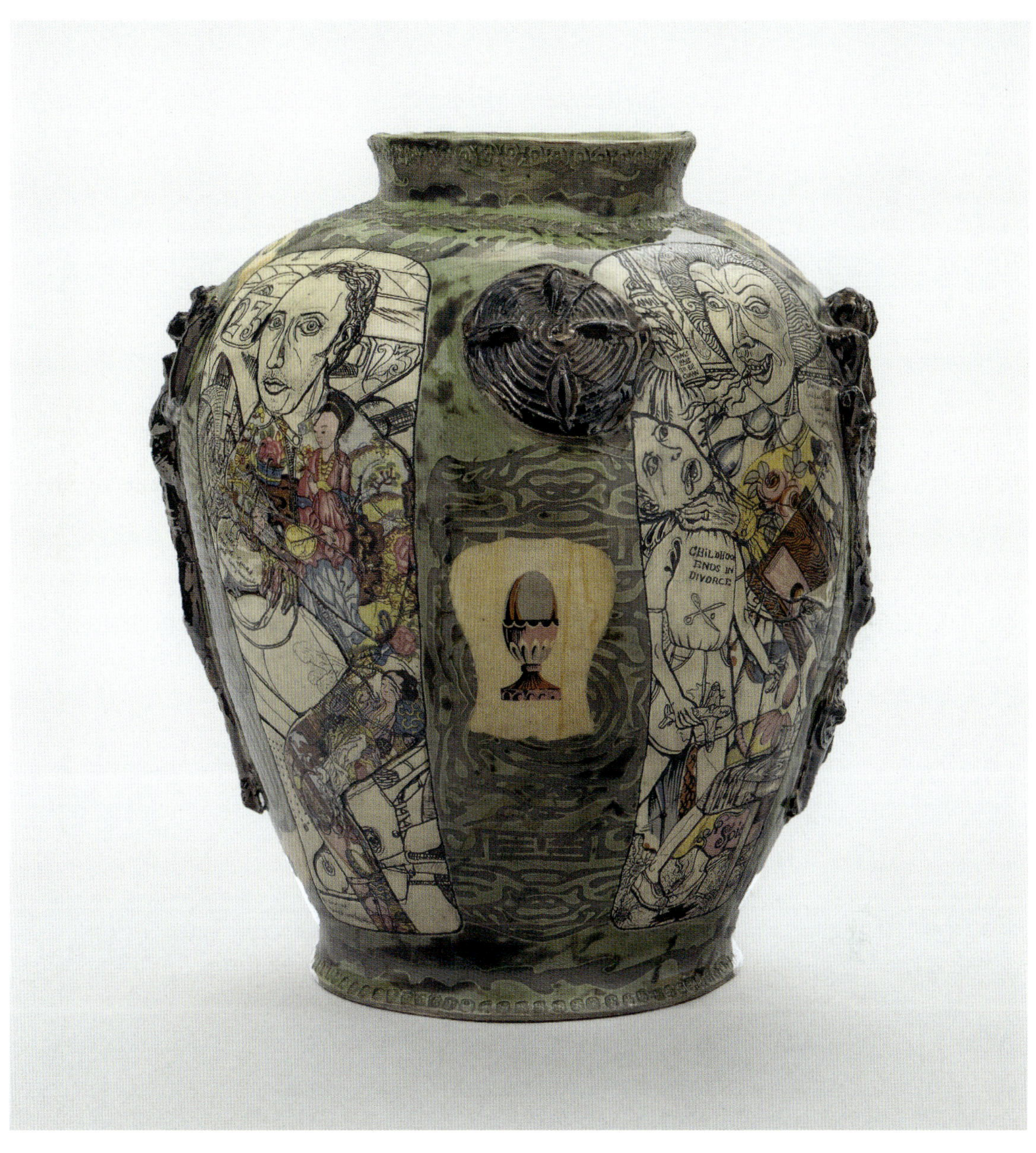

My Gods, 1994
Glazed ceramic, 40 × 34.5 cm

When you're a child, your gods are whoever you're told they
should be. I was looking back to my past and inventing my own
gods. I've included a rather wrathful female god and a guy
in decorative chinoiserie leathers. An innocent child worships
gods that have aspects of its parents in them: there's a sort of
projection of parent onto god. Some people have a very screwed
up idea of god: if you have a vengeful parent you probably have
a vengeful god. The corkscrew on the pot is a fairly innocuous
object, but in this context we can project onto it the image of
a crucifix and also the hint at parental alcoholism.

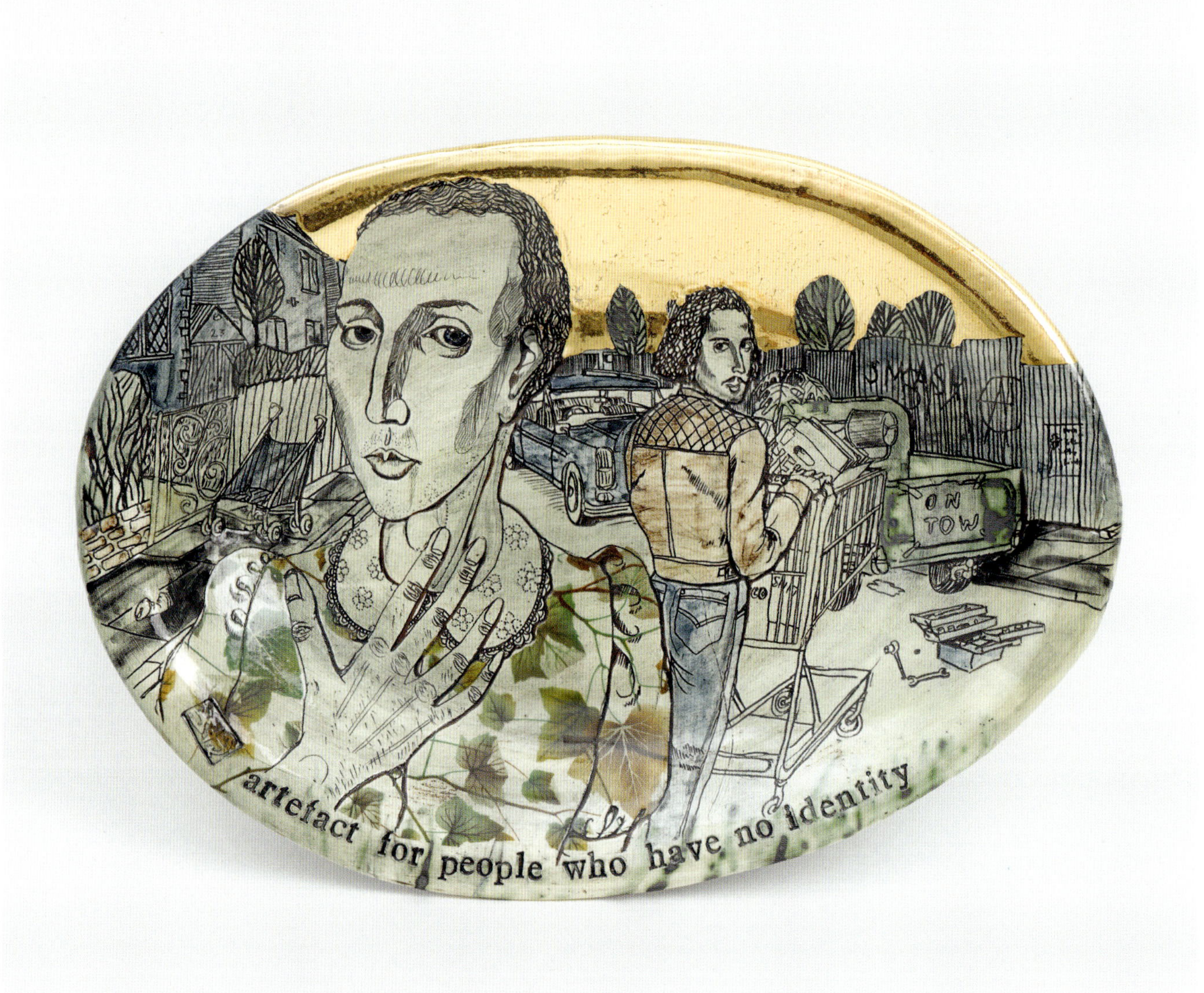

Artefact for People who have no Identity, 1994
Glazed ceramic, 26.8 × 37 cm

Judging by the style, content and techniques used on this
piece I think it was made a lot later than most of my oval
press-moulded plates, probably in the early 1990s. The street
scene in the background is reminiscent of Dyers Hall Road,
Leytonstone, where my studio was in 1987–93. A man out
wearing a girlish frock has caught the eye of another man who
is using a shopping trolley to move house. Every detail of this
artwork – the corrugated iron fence, the graffiti, the toolbox
and the baby buggy – screams at me today what my life felt like
then. The title, though, could have been coined in 2019.

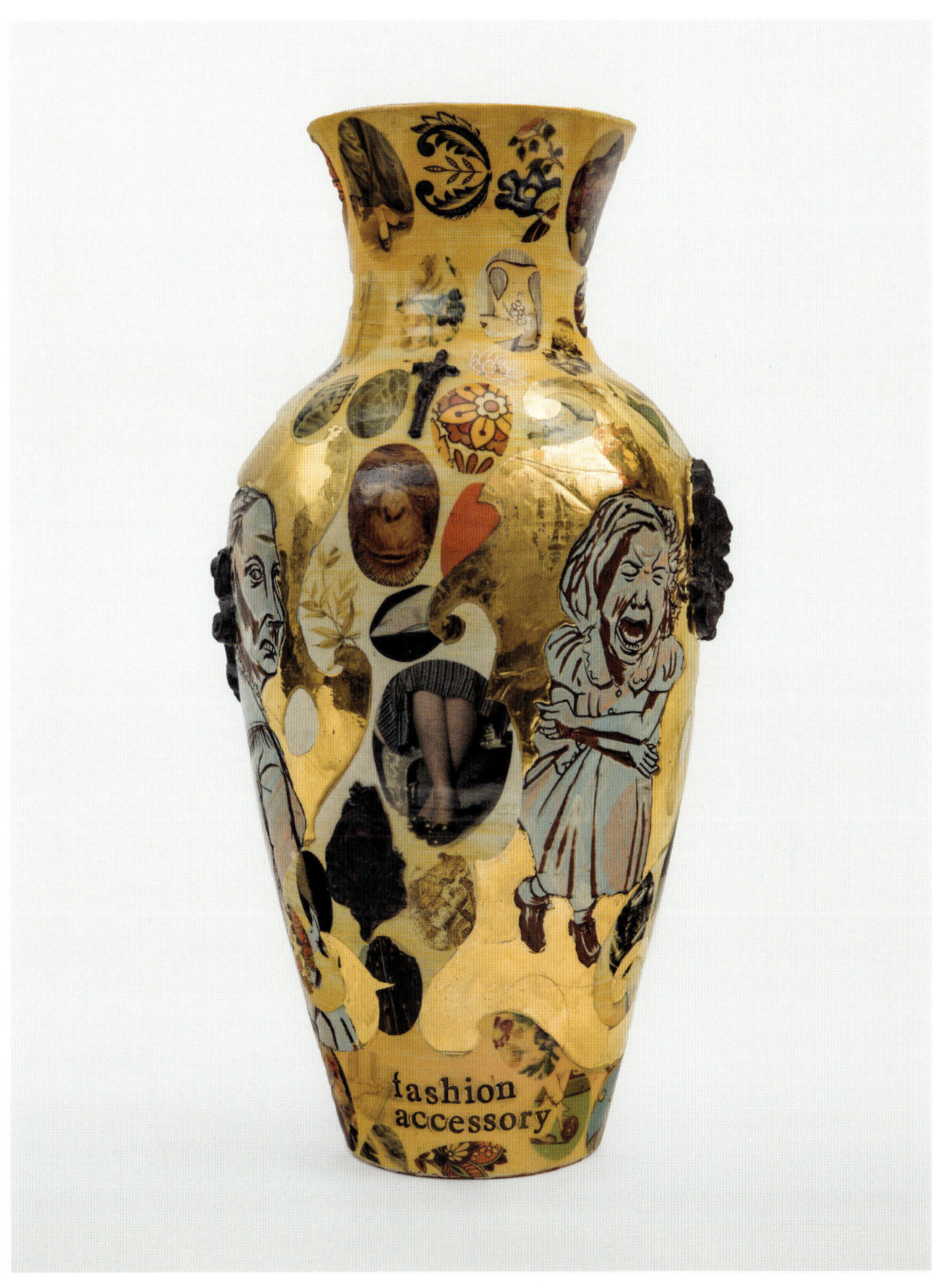

Fashion Accessory, 1994
Glazed ceramic, 36 × 54 cm

GRAYSON PERRY'S BIOGRAPHY	ART AND CULTURAL EVENTS	WORLD EVENTS
1960 · Grayson Perry born 24 March in Chelmsford, Essex		
		1961 · English model April Ashley outed as transsexual by the *Sunday People* newspaper
	1962 · Andy Warhol exhibits *Campbell's Soup Cans* at Ferus Gallery, Los Angeles	1962 · Tensions rise between the USA and the Soviet Union during the Cuban Missile Crisis Nelson Mandela is arrested and imprisoned for leaving South Africa without a passport and inciting workers' strikes
1963 · Aged 3, he contracts measles. During his illness he bonds with a teddy bear, naming him Alan Measles. The bear's first name came from his next-door neighbour		1963 · Martin Luther King, Jr. delivers 'I Have a Dream' speech during the March on Washington for Jobs and Freedom US President John F. Kennedy is assassinated in Dallas, Texas
1964–65 · His father leaves the family home after his mother has an affair with the milkman		
1965–75 · Much of his childhood is spent in fear of his bullying stepfather and with little contact from his natural father. As a coping mechanism, he retreats into an imaginary world with Alan Measles	1966 · *The Almost Complete Works of Marcel Duchamp* is shown at Tate Gallery	1966 · Mao Zedong launches China's Cultural Revolution, leading to the persecution of millions over the following decade
	1967 · David Hockney paints *A Bigger Splash* The hippie movement spreads across Europe and America during the 'Summer of Love' The Beatles release *Sgt. Pepper's Lonely Hearts Club Band*	1967 · The UK legalizes homosexuality and abortions The Six Day War: conflict between Israel and its neighbours: Egypt, Syria and Jordan
		1968 · Martin Luther King, Jr. is assassinated in Memphis, Tennessee

1979 · Leaves home to enrol on a BA Fine Art course at Portsmouth Polytechnic. Visiting lecturers include Edward Allington and Larry Knee, a sculptor who works with objects found in Victorian landfills

1980 · Exhibits in *The New Contemporaries* at the Institute of Contemporary Arts, London

1980–81 · In his second year at Portsmouth he creates *Transvestite Jet Pilots*, a mixed-media installation akin to an altarpiece

1982 · Graduates from Portsmouth Polytechnic

Participates in a five-day performance with the Neo Naturists at the B2 Gallery, Wapping

1979 · *Outsiders: An Art Without Precedent or Tradition* shown at the Hayward Gallery, London

Judy Chicago, *The Dinner Party* is displayed at the San Francisco Museum of Modern Art

1980 · Neo-Expressionism: the beginning of the decade sees the revival of figurative, expressionist painting in response to the minimalist and conceptual art of the 1970s

1981 · *A New Spirit in Painting* is shown at the Royal Academy, London

As punk becomes increasingly mainstream, Vivienne Westwood and Malcolm McLaren turn to glam rock and historical fashions in their Autumn/Winter collection, *Pirate*. This 'New Romantic' look is popularized by David Bowie, Boy George and Adam Ant

The exhibition *Objects and Sculpture* is held at the Institute of Contemporary Arts, London, and the Arnolfini, Bristol

1979 · Margaret Thatcher comes to power as Britain's first female prime minister

1980 · The Iraqi army invade Iran, triggering the Iran-Iraq War

John Lennon is murdered in New York

1981 · First reports published on what becomes the AIDS epidemic

Riots take place across Britain amid racial tension, high unemployment and deprivation

Prince Charles marries Lady Diana Spencer in a ceremony watched by 700 million television viewers

Greenham Common Women's Peace Camp begins protest against nuclear weapons outside RAF Greenham Common

1982 · Unemployment in Britain reaches three million

The Falklands War: conflict between Britain and Argentina

GRAYSON PERRY'S BIOGRAPHY	ART AND CULTURAL EVENTS	WORLD EVENTS
1983 · After graduating, he moves to a squat in Camden, London, shared with Cerith Wyn Evans and Angus Cook. During this period he makes works out of what is available, demonstrating the influence of his former tutor Larry Knee. He also works on film and performance pieces connected to the Neo Naturist group founded by his then-girlfriend Jennifer Binnie, her sister Christine, and Wilma Johnson Inspired by Christine Binnie, he takes pottery lessons at the Central Institute, where he makes his first plate, *Kinky Sex* Exhibits at Ian Birksted Gallery, London	1983 · Culture Club's *Karma Chameleon* remains number one on the charts for six weeks, making it the highest selling record of the year The counter-cultural Neo Naturist group puts on body-art performances in public spaces, gallery openings and clubs across London	1983 · US President Ronald Reagan announces his 'Star Wars' defence plan to protect the USA against a potential Soviet nuclear attack With renewed popularity after victory in the Falklands War, Margaret Thatcher wins her second general election
1984 · Begins to gain recognition for his work in ceramics. His first solo exhibition, showing pieces made in his evening classes, is held at James Birch Fine Art on Waterford Road in Fulham, London	1984 · The first Turner Prize exhibition displays works by Gilbert & George, Richard Long, Howard Hodgkin, Richard Deacon, and Malcolm Morley who wins the award Ted Hughes becomes Poet Laureate Band Aid's *Do They Know It's Christmas?* becomes the biggest selling record of the decade	1984 · Scientists discover the cause of AIDS: a retrovirus called HTLV-III Pit closures across Britain lead to a national miners' strike. The Battle of Orgreave, a violent clash between police and protesters, takes place in June An IRA bomb explodes at the Conservative Party conference in Brighton, killing five people Indira Gandhi, the prime minister of India, is assassinated by her Sikh bodyguards, leading to four days of riots and the mass murder of more than 3,000 Sikhs
1985 · Exhibits in *Gallozi e La Placa* in New York and *Artists in Essex* at Epping Forest District Museum and The Minories, Colchester A second solo exhibition is held at James Birch Fine Art, London	1985 · The Saatchi Gallery opens in London *The Pont Neuf Wrapped*: Christo and Jeanne-Claude wrap the oldest bridge in Paris	1985 · Mikhail Gorbachev becomes General Secretary of the Communist Party of the Soviet Union and introduces reform process of *glasnost* and *perestroika* Battle of the Beanfield: police clash with New Age travellers attempting to set up the Stonehenge Free Festival

GRAYSON PERRY'S BIOGRAPHY	ART AND CULTURAL EVENTS	WORLD EVENTS
		1985 · 1.5 billion television viewers in 160 countries watch *Live Aid* Microsoft launches Windows
1986 · Moves out of the Camden squat Attends evening classes in creative writing, where he meets his future wife, Philippa Fairclough Exhibits in *Mandelzoom: Controllo e destino nei modelli della giovane arte internazionale*, in venues around Viterbo, near Rome	1986 · Gilbert & George win the Turner Prize James Birch Fine Art closes	1986 · The Chernobyl disaster: accident at nuclear power station in the Soviet Union (modern Ukraine) releases radioactive materials across the USSR and Europe 'Big Bang': the stock market in London is deregulated, boosting the city's position as a financial capital
1987 · Buys his own kiln 1987–90 · Over a four-year period, has three solo exhibitions at Birch & Conran Fine Art	1987 · For the first time, Turner Prize nominations include two female artists: Helen Chadwick and Thérèse Oulton Vincent van Gogh's *Irises* (1889) sells for £30 million, setting a record price for a painting sold at auction Birch & Conran Fine Art opens in Dean Street, Soho	1987 · Margaret Thatcher wins third general election Black Monday: the US stock market crashes
1988 · Exhibits in *Two from London/Two from Texas* at Read Stremmel Gallery, San Antonio, Texas	1988 · The exhibition *Freeze*, curated by Damien Hirst, is held in a disused warehouse in Surrey Docks, London, launching the careers of Hirst, Michael Landy and Sarah Lucas The Tate Gallery holds a major retrospective of David Hockney's work	1988 · Section 28 of the Local Government Act 1988 prohibits local authorities from 'promoting' homosexuality through teaching and published material Fighting in the Iran-Iraq War ends with a ceasefire A bomb explodes on Pan American Flight 103, which crashes at Lockerbie, Scotland
	1989 · Richard Long wins the Turner Prize	1989 · Student-led protests against the Chinese government lead to shooting of demonstrators in Beijing's Tiananmen Square The Berlin Wall falls Sir Tim Berners-Lee invents the World Wide Web

GRAYSON PERRY'S BIOGRAPHY	ART AND CULTURAL EVENTS	WORLD EVENTS
1990 · Breaks contact with his mother after she tells his future wife, 'you must be desperate to marry a transvestite' Begins to work with David Gill Gallery	1990 · Britain is represented by Anish Kapoor at the Venice Biennale Birch & Conran Fine Art closes	1990 · Nelson Mandela is released after spending twenty-seven years in prison Armed forces led by Iraqi dictator Saddam Hussein invade Kuwait, triggering the start of the Gulf War East Germany and West Germany are reunited Thatcher loses support from her party after public protests against the poll tax. She resigns and is replaced by John Major
1991 · Solo exhibition held at Garth Clark Gallery, New York	1991 · Damien Hirst creates *The Physical Impossibility of Death in the Mind of Someone Living*, a tiger shark preserved in formaldehyde in a vitrine	1991 · The Gulf War comes to an end The Soviet Union is dissolved and the Cold War ends
1992 · Marries Philippa Fairclough. Their daughter, Florence, is born in the same year Solo exhibition held at David Gill Gallery, London	1992 · The Saatchi Gallery exhibits works by the group who come to be known as the Young British Artists (YBAs)	1992 · Conservative Party wins fourth general election in a row
1993–95 · Exhibits in *The Raw and the Cooked: New Work in Clay in Britain* at the Barbican Art Gallery, London, which tours to Oxford and Swansea in the UK, as well as to Japan, Taiwan and France	1993 · White Cube and Tate St Ives open to the public Commissioned by Artangel, Rachel Whiteread creates the sculpture *House*. She becomes the first female artist to win the Turner Prize	1993 · The 18-year-old Stephen Lawrence is murdered in a racist attack in South London
1994 · Begins to work with Anthony d'Offay Gallery, London, with solo exhibition *Grayson Perry: New Work*	1994 · Antony Gormley wins the Turner Prize 1995 · Oasis release *(What's the Story) Morning Glory?* Damien Hirst wins the Turner Prize	1994 · Nelson Mandela is elected president of South Africa

1996 · Second solo exhibition held at Anthony d'Offay Gallery, London

Exhibits in *Objects of Our Time* at the Crafts Council, London, which tours to Edinburgh, Manchester, Belfast, Swansea and New York

1998 · Begins psychotherapy sessions, continuing the treatment for six years

2000 · A 'coming out' party for Claire is held at the Laurent Delaye Gallery on 30 October. This ceremony marks a turning point for Claire who begins to wear the 'little girl' dresses that Perry is known for today

1996 · The world's first cloned mammal, Dolly the sheep, is born

1997 · The Turner Prize has its first all-female short list

YBAs from Charles Saatchi's collection exhibit in *Sensation* at the Royal Academy

1997 · Labour Party wins the general election; Tony Blair becomes prime minister

Diana, Princess of Wales dies in a car crash in Paris

1998 · Chris Ofili paints *No Woman, No Cry* as a tribute to murdered teenager Stephen Lawrence. Ofili wins Turner Prize

Antony Gormley erects *The Angel of the North* in Gateshead

1998 · The Good Friday Agreement is signed, marking a significant step in the peace process in Northern Ireland

Google is founded by Larry Page and Sergey Brin

1999 · Tracey Emin displays *My Bed* at the Turner Prize exhibition

1999 · In the UK, the Sex Discrimination Act of 1975 is amended to cover discrimination in employment and vocational training on the grounds of gender reassignment

THE POST-THERAPY YEARS

Perry came to public attention after winning the Turner Prize in 2003, the first potter to do so, dressing as Claire for the occasion. The same year he began to work with Victoria Miro Gallery, who continue to represent him.

Since then his work has been exhibited widely both in the UK and the rest of the world. From around 2009, Perry also returned to film, making award-winning television documentaries on such topics as identity, masculinity, rituals and British taste, and branched into architecture, designing the House for Essex in 2015. His reputation continues to grow and he has become one of Britain's best-loved artists.

Perry was elected a Royal Academician in Printmaking in 2011 and awarded a CBE in 2013. In 2015, he was appointed Trustee of the British Museum and Chancellor of the University of the Arts London. He received the 2016 RIBA Honorary Fellowship from the Royal Institute of British Architects. He lives and works in London.

TOWARDS A PRE-HISTORY OF GRAYSON PERRY

1. Grayson Perry in conversation with the author, 25 October 2001.

2. Grayson Perry and Jonathan Sidney, 'Unsophisticated Sophistication – The Paradox of Grayson Perry', *Ceramic Review*, 112 (July/August 1988), p. 24.

3. Grayson Perry in conversation with the author, 25 October 2001.

4. Grayson Perry statement in 'Wet 'n' Wild 'n' Wet', *i-D*, 13 (March 1983), p. 39.

5. Grayson Perry in conversation with the author, 25 October 2001.

6. Ibid.

7. Conversation with Louisa Buck cited in Louisa Buck, 'The Personal Political Pots of Grayson Perry', *Grayson Perry: Guerilla Tactics*, exh. cat. (Amsterdam: Stedelijk Museum, 2002), p. 98.

8. Wendy Jones, *Grayson Perry: Portrait of the Artist as a Young Girl* (London: Chatto & Windus, 2006), p. 154.

9. Chadwick cited in Waldemar Januszczak, 'Invading your space', *Guardian*, 18 November 1987, www.theguardian.com/artanddesign/1987/nov/18/20yearsoftheturnerprize.turnerprize accessed 4 April 2019. The sculpture is now sited in the Mark Hix restaurant in Shoreditch, it had previously been installed in the offices of the independent record company Some Bizarre; the work was originally performed by Silvia Ziranek and Brook Hoadley at the Acme Gallery, London, and by Chadwick herself and Philip Stanley at the Spectro Gallery, Newcastle upon Tyne, and the Ikon Gallery, Birmingham.

10. In 1981, Perry had gone to the Institute of Contemporary Arts in London to see the *Objects and Sculpture* exhibition that is often identified as announcing to a general public the shift in sculpture and included a number of the visiting lecturers to Portsmouth including Anish Kapoor and Edward Allington.

11. Conversation with the author, 1 February 2019.

12. Jones (2006), pp. 136 and 137. In the book Christine is named as 'Fiona', references that have been changed here.

13. For more on the scene at Carburton Street and Christine Binnie's position within it, see Boy George (with Spencer Bright), *Take It Like A Man: The Autobiography of Boy George* (London: Sidgwick & Jackson, 1995), pp. 145–62.

14. The Coffee Spoon was the hub for squats nearby and had been named by Christine Binnie after T. S. Eliot and the line from *The Love Song of J. Alfred Prufrock*: 'I have measured out my life with coffee spoons', though with no running water coffee was harder to get than cider. It became a venue for film screenings, performances, poetry readings and just generally hanging out.

15. Jones (2006), pp. 142–43, see also pp. 140–41.

16. Steve Strange, *Blitzed!* (London: Orion, 2002), pp. 43–44 and 62.

17. Christine Binnie in conversation with the author, 1 November 2001.

18. Cooking with Calor gas, along with the use of body paint, were the staple ingredients of Neo Naturist performance. One example of this was the performance constructed for the launch of Derek Jarman's book *Dancing Ledge* at the Diorama, London, 28 February 1984. Elisabeth Welch sang 'through a blizzard of pink petals that fluttered from the ceiling on to the assembled throng' (Tony Peake, *Derek Jarman*, London: Little, Brown, 1999, p. 321), while James Birch remembers the accompanying Neo Naturist performance for which they 'inflated a child's rubber paddling pool, poured water into it, pissed into it and then sat frying fish fingers around the side of it before throwing the book into the middle of it.' James Birch in conversation with the author, 13 November 2001.

19. David Dawson in conversation with Rob La Frenais, 'New Image and Neo-Naturism', *Performance*, 19 (October/November 1982), p. 5. Dawson ran the B2 Gallery in London from 1980 to 1984 where the Neo Naturists mounted a week-long performance in 1982 described well in this article.

20. Jones (2006), p. 171.

21. For a description of this particular 'obstacle course' see Christine Binnie, 'A Day in the Life of a Neo-Naturist', *Performance*, 42 (July/August 1986), p. 38.

22. Cited in Barry Miles, *London Calling: A Countercultural History of London since 1945* (London: Atlantic, 2010), p. 379.

23. Jennifer Binnie in conversation with the author, 3 November 2001.

24. For which see Jill Bruce cited in *Performance*, 4 (December/January 1980), p. 6. Also, Rob La Frenais, 'Magic and Performance', *Performance*, 15 (January/February 1982), p. 21. Bruce Lacey had been a visiting lecturer at Portsmouth when Perry and Jennifer Binnie were there as students and exerted a particular influence on Binnie.

25. One such performance was in Norfolk at the 1982 Fairy Fair organized by Bruce Lacey. The circumstances of this performance and their use of flour and food colouring instead of body paint is related in Christine Binnie and Wilma Johnson, 'Neo-Naturist Manifesto', *International Times*, 86:3, Full Moon (26 March – 24 April 1986), p. 15.

26. Grayson Perry in conversation with the author, 25 October 2001.

27. Ibid.

28. Ibid.

29. Jennifer Binnie remembered that 'Grayson had this thing that, even if he wasn't dressed up as a woman, he used to love getting dressed up to look really horrible. He used to buy these really horrible nylon shirts from Charity shops and it used to be quite embarrassing sometimes going out with him, it used to be quite oppressing sometimes being with somebody who always wanted to look ugly.' Jennifer Binnie in conversation with the author, 3 November 2001.

30. Joe La Placa, 'London Calling' at www.artnet.com/Magazine/reviews/laplaca/laplaca1-16-04.asp accessed 1 April 2019.

31. Grayson Perry, cited in listings, *World of Interiors* (November 1985).

32. Christine Binnie in conversation with the author, 1 November 2001.

33. Jennifer Binnie, in Louisa Buck and Liz Finch, 'An Evening of Titillation as Naughty Neo Naturist Opens Her Exhibition "Starkers"', *Ritzy* magazine, 90 (1984).

34. Miles (2010), p. 389.

35. Grayson Perry, 'Letting It All Hang Out: My Life as a Naked Artist', *The Times*, 20 June 2007.

36. James Birch in conversation with the author, 13 November 2001.

37. See Tate Archive, The Letters and Papers of Paul Nash TGA 8313/2/3/8. It is unlikely but not impossible that Perry would have knowingly adopted Banting's use of this term. The first exhibition at James Birch's gallery at Waterford Road in 1983 had been a retrospective of Banting and David Dawson maintained work by Banting at B2 at the time that he was working with the Neo Naturists, Derek Jarman, John Maybury and Trojan.

38. Jones (2006), p. 189.

39. Grayson Perry in conversation with the author, 25 October 2001.

40. Grayson Perry, *Claire's Coming Out Speech*, Laurent Delaye Gallery, London, 30 October 2000.

41. Cited in Jacky Klein, *Grayson Perry* (London: Thames & Hudson, 2013), p. 9.

42. Grayson Perry in conversation with the author, 25 October 2001.

THE ICONOGRAPHY OF GRAYSON PERRY'S 'PRE-THERAPY YEARS'

1. Inscription on *Self Portrait Cracked and Warped*, 1985.

2. Conversation with the artist, 2018.

3. Wendy Jones, *Grayson Perry: Portrait of the Artist as a Young Girl* (London: Chatto & Windus, 2006), p. 3.

4. Grayson Perry, *The Most Popular Art Exhibition Ever!* (London: Penguin, 2017), introduction.

5. Jacky Klein, *Grayson Perry* (London: Thames & Hudson, 2009 and 2013), p. 13.

6. Louisa Buck, 'The Personal Political Pots of Grayson Perry', *Grayson Perry: Guerrilla Tactics*, exh. cat. (Amsterdam: Stedelijk Museum, 2002), p. 97.

7. *Grayson Perry: The Vanity of Small Differences* (London: Hayward Publishing, 2013), p. 11.

8. Klein (2013), p. 33.

9. Jones (2006), p. 24.

10. Ibid., p. 23.

11. Klein (2013), p. 32.

12. Buck, *Guerrilla Tactics* (2002), pp. 94–95.

13. Jones (2006), p. 73.

14. Ibid., p. 75.

15. Klein (2013), p. 34.

16. Jones (2006), p. 75.

17. Ibid., p. 74.

18. Ibid., p. 48. For many cross-dressers their fantasy of outward femininity only becomes a reality when they pass unnoticed.

19. Klein (2013), p. 160.

20. Jones (2006), p. 47.

21. Ibid., pp. 48–50.

22. Ibid., p. 50.

23. Rachel Kent, 'Stockings and stealth bombs', *My Pretty Little Art Career*, exh. cat. (Sydney: Museum of Contemporary Art Australia, 2015), p. 18.

24. Grayson Perry, *The Tomb of the Unknown Craftsman*, exh. cat. (London: British Museum, 2011), p. 17.

25. Ibid., p. 17.

26. Ibid., p. 19.

27. *Grayson Perry: Guerrilla Tactics*, exh. cat. (Amsterdam: Stedelijk Museum, 2002), p. 18.

28. Klein (2013), p. 9. She quotes Tracey Emin's response to Perry's Turner Prize win: 'Grayson is very popular with the masses.'

29. Klein (2013), p. 39.

30. Ibid.

31. Ibid., p. 168.

32. Ibid., p. 52.

33. Faye Robson (ed.), *The Creative Stance* (London: common-editions, 2016), p. 14; Perry, *Tomb of the Unknown Craftsman* (2011), p. 14.

34. Klein (2013), p. 49.

35. Ibid., p. 57.

36. Conversation with the artist, 2018.

37. Klein (2013), p. 58.

38. Hilary Young (ed.), *The Genius of Wedgwood* (London: Victoria & Albert Museum, 1995), p. 102.

39. *Guerrilla Tactics* (2002), p. 14.

40. Klein (2013), p. 28.

41. *Vanity of Small Differences* (2013), p. 6.

42. Ibid., p. 11.

43. Klein (2013), p. 56.

44. Ibid., p. 60.

45. www.theguardian.com/culture/2019/mar/24/beyonce-effect-galleries-new-generation-art-devotees-picasso-jay-z

46. Buck, *Guerrilla Tactics* (2002), p. 101.

47. Grayson Perry, *Playing to the Gallery: Helping Contemporary Art in its Struggle to be Understood* (London: Particular, 2014), p. 5.

48. Andrew Wilson, 'Grayson Perry: "General Artist"', *Grayson Perry: Guerrilla Tactics*, exh. cat. (Amsterdam: Stedelijk Museum, 2002), p. 87.

49. www.theguardian.com/artanddesign/2017/jun/06/grayson-perry-the-most-popular-art-exhibition-ever-review-the-court-jester-strikes-again

50. Quoted in www.theguardian.com/artanddesign/2018/aug/14/grayson-perry-artist-discloses-details-of-estrangement-from-his-mother

Grayson Perry: Ceramics, text by Grayson Perry
(London: Birch and Conran, 1987)

Grayson Perry: Guerilla Tactics, exh. cat.
(Amsterdam: Stedelijk Museum, 2002)

Grayson Perry: Making Meaning
(Florida: Windsor Press, 2018)

Grayson Perry: The Tomb of the Unknown Craftsman, exh. cat.
(London: British Museum Press, 2011)

Grayson Perry: Vanité, Identité, Sexualité, exh. cat.
(Paris: LIENART éditions, 2018)

Grayson Perry: The Vanity of Small Differences
(London: Hayward Publishing, 2013)

Grayson Perry, *Cycle of Violence*
(London: Atlas Press, 2012)

Grayson Perry, *The Descent of Man*
(London: Penguin, 2017)

Grayson Perry, *The Most Popular Art Exhibition Ever!*
(London: Penguin, 2017)

Grayson Perry, *Playing to the Gallery:
Helping Contemporary Art in Its Struggle to Be Understood*
(London: Penguin, 2016)

Grayson Perry, *Sketchbooks*
(London: Particular Books, 2016)

Grayson Perry and Jonathan Sidney, 'Unsophisticated
Sophistication – The Paradox of Grayson Perry', *Ceramic Review*, 112
(July/August 1988)

Jacky Klein, *Grayson Perry*
(London: Thames & Hudson, 2009 and 2013)

My Pretty Little Art Career, exh. cat.
(Sydney: Museum of Contemporary Art Australia, 2015)

Wendy Jones, *Grayson Perry: Portrait of the Artist as a Young Girl*
(London: Chatto & Windus, 2006)

All works © 2020 Grayson Perry.
Images are courtesy the artist
and Victoria Miro, London/Venice,
unless stated otherwise

p. 1 Photo courtesy of Grayson
Perry © Matthew R. Lewis
www.matthewrlewisportraits.co.uk
pp. 4, 28 © Matthew R. Lewis
pp. 10, 12 (front and behind), 13, 33 (front)
Photos courtesy of Jennifer Binnie
pp. 11 (front and behind), 21, 23, 25, 27,
34 (behind) Photos courtesy of the Neo
Naturist Archive
pp. 17, 70 Photo courtesy England & Co
gallery, London
pp. 18, 19, 24, 40, 56 (front) Photos
courtesy of Grayson Perry
p. 29 Photos courtesy of James Birch
Collection, Conception James Birch
pp. 32, 34 (front), 35 Photos courtesy
of James Birch Collection, original
photographer James Birch
p. 33 (behind) Photo courtesy of James
Birch Collection, original photographer
Jane England
p. 51 © 2015 Eric Yates-Owen and Robert
Fournier, *British Studio Potters' Marks*,
Bloomsbury Academic, an imprint of
Bloomsbury Publishing Plc.
pp. 54, 55 (front and behind), 56–57
(behind) Collection of Peter Wright,
photo courtesy of Peter Wright
p. 64 Photo by Richard Gilbert
p. 156 Arts Council Collection, Southbank
Centre, London © Grayson Perry
p. 157 © Tate, London 2019

PHOTOGRAPHY
All photography Todd-White unless
stated otherwise.
pp. 2, 38, 50, 66–67, 68, 82–83, 123, 136,
137, 144, 150, 151, 152, 153 Photography
Stephen White
pp. 10, 11 (front and behind), 12 (front
and behind), 13, 21, 23, 25, 27, 33 (front),
34 (behind) Photography Andy Keate
pp. 41, 84, 86, 92, 103, 154, 159
Photography Josh Murfitt
pp. 42, 120 Photography Thierry Bal
pp. 102 Paul Marks Photography
pp. 104 Photography Dave Watts
pp. 111 Photography Prudence Cuming

pp. 113, 116, 117, 118, 135, 143, 149
Photography Luke Unsworth
pp. 122, 140, 141, 158 Photography
Jack Hems
pp. 130, 131 Photography Bruce
M. White, 2019

Every effort has been made to secure
all necessary permissions to reproduce
images within this book. Any errors or
omissions should be addressed to the
Holburne Museum.

COLLECTION CREDITS
p. 2 Collection of the artist; p. 17
Collection Pauline Amos, courtesy
England & Co gallery, London; pp. 18–
19 Installation subsequently destroyed;
p. 26 Collection of the artist; p. 37
Jane Colling; p. 38 Collection of the
artist; p. 39 Private collection; p. 41
Private collection, in memory of Lionel
Evans; p. 42 Mo Tomaney; p. 44 The
Thimblestitch and Bramble Collection;
p. 46 Private collection; p. 47 James Birch
Collection; p. 50 Collection of the artist;
pp. 66–67 Collection of the artist; p. 68
Collection of the artist; p. 69 James Birch
Collection; p. 70 Collection Pauline Amos,
courtesy England & Co gallery, London;
p. 71 James Birch Collection; pp. 72–73
James Birch Collection; p. 74 Private
collection; p. 75 The Thimblestitch
and Bramble Collection; p. 76 Private
collection; p. 77 Michael Kerr Esq.; p. 78
Private collection; p. 79 (above) Private
collection; (below) Collection Adrian
Dannatt, New York; p. 80 Collection
of Louisa Buck; p. 81 Private collection;
pp. 82–83 Collection of the artist; p. 84
Private collection, in memory of Lionel
Evans; p. 85 Hugh Warren; p. 86 Gill
Denmark; p. 87 (above) Private collection;
(below) Alicia Hills; p. 88 Collection
of sculptor Andrew Logan; p. 89 Private
collection; p. 90 Private collection,
London; p. 91 Sam Fogg; p. 92 Private
collection; p. 93 (above) James Birch
Collection; (below) Private collection;
p. 94 Collection of the artist; p. 95 Private
collection; pp. 96–97 Ralph Segreti; p. 98
Jane Colling; p. 99 Private collection;
pp. 100–101 Private collection; p. 102

Swindon Museum and Art Gallery,
purchased with the support of the Art
Fund, 2015; p. 103 Fry Art Gallery; p. 104
Collection of Sally Burgess (formerly
Clerkenwell Fine Art); p. 105 James Birch
Collection; pp. 106–107 James Birch
Collection; pp. 108–09 Private collection;
p. 110 Private collection, purchased from
the Birch Conran Gallery; p. 111 Offer
Waterman on behalf of a private collection;
p. 112 Castlegate House Gallery; p. 113 Dr
Jill Westwood; p. 114 Private collection;
p. 115 Private collection; pp. 116–17 Dr
Jill Westwood; p. 118 Jo Comino; p. 119
Private collection; p. 120 Mo Tomaney;
p. 121 Private collection, Devon; p. 122
Offer Waterman; p. 123 Collection of
the artist; pp. 124–25 Renato Pesci;
p. 126 Private collection; p. 127 Collection
Waldemar Januszczak; pp. 128–29 Ruth
Ravenscroft and Mark Smith; pp. 130–31
The Collection of Ambassador and Mrs
Edward E. Elson; pp. 132–33 Private
collection, purchased from the Birch
Conran Gallery; p. 134 Wayne Warren;
p. 135 Dr Jill Westwood; pp. 136–37
Collection of the artist; pp. 138–39 Private
collection; p. 140 Private collection; p. 141
Private collection, Devon; p. 142 Private
collection; p. 143 Dr Jill Westwood;
p. 144 Private collection; p. 145 Private
collection; pp. 146–47 Angie Koulakoglou
Collection; p. 148 Collection of the artist;
p. 149 Collection of Mark D. D. Wilson;
pp. 150—51 Collection of the artist;
pp. 152—53 Mark & Debra Eden; p. 154
Mr and Mrs Matthew Bardsley; p. 155
Siobhan Loughran; p. 156 Arts Council
Collection, Southbank Centre, London,
ACC11/2002; p. 157 Tate: Purchased with
assistance from Rob Taylor and Michael
Kallenbach 2002, T07940; p. 158 Private
collection, Devon; p. 159 Mr and Mrs
Matthew Bardsley

ACKNOWLEDGMENTS

This book coincides with an exhibition at the Holburne Museum, Bath in 2020. We are indebted to all of the lenders who have made this show possible. Thanks are due to our tour partners, York Art Gallery and the Sainsbury Centre for Visual Arts at UEA, Norwich.

Many people have helped us to bring this publication and exhibition together, for which we are hugely grateful. Particular thanks to Victoria Miro and the team at Victoria Miro Gallery (especially Erin Manns, Hannah van den Wijngaard and Valeska Wittig), Jennifer Gill, James Birch, Jennifer Binnie, Christine Binnie, Ben Fitzpatrick, Andrew Gibson, Peter Wright and Andrew Shanahan. And special thanks of course to Grayson Perry, whose enthusiasm and support for the project has been invaluable.

Catrin Jones and Chris Stephens

LIST OF CONTRIBUTORS

Grayson Perry, one of Britain's best-known contemporary artists, is also an award-winning writer and broadcaster. Winner of the 2003 Turner Prize, he was elected a Royal Academician in 2012, awarded a CBE in 2013 and in 2015 was appointed Trustee of the British Museum and Chancellor of the University of the Arts London.

Dr Chris Stephens is Director of the Holburne Museum, Bath. Before that he worked at Tate, London where he curated major exhibitions including *Barbara Hepworth: Centenary*, *Francis Bacon*, *Henry Moore*, *Picasso and Modern British Art*, and *David Hockney*. He is a leading expert on modern British art and his book *St Ives: The Art and the Artists* was published in 2018.

Andrew Wilson is Senior Curator of Modern and Contemporary British Art, and Archives at Tate Britain where he has worked since 2006; he was previously deputy editor of *Art Monthly*. The exhibitions that he has curated include *Patrick Heron* (Tate St Ives and Turner Contemporary Margate, 2018). He sat on the jury of the Turner Prize in 2003.

Catrin Jones is Curator at the Holburne Museum. She has worked at the V&A and Ashmolean Museum, specializing in historic and contemporary applied arts. Her exhibitions include *Deception: Ceramics and Imitation*, *Silver: Light and Shade* and *Grayson Perry: The Pre-Therapy Years*.

Sylvie Broussine is Assistant Curator at the Holburne Museum. She is a former Art Fund Curatorial Trainee at the National Gallery where she specialized in 17th-century Spanish painting.

R

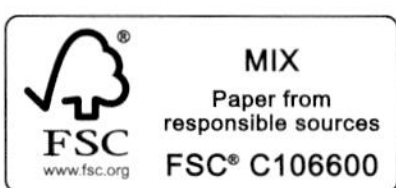
MIX
Paper from
responsible sources
FSC
www.fsc.org   FSC® C106600